# Criminal Conduct and Substance Abuse Treatment

Criminal Conduct and Substance Abuse Treatment is a project of
The Center for Interdisciplinary Studies, Inc.

Correspondence should be sent to:

The Center For Interdisciplinary Studies
899 Logan Street, Suite 207
Denver, Colorado 80203
(303) 830-8500, Fax (303) 830-8420

This document was prepared under contract numbers 957230 and 960671 with the Colorado Alcohol and Drug Abuse Division, Department of Human Services and under contract numbers 94-DB-15A-58-1 and 95-DB-15A-58-2 with the Division of Criminal Justice, Colorado Department of Public Safety from the Edward Byrne Memorial State and Local Law Enforcement Assistance Program, Drug Control and System Improvement Program Formula Grant to Colorado from the U.S. Department of Justice. Funding for this project was $91,368 (72%) federal funds and $36,327 (28%) State funds from the Offender Surcharge Fund.

Opinions are those of the authors or cited sources and do not necessarily reflect those of the Colorado Department of Human Services or the Colorado Department of Public Safety.

Kenneth W. Wanberg, Th.D., Ph.D., is a private practice psychologist and the Director of Center for Addictions Research and Evaluation (CARE), Arvada, Colorado. Harvey B. Milkman, Ph.D. is Professor of Psychology at Metropolitan State College of Denver and Director of the Center for Interdisciplinary Studies, Denver, Colorado.

Kenneth W. Wanberg ■ Harvey B. Milkman

# Criminal Conduct and Substance Abuse Treatment

Strategies for Self-Improvement and Change
## The Participant's Workbook

SAGE Publications
*International Educational and Professional Publisher*
Thousand Oaks  London  New Delhi

*For information:*

SAGE Publications, Inc.
2455 Teller Road
Thousand Oaks, California 91320
E-mail: order@sagepub.com

SAGE Publications Ltd.
6 Bonhill Street
London EC2A 4PU
United Kingdom

SAGE Publications India Pvt. Ltd.
M-32 Market
Greater Kailash I
New Delhi 110 048 India

Printed in the United States of America

*Library of Congress Cataloging-in-Publication Data*

ISBN 0-7619-0944-3 (paperback)

01   02   03   04   11   10   9   8

*Acquiring Editor:*      Margaret Zusky
*Editorial Assistant:*   Renée Piernot
*Production Editor:*     Wendy Westgate

# TABLE OF CONTENTS

**PREFACE** ...........................................................................................................................1

**PART ONE: INTRODUCTION** .......................................................................................3

    Welcome ...........................................................................................................................4

    Who Is This Program For? .............................................................................................4

    What Is Our Approach? ..................................................................................................5

    What Does This Have to Do With Our Alcohol and Drug Use? ...................................6

    What Does This Have to Do With Our Criminal Conduct? ..........................................6

    How Does the Program Bring Together My Substance Abuse and My Criminal Conduct? ..........7

    How Is the Program Set Up? ..........................................................................................7

    What Do We Expect of You? ..........................................................................................9

**PART TWO: THE PROGRAM CURRICULUM** ...........................................................11

**PHASE I: CHALLENGE TO CHANGE: INTRODUCTION AND OVERVIEW** ...............13

**MODULE 1: BUILDING TRUST AND RAPPORT** .......................................................17

    Session 1: Developing a Working Relationship.............................................................19

    Session 2: Understanding and Engaging the Change Process .....................................21

**MODULE 2: BUILDING A DESIRE AND MOTIVATION TO CHANGE** .....................25

    Sessions 3 and 4: Building Motivation to Change .......................................................27

**MODULE 3: BUILDING THE KNOWLEDGE BASE TO CHANGE** ..............................33

    *Overview of Module 3* ..................................................................................................35

    Session 5: Understanding the Role of Thinking and Feeling in Learning and Change ...............35

    Session 6: Understanding the Role of Behavior in Self-Improvement and Change .....................39

    Session 7: Basic Knowledge About Drugs ...................................................................45

    Session 8: Understanding Alcohol and Other Drug (AOD) Addiction ........................53

    Session 9: Understanding Criminal Conduct and the Influence of Drugs....................57

**MODULE 4: SELF-DISCLOSURE AND RECEIVING FEEDBACK: PATHWAYS TO SELF-AWARENESS AND CHANGE** ...............................................63

    Session 10: Learning Communication Tools and Skills ...............................................67

    Session 11: Tools of Self-Disclosure: Autobiography, Thinking Reports, Journaling and Participating in the Reflection Group ........................................71

    Session 12: Deeper Sharing: Your Deep Emotions and Your AOD Use......................75

    Session 13: Deeper Sharing: Your History of Criminal Conduct ................................79

**MODULE 5: PREVENTING RELAPSE AND RECIDIVISM: IDENTIFYING HIGH-RISK SITUATIONS** ...............................................83

    Session 14: Relapse and Recidivism Prevention I: Identifying High-Risk Situations and Understanding Relapse and Recidivism .........85

    Session 15: Relapse and Recidivism Prevention II: Learning the Cognitive-Behavioral Map for AOD Abuse and Criminal Conduct ......91

**MODULE 6: HOW DO PEOPLE CHANGE: UNDERSTANDING THE PROCESS OF SELF-IMPROVEMENT AND CHANGE** ........95

*Overview of Module 6* ........96

Session 16: Reviewing the Process and Stages of Change and Selecting Targets for Change ....97

Session 17: Ways to Change and Barriers to Change ........105

Session 18: Looking Forward: Making a Commitment to Change ........109

**PHASE II: COMMITMENT TO CHANGE: INTRODUCTION AND OVERVIEW** ........111

**MODULE 7: INTRODUCTION TO PHASE II: DEVELOPING COMMITMENT TO CHANGE** ........115

*Overview of Module 7* ........116

Session 19: Recognizing Readiness to Change: Problem Solving and Doing Something Different—It's Your Choice ........117

Session 20: Involving Significant Others ........121

**MODULE 8: IN-DEPTH ASSESSMENT: LOOKING AT THE AREAS OF NEED AND CHANGE** ....127

*Overview of Module 8* ........128

Session 21: The In-Depth Assessment: Getting the Information to Plot the Master Profile ........129

Session 22: Targets of Change and the Master Assessment Plan (MAP) ........133

**MODULE 9: STRENGTHENING BASIC SKILLS FOR SELF-IMPROVEMENT AND CHANGE: ACTING ON THE COMMITMENT TO CHANGE** ........141

*Overview of Module 9* ........142

Session 23: Coping and Social Skills Training: Basic Communication Skills— Active Sharing and Active Listening ........145

Session 24: Coping and Social Skills Training: Basic Communication Skills— Starting Conversations ........149

Session 25: Coping and Social Skills Training: Basic Communication Skills— Compliments ........151

Session 26: Recognizing and Being Aware of Negative Thoughts and Negative Thinking ........155

Session 27: Managing and Changing Negative Thoughts ........159

Session 28: Errors in Logic and Thinking ........165

Session 29: Errors in Thinking and the Entitlement Trap ........169

Session 30: Recognizing High-Risk Situations for AOD Use and CC and Refusal Training ........173

Session 31: Managing Cravings and Urges About CC and AOD Use ........177

Session 32: Assertiveness Skills Development ........181

Session 33: Deeper Problem Solving ........185

Session 34: Handling Feelings—Anger Management ........189

Session 35: Preventing Aggression and Violence ........193

Session 36: Managing Guilt, Anger and Depression: The Emotional Cycles of Rehabilitation ........199

Session 37: Developing and Keeping Intimate and Close Relationships ........203

Session 38: Understanding Values and Moral Development ........207

Session 39: Understanding and Practicing Empathy ...................................................................213

Session 40: Responsibility Toward the Community:
     Reflection and Review and Driving Attitudes and Patterns .................................217

**PHASE III: TAKING OWNERSHIP OF CHANGE** ...................................................................221

**MODULE 10: RELAPSE AND RECIDIVISM PREVENTION: REVIEW AND STRATEGIES
     FOR SELF-CONTROL AND LIFESTYLE BALANCE** ...........................................225

*Overview of Module 10* .........................................................................................................226

Session 41: Strengthening Relapse and Recidivism Prevention Skills ...............................227

Session 42: Relapse Prevention: Strategies for Self-Control and Lifestyle Balance ...........233

**MODULE 11: STRENGTHENING OUR OWNERSHIP OF CHANGE: DEVELOPING THE
     SKILLS OF CRITICAL REASONING AND SETTLING CONFLICTS** ...................239

*Overview of Module 11* .........................................................................................................240

Session 43: Critical Reasoning: Decision Making and Creativity I ...................................241

Session 44: Critical Reasoning: Decision Making and Creativity II ..................................247

Session 45: Resolving Conflicts: Negotiation and Social Skills Development ...................249

**MODULE 12: MAINTAINING SELF-IMPROVEMENT AND CHANGE: DEVELOPING A
     HEALTHY LIFESTYLE OR MANNER OF LIVING** .............................................253

*Overview of Module 12* .........................................................................................................254

Session 46: The Alternatives of Healthy Play and Leisure Time ......................................255

Session 47: The Alternative of Productive Work: Managing Work and Job Issues ...........265

Session 48: Role Modeling Change .......................................................................................271

Session 49: Preparing for Maintaining Your Changes: Exploring Self-Help Groups and
     Other Community Support Programs ...........................................................275

Session 50: Preparing for Your Program Change Support Group ....................................277

# LIST OF WORK SHEETS

1: AREAS YOU FEEL YOU NEED TO CHANGE ................................................................30

2: THE PROCESS OF COGNITIVE AND BEHAVIORAL LEARNING AND CHANGE ...........44

3: RATING SELF ON RISK FACTORS ..............................................................................61

4: ERRORS IN THINKING CHECKLIST ............................................................................62

5: YOUR TEST SCORES ..................................................................................................76

6: RECORDING PROBLEM EPISODES COMING FROM AOD USE ....................................77

7: CRIMINAL HISTORY PART OF THE LEVEL OF SERVICE INVENTORY .........................80

8: CRIMINAL CONDUCT LOG WORK CHART ..................................................................81

9: RELAPSE/RECIDIVISM LOG ......................................................................................87

10: COPING SKILLS .......................................................................................................88

11: THE RELAPSE/RECIDIVISM CALENDAR ...................................................................89

12: YOUR PATHWAYS TO ALCOHOL AND OTHER DRUG USE .........................................99

13: YOUR PATHWAYS TO CRIMINAL CONDUCT .............................................................100

14: SELF-RATING ON STAGES OF CHANGE FOR AOD USE ONLY ...................................103

## LIST OF WORK SHEETS (continued)

15: SELF-RATING ON STAGES OF CHANGE FOR CRIMINAL THINKING AND CONDUCT ONLY 104

16: PROBLEM SOLVING EXERCISE ................................................................120

17: LIST OF PROBLEMS TO WORK ON ........................................................124

18: MASTER PROFILE (MP) ..........................................................................134

19: MASTER ASSESSMENT PLAN (MAP) ......................................................137

20: HOMEWORK FOR ACTIVE SHARING .....................................................147

21: ACTIVE LISTENING................................................................................148

22: PRACTICE COMPLIMENT GIVING.........................................................153

23: RECEIVING A COMPLIMENT .................................................................154

24: NEGATIVE THOUGHTS AND THINKING ERRORS ..................................157

25: USING THE ABC RATIONAL THINKING APPROACH ..............................158

26: NEGATIVE THOUGHTS THAT LEAD TO AOD USE AND CRIMINAL CONDUCT.....................161

27: POSITIVE THOUGHT ARMING ..............................................................162

28: PRACTICING THOUGHT STOPPING .......................................................163

29: THINKING DISTORTIONS .......................................................................168

30: THE ENTITLEMENT TRAP ......................................................................171

31: LIST OF HIGH-RISK—DIFFICULT REFUSAL SITUATIONS...........................175

32: REFUSAL SKILLS ...................................................................................176

33: LOSS OF JOYS AND PLEASURES ...........................................................179

34: DEALING WITH CRAVINGS ...................................................................180

35: PRACTICING ASSERTIVENESS SKILLS .....................................................183

36: PROBLEM SOLVING ..............................................................................187

37: LOOKING AT YOUR ANGER AND ANGRY THOUGHTS ...........................191

38: IDENTIFYING TRIGGERS AND SYMPTOMS OF ANGER............................192

39: MANAGING HIGH-CHARGED SITUATIONS............................................196

40: MANAGING AGGRESSION .....................................................................197

41: IDENTIFYING AND MANAGING YOUR ANGRY, GUILTY AND DEPRESSED THOUGHTS......202

42: LOOKING AT THE RELATIONSHIP WITH YOUR INTIMATE PARTNER .........205

43: LOOKING AT YOUR CLOSENESS AND SEPARATENESS .............................206

44: GUIDING PRINCIPLES OF YOUR LIFE ...................................................209

45: LOOKING AT YOUR MORAL BELIEFS ....................................................210

46: NORMS OR THE STANDARDS OF CONDUCT .........................................211

47: PRACTICING FEELING EMPATHY FOR ANOTHER PERSON ......................215

48: MORAL DILEMMA ................................................................................216

49: DRIVING ASSESSMENT PROFILE ...........................................................219

50: CHANGING DRIVING THOUGHTS, EMOTIONS AND HABITS ..................220

51: THINKING AND ACTING SKILLS ...........................................................229

52: HIGH-RISK THINKING PATTERNS .........................................................230

53: HIGH-RISK SITUATIONS .......................................................................231

54: THE DECISION WINDOW FOR AOD USE AND CRIMINAL CONDUCT ......236

## LIST OF WORK SHEETS (continued)

55: PROPAGANDA ADVERTISEMENTS .................................................................................244

56: RELATING PROPAGANDA TO YOUR DRUG USE AND CRIMINAL CONDUCT .......................245

57: NEGOTIATION SKILLS ........................................................................................251

58: THE PERSONAL PLEASURE INVENTORY .....................................................................257

59: PERSONAL PLEASURE INVENTORY PROFILE ...............................................................261

60: LEISURE TIME ACTIVITIES...................................................................................262

61: PERSONAL TIME .............................................................................................263

62: WHAT IS YOUR WORK?......................................................................................268

63: JOB SEARCH PLAN ..........................................................................................269

64: SCHOOL AND WORK PLAN FOR THE NEXT THREE YEARS................................................270

65: YOUR STRONGEST AREAS OF CHANGE AND SELF-IMPROVEMENT........................................273

66: YOUR MOST VULNERABLE OR WEAKEST AREAS OF CHANGE AND SELF-IMPROVEMENT .......273

67: PREPARING A LIST OF SELF-HELP GROUPS ..............................................................276

## LIST OF FIGURES

Figure 1: Interaction of Thoughts, Feelings and Actions ....................................................36

Figure 2: The Process of Learning and Change ...............................................................38

Figure 3: Three Rules of Learning Behavior ..................................................................40

Figure 4: The Process of Cognitive and Behavioral Learning and Change....................................42

Figure 5: The Mental-Behavioral Pathway for Learning AOD Use Behavior: Reinforcing or
Strengthening Drug Use Behavior ...............................................................................53

Figure 6: Mental-Behavioral Addiction Cycle .................................................................55

Figure 7: Mental-Physical Addiction............................................................................56

Figure 8: The Criminal Conduct and Corrective Behavior Cycles ..........................................59

Figure 9: The Path to Talking and Learning About Self....................................................68

Figure 10: The Relapse Process ................................................................................91

Figure 11: Cognitive-Behavioral Model for Relapse and Recidivism.....................................93

Figure 12: Pathways to Changing AOD and Criminal Conduct ............................................98

Figure 13: Old or Young Woman ............................................................................106

Figure 14: Relationship Balance Between Closeness and Separateness ...............................122

Figure 15: The Assessment Framework or Picture: The Johari Window...............................130

Figure 16: The Guilt-Anger Cycle ..........................................................................201

Figure 17: Relapse Prevention: Global Self-Control Strategies .......................................235

Figure 18: Forks in the Road to Recovery ...............................................................237

# LIST OF TABLES

Table 1: Two Classes of Drugs With Their Direct and Indirect Effects................................46

Table 2: Blood Alcohol Concentration (BAC) Levels by Body Weight, Hours Over Which the Person Drinks and Number of Drinks...................................................................48

Table 3: Approximate Hours from First Drink to Zero Blood Alcohol Level ......................49

Table 4: Common Thinking Distortions or Errors in Thinking ........................................167

# PREFACE

This is the Participant's Workbook designed to accompany the Provider's Guide for **Criminal Conduct and Substance Abuse Treatment: Strategies for Self-Improvement and Change.** This workbook follows the treatment curriculum presented in Section III of the manual.

This Workbook provides an overview and objectives for each treatment module. There are 12 modules in the program. Each module has specific treatment sessions. For each session, objectives are outlined, the key ideas and concepts of each session are presented, and the classroom and homework activities are described. The Workbook provides a guide for your participation in the program. You are expected to read the content of each session and complete classroom and homework tasks. It is essential that you bring the Workbook to each Treatment Session.

# PART ONE

# INTRODUCTION

# WELCOME

Welcome to our program *Strategies for Self-improvement and Change (SSC)*. You have been selected to take part in a program that will take you on a journey of change. You may have been sent to this program because you were told that it is part of your overall plan of correcting and changing your past involvement in criminal conduct (CC). You were also seen as having an alcohol or other drug (AOD) use problem. But most important, you were enrolled in this program because you showed concern about your past criminal conduct (CC) and your past alcohol or other drug (AOD) use problems. In other words, you were seen as someone who wanted to change the direction of your life.

Yet, we know that part of you does not want to be here. We want you to tell us about that part of you. We want to understand those thoughts and feelings. But we know that part of you does want to be here and wants to change the direction of your life. We also want you to tell us about that part of you. That is the part of you that we want to support and help grow.

## Who is this program for?

This is a program of self-improvement and change for the person who has a past of criminal conduct together with alcohol and other drug use problems. There are many programs that work at helping the person who has a criminal conduct history—or a person who is called an "offender." There are many programs that work at helping people with their AOD (alcohol and other drug) problems. But this program is different. It is a program that will work at helping people with both AOD and CC problems.

As many as 60 to 75 percent of people in the criminal justice system have AOD problems. As many as 80 percent of those who are locked up for robbery, burglary or assault did those crimes when using alcohol or other drugs. So, it is clear that AOD use and criminal conduct often go together. You are in this program because you have been involved in both AOD use and abuse and criminal conduct (CC). Those of you who are participating in this program will come from different parts of our justice system. Some of you will be on probation. Others will be on parole. You may be in a group that is in a residential correctional setting. You will differ as to the kind of AOD use problems and criminal conduct you have been involved in. But all of you will have in common a history of AOD use and abuse and a history of criminal conduct.

This program of self-improvement and change is built on an approach called cognitive-behavioral therapy. Now, don't let that term throw you. Let us try to understand what cognitive-behavioral therapy means. This approach means that we make changes in our actions by changing how we think, what we believe, and how we feel. In other words, it takes place in our mind. We change how we think. We change how we act. We can put it in a simple way. It is your thoughts and your beliefs and attitudes—and not what happens around you—that cause you to feel a certain way, or cause you to do certain things.

In this program, we start with some very simple questions. What has happened in your life to bring you to where you are at this point in your life? What have been the problems that you have had as to your AOD involvement and your involvement in criminal behavior? Is your life working? Is change necessary? Who is responsible for what you do? Who is in charge of what happens to you in the future?

If what you do depends on your thoughts, your feelings and your beliefs, then this means that you can control what you do by controlling what goes on in your mind—or controlling your feelings, attitudes, beliefs and thoughts. It means you can control what you do by handling your feelings. It means you can control what you do by changing your thoughts and attitudes.

But your thoughts, your feelings and your actions all tend to affect each other. When you do a certain thing, it will lead to feelings. What you do will cause you to have certain thoughts. Yet, when we look for change and control, we are looking at our thoughts, our feelings and our beliefs. We can change our thoughts and beliefs. We can do that in our head. We can do that in the program. There is power to this kind of control and change. We want to help you to have this power. Through this control and change we achieve self-improvement.

What is it that we look at and want to change about our mind or our mental world? We will look at just a few of the things about our mental world that we want to understand and change.

We will look at what we expect. These are called our *expectations*. Our expectations have a lot to do with what we feel or how we act. If we expect that drugs will make us feel good, then we will use drugs to feel good.

This program takes place in our mind.

We will look at how we judge or evaluate ourselves, what happens to us and what we do. We call these *appraisals*. Often, how we appraise or evaluate ourselves will make a difference in our actions. Sometimes these mental judgments about ourselves and the situation we are in come quickly...so quickly we are not even aware the thoughts are happening. We call these automatic thoughts. When things don't work out for us, our automatic thought might be "Nothing ever goes my way." That is an error in our thinking. Sometimes, things do go our way.

We will look at why we believe things happen to us. We call these *attributions*. When something bad happens to us, do we say "it's someone else fault"? Or, "it's in the stars"? Or do we say "maybe it's something I've done"? We may see what happens to us as outside of us or beyond our control. Or we may see it as something within us. We can conclude that we are in control, or we can conclude that something or someone is controlling us.

We will also look at what it is that we really believe. It is our beliefs that really make a difference. If we believe "people are out to get us," our actions will be different from those we would take if we believe "most people want to treat us in a good way." It is what we call our false beliefs, or our irrational beliefs, that can lead to bad feelings or angry actions.

## What does this have to do with our alcohol and drug use?

This program teaches that our substance use is learned. It is learned because we believe that by using substances, we will feel better. We will have more pleasure. We will feel more powerful. We will feel socially and physically better. And when this happens, it makes us want to use even more. We begin to lean heavily on the use of substances. This is what it means to become addicted to substances.

We believe and expect that by using substances we will not feel bad. We will feel less tense. We will cope better with our problems. And that happens. Again, we become addicted to these beliefs about substances.

We have cravings and desires for drugs. We have urges to use substances. These become automatic. These are powerful things that keep us using alcohol and other drugs. Yet, it is in our mind that we have those cravings. Those urges. It is in our mind that we can change them so that we do not continue to use.

Then, as a result of using substances, we get into trouble—maybe trouble with the law, trouble with our mind, with our body, with other people, with our loved ones. We decide that this is not good. We need to stop. We need to change. This program of self-improvement and change will use cognitive-behavioral approaches to help us with this change. It will help us to deal with our basic beliefs and expectations which lead us to use drugs. It will help us to deal with self-defeating thoughts. It will help us to change our deep-seated beliefs which bring on defeating and destructive thoughts about ourselves and the world. It helps us deal with urges.

This program will help us do these things by teaching us some skills. Skills to deal with our urges. Skills to manage the situations in life that lead us to use. With these skills we will better handle those persons, places and things that are apt to lead us to using. Those are high-risk persons, places and things.

What this all boils down to is that this program will give us self-control. Through self-control we can improve ourselves. We can change.

## What does this have to do with our criminal conduct?

So how will this program help us with our past criminal conduct and the risk that we might again commit crimes? Just as with the use of substances, this program applies to our criminal conduct. It teaches us that we learn our criminal patterns. We change our criminal conduct and patterns through our thinking and through changing our beliefs and attitudes.

This program teaches that our substance use is learned. It is learned because we believe that the use of alcohol or other drugs will make us feel better, will give us pleasure, will make us feel more powerful. It will give us a place to fit in. We expect criminal involvement to do this for us too. And

when this happens, it makes us feel we want to do it even more. We even become addicted to our criminal thinking.

We believe and expect that by acting in criminal ways, we will be less stressed. We will cope with our problems. We will not think about the bad things that happen to us. Or we do our crimes because of the bad things that happen to us. And when these things happen, we become addicted to our criminal thinking and ways. We may believe that because of all the bad things that happen to us, we have a right to steal from or hurt others. After all, "others have hurt us."

*We may believe we have the right to hurt others.*

6

We may even develop a craving for criminal acting. Our criminal thinking becomes automatic. These are powerful things that keep us involved in criminal ways. Yet, this program teaches us that all of this starts in our mind. So, it is in our mind that we begin to change in these ways and patterns. That is, if we want to.

As a result of our criminal actions, we get into trouble. Trouble with the law. With other people. We let our loved ones down. We decide that is not good. We need to stop. We need to change. This program of self-improvement and change will use cognitive-behavioral approaches to help us to change our criminal thinking so that we will not take part in criminal actions. It will help us to deal with our basic beliefs and expectations that keep us in our criminal ways. It will help us to change our thinking and beliefs which bring on negative, defeating and destructive thoughts that can lead to criminal ways. It will teach us the skills of solving problems. We will learn skills to communicate better with others. Skills to develop friends who have a positive attitude toward themselves and others, positive in their thinking and doing. It will teach us skills to handle the high-risk persons, places and things that lead to criminal behavior.

Again, what this all boils down to is that this program will give us self-control. Through self-control we can improve ourselves. We can change.

## How does the program bring together my substance abuse and my criminal conduct?

When you enter this program, you are saying that you want to live a problem-free life as to your use of alcohol and other drugs. The best way to do this is to stay clean. When you begin to think and to act in such a way that it will lead you to going back to AOD use, you are in the first stage of *relapse*. When you go back to actual AOD use, that is relapse. When you go back to the same AOD use patterns that caused you to have AOD problems and abuse, you are in the stage of full relapse. Thus, one of our goals in this program is to help you to prevent AOD relapse.

When you enter this program, you are saying that you want to live a crime-free life. When you begin to think or act in such a way that it could lead you back to being involved in crime, you are in the first stage of *recidivism*. If you go back to criminal behavior, you are into full recidivism.

Thus, substance abuse and criminal conduct have a lot in common. Both allow us to get rewards right away. Both can make us feel good...fast and easy. But both can lead us to a lot of problems and pain in our lives and in the lives of those who are close to us.

Another way that drugs and crime fit together is through a common error of thinking. That thinking error sounds like this: "I am a victim of my own substance abuse. I did a crime because I was drunk, or I was stoned. It wasn't my fault."

You are in this program because you have been involved in substance abuse and criminal conduct. Our goal—and we know that it is your goal—is to help you avoid relapse and recidivism. We are calling this Relapse-Recidivism Prevention (RP).

## How is the program set up?

This program is one year in length. But we are going to take a step at a time. We are going to go through three phases. At the end of each phase, we will look at how you are doing and then see if you want to continue on to the next phase. You may be required to take this program because it is a condition of your probation, parole or sentencing. If this is true for you, you will still be given feedback as to how you are doing in the program. We will talk with you about how you can better make the program work for you. Now, let us look at these phases.

# ■ PHASE I: Challenge to Change

There are 18 sessions in this phase and it will last two months. We want you to do four things in this phase.

First, we want you to *build trust*: trust in the counselor or counselors who will be conducting the program, and trust in those who are in the program with you. We want you to build trust in the program itself. We want you to have this trust so that you can open up and share your feelings and thoughts. We want you to tell your story. You will not be punished or hurt by telling your story. We want you to start talking about your drug use, your past criminal behavior, your worries and fears, your problems and troubles. We want you to trust in the program and trust the desire of your counselors to help you. It may be hard for you to open up at first. You may have a lot of distrust. You may not want to share or talk. Some of you may be more open than others. Give it a try.

Second, we want you to *learn about AOD (alcohol and other drugs)* use and abuse. We want you to learn about your criminal behavior. We will teach you some important ideas and facts. Many of these things you will already know. But we want you to learn...learn...learn about you, about drugs, about antisocial and criminal behavior. We are using the word *antisocial* to mean behavior that goes against the rules and the good of society. Your criminal actions have been antisocial.

Third, we want you to be more *aware of yourself, of your AOD use and CC (criminal conduct)* thinking, feelings and actions. We want you to make a commitment to a long-term change in your thinking and your believing and your acting.

Finally, we will spend time helping you to *understand* what would lead you to relapse and/or *recidivism (RR)* and how to avoid RR. We will call this relapse-recidivism prevention (RP). This will be a very important part of this phase of the program.

# ■ PHASE II: Commitment to Change

This phase is 22 weeks. Now we want you to sort out your problems, to *put labels* on your *thoughts, your feelings and your actions.* In this phase, you will *look at yourself in more depth.* You will look at yourself in a mirror through your counselors and your peers in the program. You will be *confronted as to who you are and what you do.* You will *make a decision to change* and *take action* to change. You will test out and practice changes in your actions. You will become much more aware of yourself, your AOD use and your CC. You will be miles ahead of other people as to being aware of who you are. You will learn what you want and need to change about yourself. In this phase you *will take part in special skill building programs to develop self-control and to change*—to improve your life. You will get stronger in your desire and ability to live a drug-free and crime-free life.

# ■ PHASE III: Taking Ownership of Change

This phase is about three months long. You will spend two weeks to review your practice of recidivism and relapse prevention. You will spend two weeks in learning about developing alternative lifestyles and activities that will help you to maintain the changes you have made. You will also spend some time looking at work and job issues. Our last formal session will look at how you can become a guide or mentor for others who have had life problems similar to yours and who are also going through programs of change and self-improvement.

You will then spend two months in a support group to strengthen your actions to live drug free and crime free. You will now put together what you have learned and make those things work for you. You will feel the power of the ideas, the skills, the thoughts and the actions you have learned. You will begin to feel the ownership of your change. It belongs to you. It is yours. And the strength of that will come as you share that power with others as a guide or mentor or tutor. You will have a chance to become an example for others. You will find new pleasure from comfortable and responsible drug-free and crime-free living.

We live in a world with rules and guidelines. The same is true in this program. Here are these guidelines. They have only one purpose: To make the program mean more to you.

**1.** ### Abstinence: To Be Alcohol and Drug-Free and Crime-Free

While in this program, we expect your goal to be alcohol and drug free. You are expected to be crime-free. You may relapse in your thinking. You may even test out whether you can drink or use drugs. You may find yourself on the path of doing more crimes (e.g., beginning to spend time with old friends who commit crimes), but you are expected to stop at that lapse point. Even if you have a lapse (say in your thinking or who you spend time with), we want you to stay in the program. However, you are asked to not come to a session if you have been using alcohol or other drugs. You may be asked to give a urine or breath sample. If you test positive, you will be asked to return home after setting up an appointment with your counselor to discuss your relapse and how you can continue the program drug and alcohol free. You may, at times, have mixed feelings about all of this. But you will begin to feel the power of this self-control.

**2.** ### Be on Time and Attend All Groups

You are asked to be on time. If you must be late or absent, you are asked to let your counselor know ahead of time. You will be expected to attend all sessions. You may ask to be excused from the program for important reasons. If you are having some problems in attending, you are asked to talk with your counselor and the group. Attending all groups on time will allow you to feel the power of self-control.

**3.** ### Taking an Active Part in the Program

You are expected to be an active member of the group. This means you take part in the discussions. You do the homework. You show you want to change.

**4.** ### Keeping All You Hear to Yourself: Confidentiality

This is important to the group. We want you to promise to keep what you see and hear in the group to yourself. You need to know that the counselors in this program will keep in confidence what you share and tell. If you need to have a report on how you are doing in the group sent to your adult criminal justice supervisor, you will need to give written consent for this. You need to know that your counselor can break this promise to keep what you say and do in confidence if your counselor is concerned about your safety or the safety of others—if you are in danger of hurting yourself or others.

**5.** ### Eating and Smoking in Group

You will not be able to smoke in the group. Your group can decide if you can have beverages in group and what kind of breaks you will have.

**6.** ### Cravings and Slips

You may have cravings or slips into AOD use. We want you to talk about these cravings and urges.

**We are now ready to start the program. Good Luck.**

# NOTES:

# THE PROGRAM CURRICULUM

You will now start a journey of self-improvement and change. This may be one of the biggest journeys of your life. This Workbook is your guide for this journey. It is set up to help you get the most out of each program module and each session in these modules. You were given the outline of the program in Part I of this Workbook. There are three sections in this workbook to match the three phases of the program.

There will be a short introduction to each phase of the program. Then, we will introduce you to each module of the program. Most modules have several sessions. The important ideas and facts for each session will be given to you. Many sessions will have exercises. Sometimes these will be part of your homework. Sometimes you will do them in your group.

After most sessions, you will be asked to fill out a form to rate or evaluate each session. It is important that we get your ideas and thoughts about each session.

Your counselor will rate or evaluate what you do in the program. You will get a score from that rating. This score will tell us how you are doing. Your total score will be important in helping you and your counselor to decide how ready you are for Phases II and III of the program.

# PHASE I

## CHALLENGE TO CHANGE
### INTRODUCTION AND OVERVIEW

*We will learn about the cycles and patterns of substance abuse and criminal conduct.*

# PHASE I:
# CHALLENGE TO CHANGE

This part of your program sets the stage for self–improvement and change. We will spend two months together, twice a week in this phase. Our first job will be to get to know each other. Then we will start to understand how we make self-improvement and change. We will spend the first week doing this.

Our next step in this part of the program will be to get inspired or motivated to change. Part of getting inspired is to give serious thought to whether you need to or want to change. We will want you to look at what changes you have already made. How did that work for you? Maybe we haven't really thought about changing. Or if you have, maybe you haven't gotten inspired or pumped up to change. Before an athlete can play a good game, he or she has to train for that game. Training involves using the skills and strengths that one already has and then building on these strengths and skills. But training requires effort. Effort requires inspiration and motivation. This is what we want you to do. Look at your skills and strengths. Look at the changes you have made. Then, we want you to get inspired to get ready to change or to strengthen the changes you have already made. We will take two full weeks to do this.

Once we get ready to start training for change, we need to learn about those areas where we are going to make changes. We need to learn about ourselves. We can't change or correct ourselves if we don't have knowledge about what it is we are trying to do. Much of this phase involves learning, or learning what we need to know. What do you need to know? You need to know something about alcohol and drugs and the cycles of addiction. You will need to know about criminal conduct and the cycles of criminal behavior. It will be important to learn about how change takes place. You will get some basic information about drugs, drug use and drug abuse. You will understand how thinking and acting fit into self-improvement, self-control and change. You will learn about the cycles and patterns that offenders and people with a history of criminal conduct get into. You will then begin to learn more about who you are and what you are. We will spend five two-hour sessions doing these things.

Phase I will also involve you sharing your story and talking about you. It is through talking about yourself—or what we call self-disclosure—that you become aware of yourself and who you are. We will spend five two hour sessions doing just that. To do this, you will learn basic communication skills to self-disclose. We will look at our thinking errors, at our feelings and emotions, and at our history of AOD use and abuse and our criminal conduct. To help you do this, you will be asked to write your own history—or your autobiography. You will learn the tools of sharing yourself—the tools of writing thinking reports and writing in a journal. An important part of Phase I will be to focus on understanding and preventing relapse (returning to thinking and actions that lead to alcohol and other drug use) and recidivism (returning to thinking and actions that lead to criminal conduct).

At the end of this phase, we will help you look at the specific things about yourself that you want or need to change. We call these "targets of change." Then, we will challenge you to go on to Phase II of the program.

## Here are our goals and objectives for Phase I:

**Understanding and Skill Development:**

◆ Learn the basic ideas of Cognitive-Behavioral Treatment (CBT): That patterns of criminal conduct (CC) and alcohol and other drug use (AOD) and abuse are the result of your style of thinking about yourself and the world and that we improve the course of our life by controlling how we think about ourselves and the world;

◆ Learn basic facts about the patterns and cycles of CC and how people develop and continue these patterns;

◆ Learn basic facts about the patterns and cycles of AOD abuse and how people develop and continue these patterns;

◆ Learn how to recognize the warning signs of relapse and recidivism and to prevent returning to thoughts and actions which lead to relapse and/or recidivism;

◆ Learn about the stages that people go through when making changes;

◆ Learn how to write Thinking Reports and keep a personal journal of thoughts and attitudes about cravings and urges for both CC and AOD abuse;

◆ Learn your own patterns of thinking that lead to CC and AOD abuse;

◆ Learn about your own personal characteristics that lead you to CC and AOD abuse.

## Here is what we expect you to do in the program:

◆ That you attend at least 90% of all meetings. Being on time and doing homework assignments are required for all sessions.

◆ You are expected to cooperate with staff and other clients in these ways:

1) By acting in a self-directed, businesslike manner while helping others to complete the tasks of Phase I.

2) Talk about and share your thoughts and feelings (self-disclosure) in group and in your Thinking Reports.

3) Put to work different ways of thinking and acting which prevent you from relapse into AOD use or into criminal conduct.

# NOTES:

_____

_____

_____

_____

**NOTES:**

# MODULE
# 1

## Building Trust and Rapport

# MODULE 1: BUILDING TRUST AND RAPPORT

## Session ❶ : Developing a Working Relationship

### 1. Objectives of Session:

> ⠠⠕ Look at what we are calling the Cognitive-Behavioral Treatment (CBT) Strategies for Self-Improvement and Change (SSC);
>
> ⠠⠕ Get acquainted with each other and look at the outline of the program;
>
> ⠠⠕ Be shown what you will need to do to complete Phase I of this program and we will go over the program guidelines and ground rules;
>
> ⠠⠕ Begin to build trust and respect among participants and with your counselors.

### 2. Understanding approaches for self–improvement and change:

Addiction to alcohol and other drugs (AOD) and criminal conduct (CC) have much in common with each other. Both give us rewards right away. We get a rush or high from the act itself. Both are usually followed by feelings or thoughts which are not pleasant such as anxiety, guilt, social disapproval or punishment. We can go back (relapse) into drinking or return to criminal conduct when we place ourself in high-risk situations or when we allow ourselves to engage in certain patterns of thinking and feeling.

There are two main purposes of this program for the substance abusing offender (SAO):

a. to learn the basic skills and ways to spot the thoughts and actions that lead to substance abuse and crime;

b. to develop the skills to change destructive patterns of thought and behavior.

The sessions will help you to learn the skills for handling and coping with high risk situations that lead to substance abuse and crime. All group discussions, exercises and homework assignments have been set up to explain and illustrate how the basic CBT ideas and skills can be used to prevent relapse into AOD use and recidivism into criminal conduct.

You will be asked to practice the skills taught in this program outside of the group, especially in situations that are high risk for AOD (alcohol and other drug) use or criminal conduct (CC). Exercises practiced during group sessions are often intense so that members can use the skills in real-life situations.

### 3. Introduction to program exercises:

You will be asked to take part in many exercises in order to successfully complete this program. They are set up mainly for you to improve your life-management and coping skills.

### 4. Beginning to build trust and rapport or harmony:

One way to begin to build trust and rapport (or harmony) is to get to know each other. We will introduce ourselves and find out who we are and what we are about. You will be asked to do several exercises. Begin by sharing:

a. Facts about yourself including your age, where you work, and who are the significant people in your lives;

b. What brings you to the program;

c. What you want to get out of the program;

d. Your concerns or worries about being in the program.

**5. Now you will discuss the Strategies for Self-Improvement and Change (SSC) program guidelines and ground rules. These are given in Part I of this Workbook.**

**6. Being alcohol- and drug-free:**

Although we may be jumping into this quickly, let us now think about our not using (abstaining) from alcohol and other drugs (AOD). It may be strange for you to make a promise or commitment to this. Let's talk about it. Think of what will make this difficult for you. Are you afraid of this commitment? What are your thoughts and feelings about it?

## Your homework for this week:

- Be ready to talk about these topics during the next session:

  ⇨ The SSC course outline;

  ⇨ Completion requirements for Phase I;

  ⇨ Program rules and guidelines.

- Think about what you want most in this program.

- Read over material for Session 2 in this Module.

# NOTES:

_____

_____

_____

_____

_____

_____

_____

_____

_____

_____

## Session ❷: Understanding and Engaging the Change Process

### 1. Objectives of Session:

> ⟱ Learn the facts and ideas this program is built on;
>
> ⟱ Learn the three phases of treatment;
>
> ⟱ Review the goals and objectives of Phase I treatment;
>
> ⟱ Continue to build trust in each other and in our group;
>
> ⟱ Review the program guidelines and ground rules.

### 2. Two basic ideas on which this program is based:

a. That our thoughts and beliefs lead to criminal conduct (CC) and alcohol and other drug (AOD) use and abuse;

b. That criminal conduct and AOD use and abuse mix together to boost or promote further involvement in both criminal conduct and AOD abuse.

### 3. Change and self-correction in criminal conduct (CC) and AOD use takes place when we:

a. Change and get control of the thoughts (mental sets) and beliefs which lead to CC and AOD use;

b. Put our changes in our thinking and mental sets into action;

c. Feel the reward and power of the changes in our thinking and the changes in our behaviors and actions.

### 4. You will be asked in this session to:

a. Share what past AOD or CC treatment or therapy programs you have been involved in and whether they helped;

b. Talk about your basic ideas and beliefs about criminal conduct, drug abuse, and self-improvement.

c. See where you are as to which of these stages of change you might be in:

    1) I really haven't thought much about making serious change in my life;

    2) I've given it some thought;

    3) I think I want to change, but I'm not sure;

    4) I want to change.

d. Learn how thoughts lead to feelings and actions. Give a personal experience that explains this;

e. See how substance abuse and crime get mixed together. Give a personal experience;

f. Talk about trust. How do you know who you can trust? How do you start trusting someone new? How do you see the lack of trust as part of a criminal and drug-abusing lifestyle?

## Your classroom or homework for this week:

- Be prepared to explain what is expected of you in order to successfully complete Phase I, Challenge to Change.
- Write a short paragraph on "The importance of trust in living a crime-free, drug-free life":

• Write a short statement of how improving yourself and changing will keep you from further criminal conduct and AOD use and abuse:

_____

_____

_____

_____

_____

_____

_____

_____

_____

_____

• Describe one situation in which a thought you had led you to committing a crime:

_____

_____

_____

_____

_____

_____

_____

# NOTES:

# MODULE 2

**Building a Desire and
Motivation to Change**

# MODULE 2: BUILDING A DESIRE AND MOTIVATION TO CHANGE

## Sessions ❸ and ❹: Building Motivation to Change

### Here is what we would like to accomplish in this Module:

◆ Have a better understanding of how our attitudes, beliefs and thinking patterns control how we act and behave;

◆ Understand that we will have mixed feelings about changing and that a big part of us will stubbornly resist changing;

◆ Know that people who have become addicted to alcohol and other drugs and who have a history of criminal conduct often put up blocks to change;

◆ Get inspired and enthused about changing;

◆ Come to feel the power of our freedom of choice in the change process.

**In the next two sessions, we will look at five important ideas that are the foundation on which this program is built. These are new ways of thinking.**

   1. **Our attitudes, beliefs and thinking patterns control how we act toward people and situations that are important in our everyday life.** We make changes in our lives only when we change our attitudes, beliefs and thoughts.

      a. An **attitude** is a thought, feeling or orientation for or against a situation, person, idea or object outside of ourselves. An attitude directs how we think, feel and act. An attitude will cause you to line up in a certain way to something or someone outside of you. An attitude is usually hooked into feelings or emotions. Attitudes are described in terms of "good" or "bad." "People who boss me around make me angry."

      b. A **belief** is a value or idea we use to judge or evaluate outside events, situations, people or ourselves. A belief will bond you to or tie you to the outside event. It is more powerful than an attitude but will direct our attitudes toward things or people. "All people are created equal." "We believe in the team." It is a "truth" or a conviction. It is usually 100 percent. We hold on to beliefs.

      c. A **thinking pattern or thought habit** is a mental reaction already inside our head that happens automatically. They are already formed inside of us. It could be how we think about things or how we see or perceive things or what we think about things. They occur automatically when things happen to us or when we come up against things outside of us. It is a response to things outside of us or feelings and beliefs inside of us. A thought pattern may be made up of both our attitudes and beliefs. Our response to someone who cuts in front of us when driving may be "people are jerks." Or, when we perceive someone to ignore us, our automatic response might be "she doesn't like me."

*Our attitudes, beliefs and thinking patterns control how we act and behave.*

27

2. **We resist or defend against change.** When we fight against changing ourselves, our attitudes, beliefs and thinking, what we are really doing is defending our view of ourselves. We hold on to beliefs. "I've never had a fair chance in life." We call this a *Belief Clutch*. It is a "do or die view of ourselves" that we have held for years. Sometimes we call this resistance or denial. It is our view of ourselves. This view can change. But in order to change, we have to want to change. We have to be motivated to change...to be eager to change.

3. **We have mixed feelings about change.** We go back and forth about change or we are hesitant to change. We call this **ambivalence.** To make changes, we have to change or give up thoughts, feelings or actions that support our use of alcohol or other drugs or our taking part in criminal conduct. Sometimes those thoughts or views of ourselves bring us pleasure and comfort. Sometimes they give us excuses for what we do. We get over our wavering or **ambivalence** to change when we learn that the thoughts, feelings and actions lead to more pain and discomfort. It is then that we stop wavering or stop being hesitant. Once we know that holding on to those thoughts and actions causes us more pain than pleasure we give them up.

4. **We go though steps or stages when we make change.** Change is not an event. It is ongoing. It is a process. We change in steps.

   a. A first step is we think about change. We may even get ready to change. We may even say or begin doing some changing. In our Strategies for Self-improvement and Change (SSC) we will call this the **Challenge to Change.**

   b. Our next step is that we decide we want to change. We even put time and energy into it. We come to this program. We begin making changes. We even feel the power of change. We learn skills to change. We master change in SSC and we call this **Commitment to Change.** We pledge to change.

   c. Our next step is that we learn ways to keep the change going. We learn what it means to really go back to the old ways. We find that the changes we make and made are ours. The change, the skills and the power of change belong to ourselves. We learn: "It is mine. I own it." In SSC, we call this **Taking Ownership of Change.**

5. **In your best interest and the long-term look.** We take part in using drugs or crime many times on the spur of the moment. We don't think "what is in my best interest? What are my long-term interests?" We fail to think "I want a family but I can't if I'm in jail." Taking the "long term look" will help us think about what are the results or consequences of what we think and then what we do.

Your classroom or homework assignment for Session 3:

- Write down one *Belief Clutch* that you have held on to which has led to criminal conduct. Have you made changes in that belief?

_____

_____

_____

_____

_____

- Write down one *Belief Clutch* that you have held on to which has led to alcohol and other drug use (AOD). Have you made changes in that belief?

_____

_____

_____

_____

- Using the Change Work Sheet on page 30:

  1) List areas you feel you need to change.

  2) In what parts of this area do you resist or fight change?

  3) What stage of change are you in concerning this area?

  Take some time to complete this work sheet. Bring it to your next session so that we can discuss it. Be as honest as you can in doing this homework.

## Your homework or classroom assignment for Session 4:

- Do a Situational Assessment that describes a situation or event in your life important to you:

_____

_____

_____

- What are your thoughts and beliefs that you use in this situation?

_____

_____

_____

- What was the result or outcome in that situation?

_____

_____

_____

**WORK SHEET 1**

AREAS YOU FEEL YOU NEED TO CHANGE

| AREAS YOU NEED TO CHANGE | HOW DO YOU RESIST CHANGE | STAGE OF CHANGE YOU ARE IN |
|---|---|---|
| | | |
| | | |
| | | |

- If you changed your thoughts or beliefs, would the situation have worked out differently?

_____

_____

_____

- Read introduction to Module 3 and material for Session 5.

# NOTES:

# MODULE
## 3

**Building the
Knowledge Base
to Change**

# MODULE 3: BUILDING THE KNOWLEDGE BASE TO CHANGE

## Overview of Module 3

In order to change, we must have a certain amount of knowledge and awareness of what we are going to change. The purpose of this module is to develop a knowledge base in the areas of alcohol and other drug (AOD) use and in the area of criminal conduct (CC). Here is what we want to get done in this learning module:

◆ Understand how thinking and emotions fit into self-improvement and change;

◆ Understand how our behavior and actions fit in with learning self-improvement and change;

◆ Learn some basic facts about AOD use and abuse;

◆ Learn how people get addicted to alcohol and other drugs;

◆ Understand criminal conduct and the offender cycle and how AOD abuse and criminal conduct fit together.

## Session ❺: Understanding the Role of Thinking and Feeling in Learning and Change

### 1. Objectives of Session:

➠ Learn how our mental (cognitive) events and thinking help us to learn and to change;

➠ Understand and learn five rules about thinking and acting.

### 2. The rules of thinking and acting:

a. **Rule One: That your beliefs, attitudes and thoughts—not what happens outside of yourself—control your actions, your emotions and your relationships with people.** It is through controlling what goes on inside our head that we are able to control our actions toward the outside world. Review the meaning of attitude, belief and thought pattern in Module 2.

b. **Rule Two: That each person perceives (sees) the world and themselves differently. How we see the world, outside events and ourselves, is set by our attitudes and beliefs.** Two people can look at an event or a particular scene and see, feel and think different things. "Two men looked out from prison bars; one saw mud, the other saw stars." This leads to some very important ideas:

1) We make choices about what we think about the world. Our thoughts and actions are based on choice.

2) No one view of the world is right or wrong. Yet, we do form common ideas or beliefs about the world. These become rules or laws. Then, as a group, we say that this is true, or this is right, or this is wrong. It is when our actions resulting from our beliefs and our thinking patterns go against these common rules or laws that our thoughts and actions lead us into problems.

c. **Rule Three: That our thought patterns or thought habits (automatic thoughts) about the outside world and about ourselves can become twisted and distorted.** These are called errors in logic or "cognitive (mental) distortions." These errors or twisted thoughts can lead to disturbed behaviors or emotions. We will spend time in this session and in other sessions looking at these thinking errors or thinking distortions.

d. **Rule Four: That thoughts, emotions and actions affect each other or they interact:** Emotions and moods can lead to certain thoughts; actions can influence how one thinks or feels; emotions can lead to certain behaviors. The diagram in Figure 1 below explains this.

## Figure 1

**Interaction of Thoughts, Feelings and Actions:**

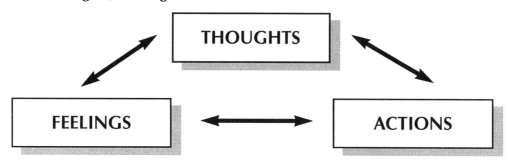

Again, remember Rule One: Your actions and feelings are **not controlled** by what happens outside of you. Your beliefs, your attitudes and your thoughts control your feelings and your actions.

e. **Rule Five: What happens outside of you will bring certain thoughts based on your beliefs and attitudes. Those automatic thoughts can bring on certain feelings; possibly a behavior or an action response.** That action response may be maladaptive. It may violate the rights and privileges of others. It may lead to criminal behavior or excessive drinking. Or the action response may be a positive coping behavior. But we have a choice before we act. The choice is how we think about the event or how we feel about the event. Then, we have a choice of how we act. Figure 2 gives us a picture of this process.

**Exercise**: Describe an event or situation you have experienced in the past and then list your beliefs, attitudes and thinking patterns associated with that event or situation.

EVENT:

_____

_____

_____

BELIEFS, ATTITUDES AND THINKING RELATED TO THE EVENT:

_____

_____

_____

## Classroom exercises or homework:

- Identify an attitude or belief which has led to your use of alcohol or other drugs (AOD).

______________________________________________

______________________________________________

______________________________________________

- Identify an attitude or belief which has led to criminal conduct.

______________________________________________

______________________________________________

______________________________________________

- During the week between sessions, identify a situation which has led to automatic thoughts. What was a twisted thought you had in relationship to that event (thinking distortion)? What was a straight thought related to the event?

**EVENT** ______________________________________________

______________________________________________

______________________________________________

______________________________________________

**THINKING ERROR** ______________________________________________

______________________________________________

______________________________________________

______________________________________________

**STRAIGHT THOUGHT** ______________________________________________

______________________________________________

______________________________________________

______________________________________________

- Read material for Session 6.

**Figure 2**

**The Process of Learning and Change**

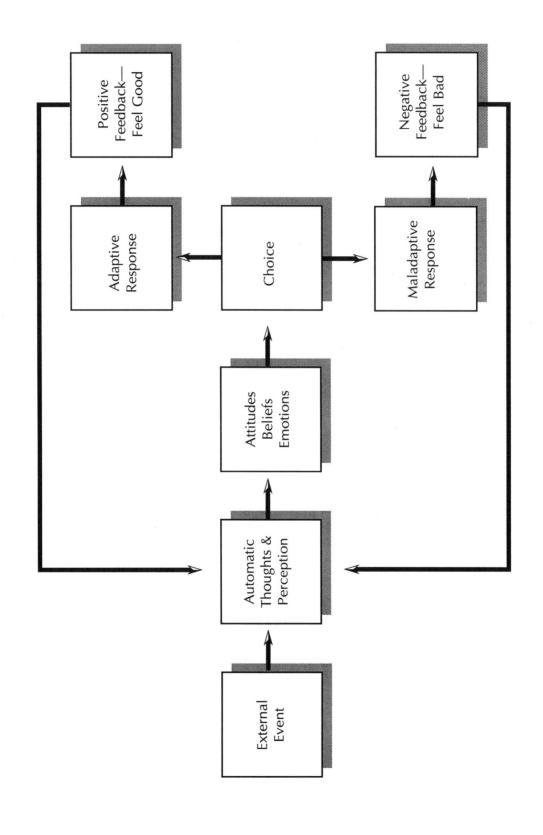

# Session ⑥: Understanding the Role of Behavior in Self-Improvement and Change

## 1. Objectives of Session:

> ➠ Learn and apply the rules of how we learn behavior;
>
> ➠ Understand how the learning of behavior fits into cognitive-behavioral change.

## 2. Review: how our thoughts, beliefs and feelings get reinforced or strengthened:

In our last session, we used Figure 2 to help us understand that thoughts, feelings and beliefs are reactions to outside events that we experience. We also saw that if our action or response resulting from our thoughts or beliefs leads to a positive outcome, our inside mental events (thoughts, beliefs) are strengthened or reinforced. We might get positive feedback from our behavior, and this then reinforces or strengthens a positive view of ourselves and of other people. "I handled that well."

If an action or response resulting from our thoughts or beliefs leads to a negative response from others, our thoughts and beliefs may still get strengthened or reinforced. For example, if our thoughts and beliefs lead us to criminal conduct, the outside world punishes us. This might just reinforce our inside-the-mind belief that "people are out to get me."

Our thoughts, feelings or beliefs may not always result in an action or behavior. When our inside-the-mind responses (thoughts, beliefs) do lead to an action or behavior, then that action or behavior may be reinforced or strengthened. That is, the behavior will repeat itself under the same situations. The behavior is learned. But, how does this learning take place? How do our actions get reinforced or strengthened? Let us look at this.

## 3. The rules of how behaviors or actions are learned:

Once an action response takes place, one of several things can occur. First, the behavior may never repeat itself. Second, the behavior may repeat itself, but not on any steady basis or in any consistent pattern. Third, the behavior may form a pattern or what we call a **behavior habit or action habit.** This is comparable to a thought pattern or what we have called automatic thoughts.

In the last session, we learned the rules that decide how our thoughts, feelings and beliefs get strengthened to form thought patterns. There are also rules that decide or govern how our actions or behaviors are strengthened or reinforced and form habits or behavior patterns. These three rules are described below and pictured in Figure 3.

a. **Learning Rule I—Turning on positive events:** If a behavior turns on something positive such as a pleasant feeling or a sense of well-being, that behavior gets reinforced. It will repeat itself. It may become a habit. This is the *warm fuzzy* rule. When an action or response turns on a warm fuzzy, that response gets reinforced. If drinking alcohol makes us feel good or gives us "warm fuzzies," then drinking is reinforced. We will do it again to feel good.

b. **Learning Rule II—Turning off cold pricklies:** If a behavior turns off a "cold prickly"—something unpleasant, stress, pain, a negative event—that behavior gets reinforced and will be learned. It will become a habit. We will call this the *Cold Prickly Rule Number 1.* This is the most powerful way to reinforce or strengthen behavior. When we feel stress we drink. The stress goes away. This reinforces the drinking.

c. **Learning Principle III—Turning on negative events:** If a behavior turns on a cold prickly—an unpleasant event, pain, stress or something negative—that behavior is weakened, and will probably not occur at some point in the future. We will call this the *Cold Prickly Rule Number 2.* We drink too much. We get sick, have a severe headache or hangover. This rule says we should not drink again. We do. Why?

## Figure 3
### Three Rules of Learning Behavior

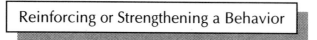

**Learning Rule I: Turning on Warm Fuzzies**

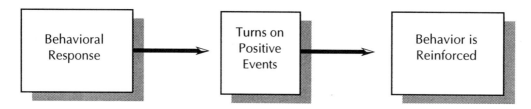

**Learning Rule II: Turning off Cold Pricklies**

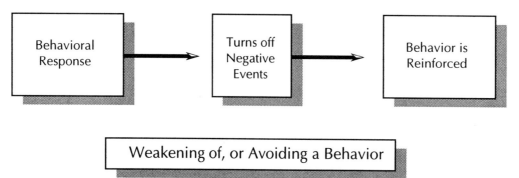

**Learning Rule III: Turning on Cold Pricklies**

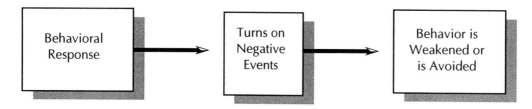

Learning Rule III doesn't always work. Why do people continue actions or behaviors which cause them a lot of pain and problems? Why would you drink to excess a second time if you had a seizure from drinking? Or if you are told that drinking is destroying your liver? Remember the power of Rules I and II above. The behaviors we do to turn on "warm fuzzies" or turn off "cold pricklies" give immediate reward even though those behaviors can lead to negative outcome or pain. This is true for actions that lead to quick rewards or pleasant events, or behaviors that take away strong negative or unpleasant experiences. The behavior that leads to a reward we get right away is very powerful. It even causes us to not think in a clear or rational manner.

You go to a bar to drink to "drown" your sorrows or worries. These sorrows are painful right now. You want relief right now. That is more important than knowing that you will have a hangover tomorrow. Or you may get a DUI tonight. You steal from a store to get a reward right away. This overrides the long-term outcome of being placed in jail.

There is another reason why *Learning Rule III* doesn't always work. The negative or bad results from a behavior also strengthen or reinforce our automatic thoughts and beliefs as shown in Figure 2. We get drunk. We let our family down. That may strengthen or reinforce our belief that "I'm no good." We will get drunk again just to support that old belief "I'm no good."

**4. How thinking and acting lead to the process of learning:**

Now, let's put together the puzzle of how thinking and acting lead to the learning of thinking patterns or habits (automatic thoughts) and behavior or action habits. Figure 4 gives us a picture of this process. Figure 4 is the same as Figure 2 up to the point of where the behavior or actions take place. Now, we do not say whether the behavior is positive or negative, good or bad. The action or behavior can be any response such as drinking, talking to a friend or committing a crime. It is what the behavior does for the person that counts. The behavior may turn **on** a warm fuzzy. It may turn **off** a cold prickly. It may turn on a cold prickly. The result of the first two is that the behavior is strengthened—or it is learned. It will occur again. It will become an action habit. But regardless of the outcome of the behavior—positive (adaptive) or negative (maladaptive), good or bad—the inside-the-mind stuff is reinforced or strengthened. The thought habits, the beliefs, the feelings, and the attitudes are strengthened. They are reinforced—they are learned. They become thought habits or automatic thoughts.

# NOTES:

_____

_____

_____

_____

_____

_____

_____

_____

**Figure 4**

**The Process of Cognitive and Behavioral Learning and Change**

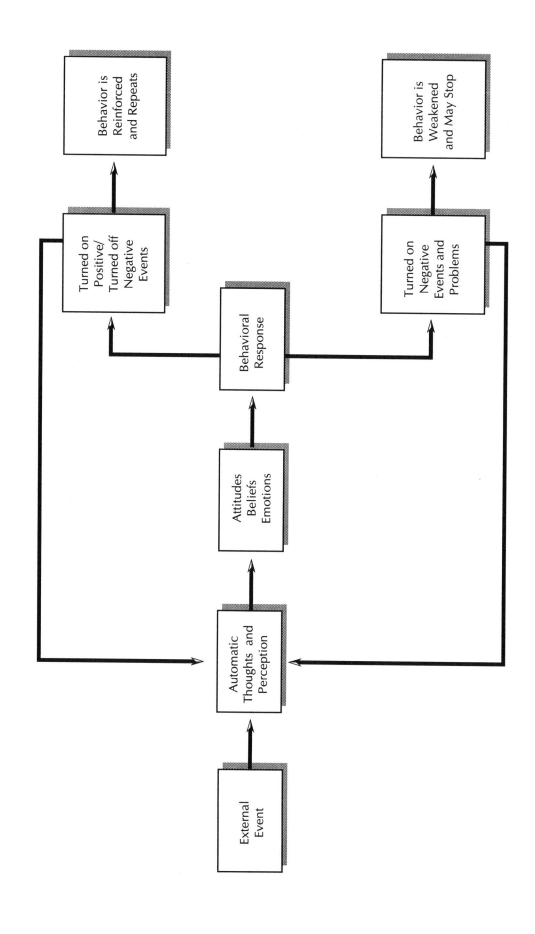

a. Complete the blank copy of Figure 4—Work Sheet 2. Give an external event, an automatic thought (thought habit), an underlying belief and related feelings and then a behavioral response (behavioral habit). Complete the whole figure. Your counselor will help you. Have it apply to something that happened to you.

b. Describe an event or circumstance that led to a positive or adaptive response and then record the thoughts, feelings and emotions around the positive results of the adaptive response.

_____

_____

_____

_____

_____

_____

_____

_____

_____

_____

_____

_____

_____

_____

_____

c. Read material for Session 7 in Workbook.

# WORK SHEET 2

## THE PROCESS OF COGNITIVE AND BEHAVIORAL LEARNING AND CHANGE

Complete this picture. Take an event that you recently experienced. Then note your automatic thoughts that came from that event. Then note your feelings and beliefs. What was your behavior? Fill in the rest of the squares.

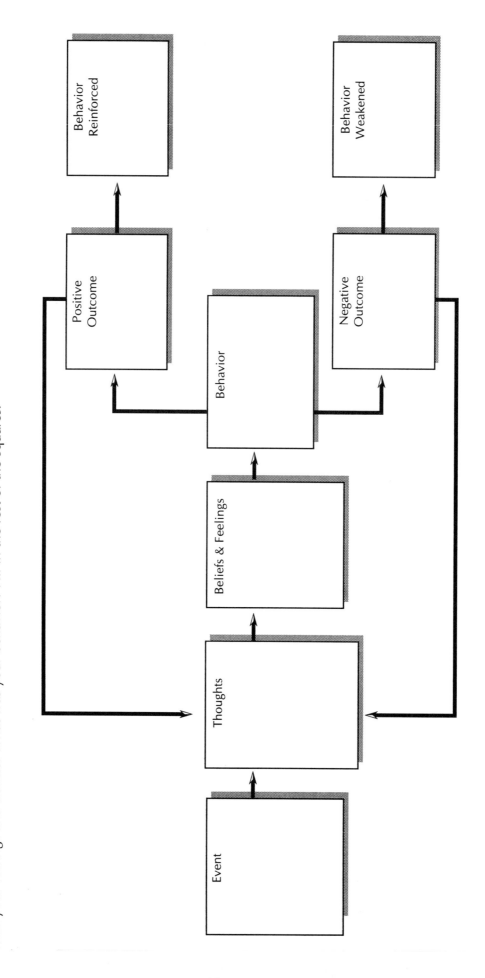

## Session ⑦ : Basic Knowledge About Drugs

### 1. Objectives of Session:

> ➨ Give your view of addiction;
>
> ➨ Learn some basic facts about alcohol and other drugs;
>
> ➨ Learn how alcohol affects the body.

### 2. For thought and discussion: What is and what causes alcohol and drug addiction?

### 3. Here are some basic things about drugs that people who have developed AOD problems need to know in order to make changes in their AOD use.

a. **About Drugs.**

1) **Definition of Drug:** A drug is a substance that changes or alters the way a person feels, thinks or acts.

2) **Drugs work because they have an effect on both the person's nervous system by changing the flow of electricity and the release of the body's natural nerve chemicals called neurochemicals.**

3) **There are two kinds of drugs: There are drugs that slow down the nervous system and there are drugs that speed up the working of the nerves.**

- Drugs that slow down the nervous system are called **suppressors**, sedatives or downers: alcohol, barbiturates, tranquilizers and opioids such as heroin.

- Drugs that speed up, excite or pick up the nervous system are called **enhancers**, stimulants or uppers. Some of these drugs speed up the body and mind: speed (amphetamines) and cocaine. Some of these drugs speed up only the mind: acid, PCP.

4) **Drugs have a direct and an indirect effect on people:**

- The direct effect (during use effect) is what happens when you are on the drug: may be physical (alcohol causes sleepiness); may be psychological (alcohol makes you feel good).

- The indirect effect is what happens after the drug is no longer in the body. The body reacts to its absence. This is the abstinence reaction to be discussed more below. Indirect effect of alcohol: unable to sleep. Direct effect of cocaine: unable to sleep.

5) **Different kinds of drugs will have different direct effects and different indirect (withdrawal) effects.**

- Direct effects of a drug will be different and usually the opposite of an indirect effect of a drug. When alcohol is in the blood, it slows down the nervous system (go to sleep). When it is gone, the nervous system speeds up and you might shake or can't sleep. When cocaine is in the body, the nerves speed up. When cocaine leaves the body, the nervous system slows down.

- Both the direct and indirect effects of a drug can cause problems.

- Table 1 provides the direct and indirect effects from the two different types or classes of drugs.

## Table 1

### Two Classes of Drugs With Their Direct and Indirect Effects

| SYSTEM SUPPRESSORS OR DEPRESSANTS | SYSTEM ENHANCERS (STIMULANTS) | |
|---|---|---|
| | MENTAL–ENHANCERS | MENTAL–PHYSICAL |

| SYSTEM SUPPRESSORS OR DEPRESSANTS | MENTAL–ENHANCERS | MENTAL–PHYSICAL |
|---|---|---|
| Alcohol | Cannabis | Amphetamines |
| Sedatives (Barbiturates) | Hallucinogens (speed) | Cocaine |
| Inhalants (small amounts) | Phencyclidine (PCP) | Caffeine |
| Opioids (heroin) | MDMA (Ecstasy) | |
| Tranquilizers | | |

### Direct Effects

- drowsiness
- slurred speech
- lack of motor coordination
- confusion
- aggressive actions
- poor work performance
- auto accident
- driving while intoxicated
- decrease of social & interpersonal involvement
- depression

### Indirect Effects

- hyper and excited
- stimulation
- agitation & irritability
- hallucinations/delusions
- anxiety, fear, panic
- shakes and tremors
- unable to sleep (insomnia)
- interpersonal impairment
- work impairment
- decreased responsibility to others

### Direct Effects

- insomnia
- weight loss
- tremors
- hyperactivity
- panic
- poor work performance
- hallucinations/delusions
- aggressive actions
- inappropriate social & interpersonal behavior
- stimulation

### Indirect Effects

- sedation and slowness
- depression
- fatigue
- guilt
- indifference, lethargy
- body slows down
- sleeping too much
- interpersonal impairment
- work impairment
- decreased responsibility to others

6) **When drugs are taken, they make the body toxic:**

Drugs toxify or poison the body. When the drug ("drug" also includes alcohol) has been in the body for a time, the body has to detoxify when the drug leaves the body. This can cause a shock to the body. We call this the abstinence reaction or withdrawal. Sometimes this reaction is only mental; often it is a direct physical response of the body. It can be dangerous. The reaction can be so strong that the nervous system can have a very strong shock even to the point where it will result in an epileptic seizure.

7) **Your tolerance for drugs can increase and you can become physically and psychologically dependent on drugs:**

As you use certain drugs, you may need more and more of the drug to get the same reaction; or you may find that the same amount of drug will give you less of what you expect from the drug. This is what we call tolerance. It varies from drug to drug. Where two drinks may have brought on a "buzz" or a feeling of relaxation, after some time of using alcohol, you may find that you need three drinks to get the same "buzz" or to feel the same amount of relaxation. A daily quart of vodka may be required to get the same effect as once did a half pint of vodka. You may need as much as ten times the amount of some narcotics (heroin) to get the same effect. This is one reason why people get dependent on drugs.

*You may need more of the drug to get the same reaction.*

8) **Mixing two drugs in the body at the same time may increase the strength of one or both drugs. We call this drug interaction.**

A drug may get stronger because another drug is in the body. This can be very dangerous. The presence of alcohol and a barbiturate in the body at the same time lowers the fatal dose of the barbiturate by 50 percent.

**b. About alcohol:**

Because alcohol is one of the most commonly used drugs, we will look at some specific facts about alcohol.

1) Alcohol is a sedative-hypnotic drug: it puts you to sleep. It is a system suppressor—a downer.

2) Alcohol per drink: One drink equals about one-half ounce (12 grams) of pure alcohol. One drink is:

   a) a 12-ounce can of beer;

   b) a 4-ounce glass of wine;

   c) one mixed drink: one ounce of 80 proof (40 percent pure alcohol) or one half ounce of pure alcohol.

3) Alcohol in the body is measured through the Blood Alcohol Concentration (BAC). BAC is the percentage of alcohol in the body. A BAC of .10 means that you have one tenth of one percent of alcohol in your body. That doesn't sound like much, but look below:

4) Our response to different BAC levels:

    a) .02-.03: Feel relaxed and decreased judgment;

    b) .05: not walk normally; decreased judgment; perform poorly; in Colorado legally impaired.

    c) .08: Definite driving impaired; legally drunk in some states.

    d) .10: Clearly not able to function normally; lack of muscle control; poor coordination; poor judgment; decreased emotional control. This is legally drunk.

    e) .15: more severe impairment as in d) above; 25 times more likely to have fatal accident.

    f) .20: all of the above including amnesia, blackouts; 100 times more likely to have fatal accident.

    g) .30: most will lose consciousness or pass out;

    h) .40: almost all will lose consciousness;

    i) .45-.60: fatal for most people.

5) The level of BAC depends on the weight of the person, the number of drinks and the length of time over which these drinks are taken. Table 2 provides the approximate information for number of drinks within three time periods which will result in either a .05 or a .09 BAC. This table is generalized to men and women. Table 3 provides information regarding approximate number of hours from the first drink to a zero BAC based on varying number of drinks for both men and women.

## Table 2

**Blood Alcohol Concentration (BAC) Levels by Body Weight, Hours Over Which the Person Drinks and Number of Drinks (men and women will vary)**

| BAC based on number of drinks and body weight | | | | | | | | |
|---|---|---|---|---|---|---|---|---|
| Number of hours of drinking | 120 lbs | | 140 lbs | | 160 lbs | | 180 lbs | |
| | BAC | | BAC | | BAC | | BAC | |
| | .05 | .09 | .05 | .09 | .05 | .09 | .05 | .09 |
| One hour | 2* | 4 | 2 | 4 | 3 | 5 | 3 | 5 |
| Two hours | 3 | 5 | 3 | 5 | 4 | 6 | 4 | 6 |
| Three hours | 4 | 6 | 4 | 6 | 5 | 7 | 5 | 7 |

*refers to number of drinks for time period

## Table 3

### Approximate Hours from First Drink to Zero BAC Levels—for men

| Number of drinks | Your weight in pounds | | | | | | | |
|---|---|---|---|---|---|---|---|---|
| | 120 | 140 | 160 | 180 | 200 | 220 | 240 | 260 |
| 1 | 2* | 2 | 2 | 1.5 | 1 | 1 | 1 | 1 |
| 2 | 4 | 3.5 | 3 | 3 | 2.5 | 2 | 2 | 2 |
| 3 | 8 | 5 | 4.5 | 4 | 3.5 | 3.5 | 3 | 3 |
| 4 | 8 | 7 | 6 | 5.5 | 5 | 4.5 | 4 | 3.5 |
| 5 | 10 | 8.5 | 7.5 | 8.5 | 6 | 5.5 | 5 | 4.5 |

*refers to number of hours before reaching a BAC of zero

### Approximate Hours from First Drink to Zero BAC Levels—for women

| Number of drinks | Your weight in pounds | | | | | | | |
|---|---|---|---|---|---|---|---|---|
| | 120 | 140 | 160 | 180 | 200 | 220 | 240 | 260 |
| 1 | 3 | 2.5 | 2 | 2 | 2 | 1.5 | 1.5 | 1 |
| 2 | 6 | 5 | 4 | 4 | 3.5 | 3 | 3 | 2.5 |
| 3 | 9 | 7.5 | 6.5 | 5.5 | 5 | 4.5 | 4 | 4 |
| 4 | 12 | 9.5 | 8.5 | 7.5 | 6.5 | 6 | 5.5 | 5 |
| 5 | 15 | 12 | 10.5 | 9.5 | 8 | 7.5 | 7 | 6 |

*refers to number of hours before reaching a BAC of zero

6) Alcohol dissolves in water. About 98 percent is broken down in the digestive system; 2 percent leaves the body through the breath and urine.

7) An average drink of one half ounce pure alcohol has about 80 to 90 calories. Four drinks make up 325 calories based on pure alcohol. One beer, one glass of wine or one mixed drink can give the body about 200 calories.

8) Drinkers are often classified based on the amount of alcohol used on one occasion:

    a) Light drinker: one drink.

    b) Moderate drinker: two to three drinks.

    c) Heavy drinker: four to five drinks.

    d) Excessive drinker: six or more.

9) The frequency of drinking is often classified as follows:

    a) Infrequent: Less than one time a month;

    b) Occasional: Less than one time a week;

    c) Frequent: One to three times a week;

    d) Consistent: Four to five times a week;

    e) Daily/sustained: six to seven times a week.

10) What type of drinker have you been? Find this out by putting together how often you drank with the amount you drank. For example, if you drank two to three drinks one to three times a week, you would be classified as a Frequent-Moderate drinker.

11) You will get more drunk and have less control over alcohol if you weigh less, are female, have no food in the body, have little sleep, drink over a longer period of time and are relaxed. A person who has been drinking for several years and who has had six or seven drinks may not look drunk or intoxicated but may have a BAC of .10. This is due to what we call behavioral tolerance.

12) Impact on the body:

**Liver:** The liver can become diseased when there is a buildup of fatty tissue in the liver. Fatty tissue separates the cells. Fatty tissue builds up when you drink a lot or even moderate amounts a day. When fatty tissue separates the cells, less blood gets to the cells. The cells die. This leads to what we call cirrhosis. This is the replacing of dead liver cells with scar tissue. Drinking more than six drinks per day will increase the risk of liver disease and cirrhosis.

**Your stomach and digestive organs:** Alcohol irritates the stomach lining and this can lead to development of ulcers. This can occur in moderate to heavy drinkers, depending on how vulnerable the person is to stomach ulcers. This risk increases if alcohol is used with other stomach irritants such as aspirin.

**Your heart and blood system:** Heavy to excessive amounts of alcohol, particularly associated with smoking, can increase risk of heart problems and can increase blood pressure. One to two drinks a day will most likely not increase risk of heart problems or high blood pressure.

**Our brain and nerves:** Heavy to excessive amounts of alcohol can hurt the brain and our body nerves. The brain has a way of blocking alcohol from getting to it if the alcohol amount is small. This is the blood brain barrier. But several drinks can break this barrier. When this barrier is broken, the brain cells may be hurt or damaged by the alcohol. Excessive drinking can damage nerve cells in all parts of the body. Excessive drinking can damage the nerve cells in the hands, feet and other body extremities noted by the tingling of the fingers and feet.

13) Breaking down the alcohol: The body breaks down the alcohol. We call this the metabolism of alcohol. The breakdown of alcohol depends on gender and body fat. A person with a lot of body fat will break down alcohol at a slower rate. That person may actually end up with a higher blood alcohol concentration (BAC). Table 3 shows that if a heavier person drinks the same as a lighter person, the heavier person may have a lower percent of alcohol in his or her blood. But, if the heavier person has more body fat, the heavier person may end up with a higher BAC level. The person with high body fat may also have a greater risk of alcohol damaging or harming the body. Because women have a higher percentage of body fat, they may be at more risk for developing physical problems from drinking.

14) The frequent-heavy to frequent-excessive drinker has a much higher risk of alcohol harming the body.

## Homework assignment:

a. Read the material for Session 8.

b. Complete the Drug Knowledge Test in the Workbook.

**DRUG KNOWLEDGE TEST (To be completed as part of homework)**

Answer true or false for each of the following questions:

T    F    1. Alcohol is a stimulant.

T    F    2. Cocaine is a stimulant.

T    F    3. When you come off of alcohol, you are relaxed.

T    F    4. Alcohol is not a drug.

T    F    5. Most drugs speed people up.

T    F    6. The indirect effect of a drug is usually just the opposite of its direct effect.

T    F    7. Tolerance is when you need more of the drug to get the same feeling.

T    F    8. If you drink when you have another sedative in you, you will probably get drunker.

T    F    9. One can of beer, one glass of wine and one mixed drink will have the same amount of pure alcohol.

T    F    10. If you have a Blood Alcohol Concentration of .10 you are legally drunk.

T    F    11. A heavier person can always drink more and get less drunk than a lighter person.

T    F    12. A light drinker is one who drinks about four or five drinks a day.

T    F    13. You need to drink about 10 drinks a day before alcohol will damage your body.

T    F    14. If you have a Blood Alcohol Concentration of .20, you are twice as likely to have a fatal accident.

T    F    15. Drugs which change your moods, thinking or actions make the body toxic.

# NOTES:

## Session ⑧: Understanding Alcohol and Other Drug (AOD) Addiction

### 1. Objectives of Session:

> ➠ Learn about two paths or ways that lead people to become addicted to drugs and see how these two pathways lead to the cycles of addiction. These two paths and their addiction cycles are based on the principles of cognitive-behavioral learning and change taught in Sessions 5 and 6.
>
> 1) The mental-behavioral cycle;
>
> 2) The mental-physical cycle.
>
> ➠ See these two pathways and their cycles of addiction fit you. If so, how?

### 2. Pathways to the addiction cycles:

We will first look at two different paths that lead to two cycles of addiction. Then we will see how these fit your own use of drugs and your drug addictions.

#### a. The mental-behavioral addiction cycle:

We saw in Figure 3 of Session 6 of this Module two ways that people learn behavior (Learning Rules I and II). If we **expect** that something we do (behavior) will make us feel good, and it does, then we will do it again. If we **expect** that a behavior will take away something unpleasant (stress, tension), and it does, we will do it again. Figure 5 shows us how drug use fits this learning idea.

If a person expects something positive to come from using a drug and this happens, then AOD use is strengthened and will repeat itself. It becomes a behavior habit. The positive things might be feeling relaxed, feeling "on top of the world," emotional and sexual pleasures, or improved thinking.

Second, if a person expects a drug to shut down or turn off or decrease unpleasant or negative life experiences, and this does happen, then the use of that drug is strengthened and will repeat itself. Again, AOD use becomes a behavior habit. Such unpleasant things might be stress, unpleasant memories, job or marital problems, or the bad results from using the drug itself. In this way, the person uses a drug to cope with or handle the stress of life.

## Figure 5

### The Mental-Behavioral Pathway for Learning AOD Use Behavior: Reinforcing or Strengthening Drug Use Behavior

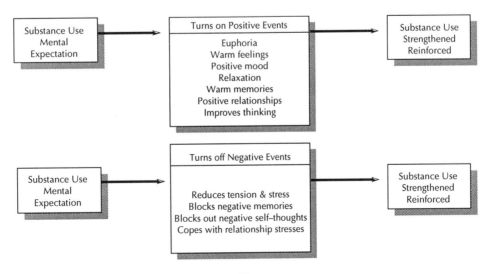

53

**Mental-behavior addiction cycle:** The pathway pictured in Figure 5 can lead to the mental-behavior addiction cycle pictured in Figure 6.

Our life situation (Point A in Figure 6) leads to a need or desire to increase pleasure or decrease discomfort. We expect that drug use will do this for us. So we use a drug (Point B). The outcome is as we expect: we find an increase in pleasure or decrease in discomfort (coping). The use of the drug is strengthened or reinforced (Point C). Most people never go beyond the Point A to C path. This path, however, can lead to the addiction cycle. Let us look at this cycle.

For some people, as a result of using a drug to feel good or to not feel bad, the use of the drug causes them problems (Point D). Now there is a need to cope with the problems and stress that comes from drug use itself. What's the best way to do this? Use more drugs (Point E of Figure 6). This just leads to further problems and stress from drug use (Point F). You use drugs to handle these problems (Point G) resulting from this further use. The life situation problems not AOD related continue to occur, and the individual now needs to use drugs to deal with those problems, plus problems resulting from AOD use. This completes the addiction cycle.

Example: You stop off at the bar to have a few beers to handle your life problems. This works for you. One day, you get arrested for driving while intoxicated. You get convicted. Now, you find a great amount of stress from getting a DUI. You find that one way you can handle the stress is to drink. You have always drunk to handle your problems. So now you drink to handle the problem that came from drinking. This drinking leads to further problems. Now you drink to handle the problems that came from drinking. You also drink to handle your life problems. This is the addiction cycle.

Some get help at Point D in Figure 6 when the first problems from AOD use start. Others wait until the problems begin to build up. Still others wait until they are so deep into the addiction cycle that AOD use becomes their way of life. Now, the person uses drugs because he or she uses drugs. An old proverb sums it up: "A man takes the drink. The drink takes the drink. Then the drink takes the man."

b. **The mental-physical addiction cycle:**

You may use a drug—such as alcohol—for its direct effect—to relax and to reduce mental and body stress. But when the drug goes out of your body, the indirect effect or withdrawal from the drug is just the opposite. For alcohol, the indirect results would be stress, agitation, anxiety and mental and body tension. But that's why you may have drunk to begin with—to get rid of tension and stress. We call this the REBOUND from the result of using the drug. Now you may drink to "cure" the symptoms or rebound coming from withdrawal from drinking. Mentally, you expect the drug to do this. Physically and chemically, it does do this. Now you may be using the drug only for the purpose of "curing" the discomfort of the rebound or withdrawal from use. To maintain a balance in body tension, you must continue to drink. This is addiction. Or, you may have to stop using the drug long enough to work through the distressful condition of withdrawal, and develop a drug-free state of balance. This is the first step of treatment.

This mental-physical cycle can be applied to other drugs such as cocaine. The direct results of cocaine are hyperness, stimulation, agitation and tension. When the drug goes out of the body, the rebound or withdrawal process results in depression and tiredness. You crash. How do you deal with the rebound (crash)? Take more cocaine. The cocaine addicted person begins to use cocaine to "cure" the rebound from its use. **In simple terms, mental-physical addiction is using the drug to "cure" the mental and physical pain from rebound or withdrawal from the drug. The user expects this. The addiction cycle is reinforced. This is pictured in Figure 7.**

# Figure 6
## Mental-Behavioral Addiction Cycle

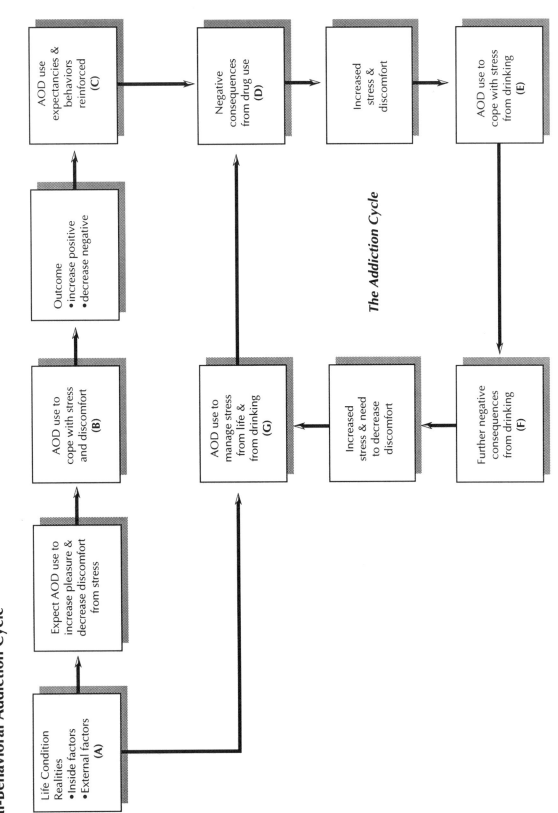

Adapted from Wanberg/Wanberg, (1974, 1990).

55

# Figure 7

**Mental-Physical Addiction**

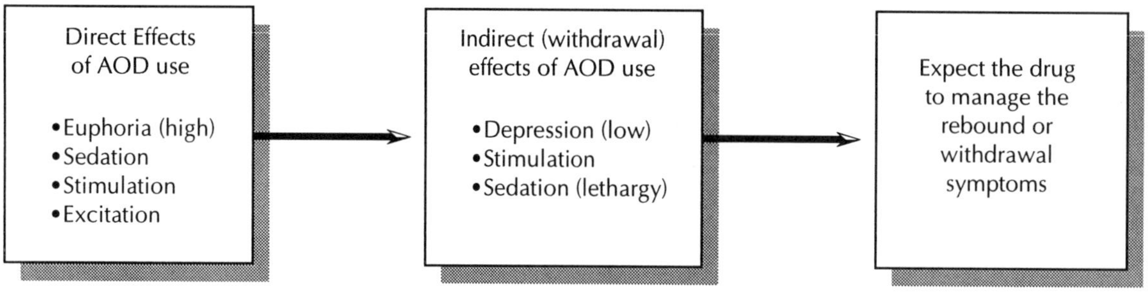

| Direct Effects of AOD use | Indirect (withdrawal) effects of AOD use | Expect the drug to manage the rebound or withdrawal symptoms |
|---|---|---|
| • Euphoria (high)<br>• Sedation<br>• Stimulation<br>• Excitation | • Depression (low)<br>• Stimulation<br>• Sedation (lethargy) | |

**Direct Effects:** _____

_____

_____

**Indirect Effects:** _____

_____

_____

**Manage Withdrawal:** _____

_____

_____

## Homework assignments:

a. Think about your own drinking and drug use pattern. How does your pattern fit Figure 6? How about Figure 7? Can you see yourself fitting these cycles? Use Figure 6 as a Work Sheet to identify the specific ways you fit the various rectangles in the figure. For example, what are your life conditions or problems that lead you to drink alcohol or use other drugs (Rectangle A in Figure 6)? Write down under the rectangle what these are. For example, are they not being happy in your job, not being able to pay your bills, etc.? For point B in Figure 6, what is your pattern of AOD use that you get into which helps you cope with your life stresses or problems? Continue to follow the cycle and write down how you fit each of the points in the Figure 6. Do the same with Figure 7. Take one drug that you use, such as alcohol. Identify for yourself what are the direct results of alcohol use (first block in Figure 7), what withdrawal or indirect results (second block) and how you use alcohol to manage the results of withdrawal, such as drinking in the morning.

b. Read the material in the workbook for Session 9 to prepare for the next session.

# Session ❾: Understanding Criminal Conduct and the Influence of Drugs

## 1. Objectives of Session:

> ➡ Understand the thinking patterns that lead to our criminal conduct;
>
> ➡ Understand the criminal conduct and offender cycles;
>
> ➡ Understand the relationship between criminal conduct and AOD use and abuse.

## 2. Review of the AOD addiction cycle:

We have seen that AOD use and abuse are learned behaviors. These behaviors are responses to our outside world and what goes on inside of us. We expect that alcohol and other drugs will help us cope with life problems and the stress and discomfort resulting from these problems. Our AOD use expectations and behaviors get strengthened and reinforced when AOD does help us deal with the problems and stresses of living. However, at some point in the individual AOD user's life, AOD use produces negative consequences—problems in living. It is when the individual begins to engage in AOD use to cope with the problems from use that the AOD addiction cycle begins.

## 3. Understanding criminal conduct and the offender cycle:

Just as with AOD use, criminal conduct is also learned. Engaging in criminal behavior is a way that some people handle events of their outside world and the world inside their mind. Just as with AOD use, our criminal conduct can turn on positive feelings and events, or it can turn off stress and unpleasant events. Thus, our criminal conduct, and our expectations and thoughts that lead to criminal conduct, get reinforced. They form thought habits (automatic thoughts) and action habits (behavioral patterns). Just as irresponsible AOD use will lead to negative consequences, irresponsible actions in the community such as criminal conduct will lead to negative consequences.

Negative consequences or punishment resulting from criminal conduct can weaken or even stop the behavior. But, it can also strengthen this behavior because it reinforces the internal automatic thoughts and beliefs of the individual. For example, being punished for a crime may just reinforce the person's belief that "nothing is fair," or "the world is out to get me." Just as with AOD use, the individual will engage in criminal conduct to cope with the negative consequences and stress that come from criminal conduct itself.

*Being punished for a crime may reinforce the person's belief that "nothing is fair."*

### a. What is criminal conduct?

Criminal conduct represents thinking, feelings and actions that put a person at risk of becoming a focus of the attention of adult criminal and juvenile justice professionals.

1) From a **legal view**, it is an act not allowed by a city, state or nation and is punishable by law;

2) From a **moral view**, it goes against the norms of a religion or a belief of what people see as right or wrong;

3) From a **social view**, it is an act that goes against the customs and traditions of the community and is punishable by the community;

4) From a **psychological view**, it is antisocial in that it brings pain and loss to others but is rewarding to the criminal.

b. **What can lead a person into criminal conduct? Past risk factors:**

There are things that happen to people in their past that can increase their risk of being involved in criminal conduct. These are the first six things listed in Work Sheet 3 below. Check whether they were no risk, low, moderate or high risk for you. These are things you can't change. But we can understand them. We can change our thoughts, beliefs and attitudes about them.

c. **What are the present risk factors that lead to criminal conduct?**

What happens to people in their present life that brings them to be involved in criminal conduct? We call these dynamic risk factors. They are also called criminogenic needs. Work Sheet 3 below provides a list of these risk factors from the present. For each risk factor, check whether it is no risk, low, moderate or high risk for you. Are there others not listed in the Work Sheet? These are things that you can change.

d. **Errors in thinking can lead to criminal conduct:**

Errors in thinking are thought-habits or automatic thoughts that can lead to criminal conduct. They are required by the person with a history of criminal conduct to live a criminal life. They distort the true reality of living, but they are also basic to criminal conduct. Work Sheet 4 gives us a list of these errors. Check how they apply to you.

e. **The criminal conduct cycle:**

Just as with AOD use and abuse, there is a cycle of criminal conduct (CC). Sometimes we call this the Offender Cycle. By taking part in criminal activities, the cycle gets reinforced (thought habits and action habits form around this cycle). Figure 8 provides a picture of this cycle. Even though people will differ as to particular thinking and action responses in this cycle, this cycle will apply to most people who engage in criminal conduct. You will go over this cycle carefully in your session. Here is what is important:

1) Before criminal acts take place, there are mental reactions to our outside world and the world inside our minds;

2) People who become involved in CC choose to do so; they make a conscious choice as to the type of criminal conduct and who they will victimize;

3) Once a criminal act takes place, it sets off new mental reactions which make the criminal thinking stronger;

4) When the mental reactions to the criminal act become stronger, then the criminal conduct is made stronger. The criminal conduct is reinforced.

**You change or correct this cycle in three ways:**

*First,* correction and change takes place in your mental reactions to the what happens outside of you. You can replace your criminal thinking with what we call **prosocial thinking**. This is positive social action. This is thinking that says "I want to follow the laws of society. I want to be a positive part of my community."

*Second,* you can change or correct your actions. You can choose to do something different. You can use actions that are not criminal conduct.

*Third,* you can make changes in the events or things outside of you that set off the criminal actions. For example, you can avoid situations that are high risk for being involved in criminal conduct. We would call these preventive measures. However, we are not able to shelter ourselves from all outside and inside events which lead to mental reactions that lead to criminal conduct.

# Figure 8

## The Criminal Conduct and Corrective Behavior Cycles

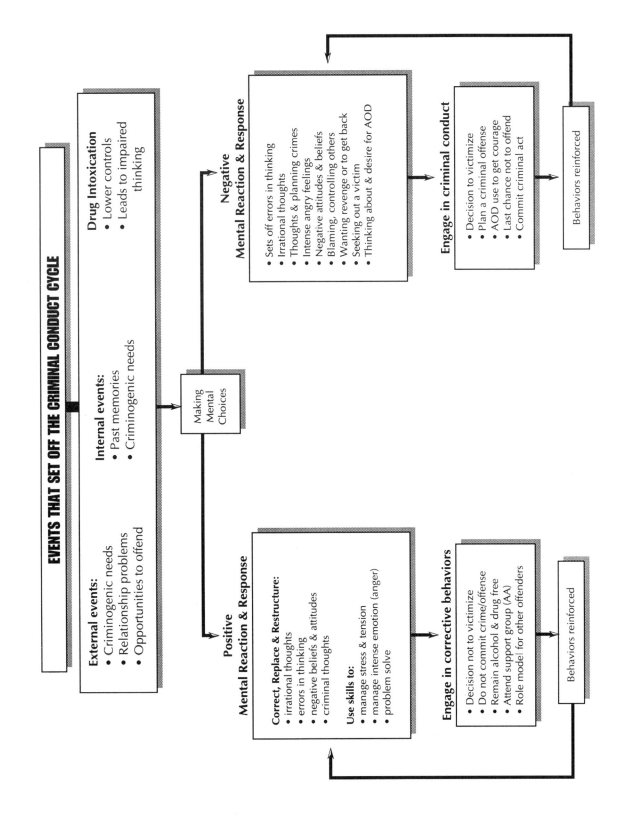

### EVENTS THAT SET OFF THE CRIMINAL CONDUCT CYCLE

**External events:**
- Criminogenic needs
- Relationship problems
- Opportunities to offend

**Internal events:**
- Past memories
- Criminogenic needs

**Drug Intoxication**
- Lower controls
- Leads to impaired thinking

Making Mental Choices

**Negative**
**Mental Reaction & Response**

- Sets off errors in thinking
- Irrational thoughts
- Thoughts & planning crimes
- Intense angry feelings
- Negative attitudes & beliefs
- Blaming, controlling others
- Wanting revenge or to get back
- Seeking out a victim
- Thinking about & desire for AOD

**Engage in criminal conduct**

- Decision to victimize
- Plan a criminal offense
- AOD use to get courage
- Last chance not to offend
- Commit criminal act

Behaviors reinforced

**Positive**
**Mental Reaction & Response**

**Correct, Replace & Restructure:**
- irrational thoughts
- errors in thinking
- negative beliefs & attitudes
- criminal thoughts

**Use skills to:**
- manage stress & tension
- manage intense emotion (anger)
- problem solve

**Engage in corrective behaviors**

- Decision not to victimize
- Do not commit crime/offense
- Remain alcohol & drug free
- Attend support group (AA)
- Role model for other offenders

Behaviors reinforced

Remember: what is most important is that true change and self-correction comes when you handle the mental reactions. Change comes when you change your thinking and beliefs. Change comes when you learn the skills that will help you to choose positive social actions.

f. **Relationship between the Addiction Cycle and the Criminal Conduct Cycle:**

Alcohol and other drug use feeds into and makes stronger the criminal behavior and the criminal conduct cycle. It can do this in these ways:

*Alcohol and other drug use feeds into and makes stronger the criminal behavior and the criminal conduct cycle.*

1) Alcohol and other drugs may be part of the events that set off criminal thinking. AOD intoxication lowers self-control, stops good judgment and gets us into irrational beliefs and errors of thinking;

2) Drugs are often a part of situations of high risk for criminal activity;

3) AOD use and influence can stop the person from using positive and corrective mental activities. It can block the use of skills to stop relapse and recidivism. It can cause the person to pass up self-correction;

4) AOD use and intoxication can strengthen errors in thinking which excuse criminal conduct. They can prevent the person from having fear and guilt before committing the criminal act. They can block fear and guilt, which should follow a criminal act.

## Classroom or homework assignments:

a. Complete Work Sheets 3 and 4

b. Read material for Module 4.

# NOTES:

_____

_____

_____

_____

_____

_____

_____

# WORK SHEET 3

## RATING SELF ON RISK FACTORS
## CHECK OR RATE THE RISK FACTORS AS TO HOW THEY APPLY TO YOU.

| RISK FACTORS FROM THE PAST | NONE | LOW | MODERATE | HIGH |
|---|---|---|---|---|
| Involved in juvenile delinquency | | | | |
| Disruptive family development | | | | |
| Poor school adjustment/school failure | | | | |
| Early use of alcohol/other drugs | | | | |
| Involved with delinquent friends | | | | |
| Rejected by average peers/classmates | | | | |

| RISK FACTORS IN THE PRESENT | NONE | LOW | MODERATE | HIGH |
|---|---|---|---|---|
| Antisocial/criminal friends/peers | | | | |
| Have criminal role models | | | | |
| Self-centered thinking | | | | |
| Criminal thinking | | | | |
| Criminal beliefs | | | | |
| Lack social/relationship skills | | | | |
| Have angry/aggressive attitude | | | | |
| Have angry/aggressive feelings | | | | |
| Act on the spur of the moment | | | | |
| Don't have family closeness | | | | |
| Go against authority/rebellious | | | | |
| Get rewards through doing crimes | | | | |
| Blame others for your actions | | | | |
| Lack of good moral thinking | | | | |

# WORK SHEET 4

## ERRORS IN THINKING CHECKLIST
## CHECK LIST FOR YOUR USE IN THESE ERRORS IN THINKING.

| ERRORS IN THINKING | DON'T USE | USE SOMETIMES | USE A LOT | USE ALL THE TIME |
|---|---|---|---|---|
| Power thrust: Put people down | | | | |
| Seeing things only your way | | | | |
| Blaming others: Victim stance | | | | |
| Feel superior to others | | | | |
| Lack concern for how others affected | | | | |
| Think; can't trust anybody | | | | |
| Refuse something you don't want to do | | | | |
| Want what you want right now | | | | |
| Take what you want from others | | | | |
| Refuse to lean on other people | | | | |
| Put off things to tomorrow | | | | |
| I don't have to do that | | | | |
| Won't change your ideas | | | | |
| Think in black and white terms | | | | |
| Mountains out of molehills | | | | |
| Feel singled out | | | | |
| Think: They deserve it | | | | |
| Think: I feel screwed | | | | |
| Tune out what you should hear | | | | |
| Think about forbidden things | | | | |
| Demand from others but don't give | | | | |
| Thinking about criminal things | | | | |
| Lying or exaggerating the truth | | | | |

# MODULE
# 4

## Self-Disclosure and Receiving Feedback:

## Pathways to Self-Awareness and Change

# MODULE 4: SELF-DISCLOSURE AND RECEIVING FEEDBACK: PATHWAYS TO SELF-AWARENESS AND CHANGE

## What this Module is about:

Self-awareness—being aware of ourselves—is a key to opening the door to change our thinking, feelings and actions. There are two pathways to self-awareness. One is through self-disclosure—sharing and disclosing our personal experiences and problems. The other is to have others give us feedback—which is having others tell us what they see and feel about what we have shared and disclosed.

Self-disclosure is not easy since during much of our lives we have been told to not talk about our feelings and problems. Or, if we did express our feelings and thoughts, we often were put down or even punished for what we said. Often we were told not to get angry or to be happy when we were sad. If we did show our feelings, it was after we stored them up and then they came out by "blowing up" or throwing a tantrum or we would just pout and get sullen.

Also during our years of childhood and youth, we most likely were not taught ways to tell our thoughts or show our feelings in healthy ways. We were often taught to blame others, since that is the way most adults solve their frustrations and problems. Or, we learned to solve problems by someone being right and someone being wrong. We still hold on to the old ways of showing our feelings and thoughts by losing our temper when upset, or by getting depressed when we don't get our way.

In this program of self-improvement and change, we want you to talk about yourself, express your feelings and thoughts, explore your past and present feelings, explore your thoughts and actions and tell us your story.

Being open to getting feedback from others is also difficult. Most of the time, what we get from people is not feedback but is a reaction to what we have done. It is usually a judgment of us. Telling us we are wrong. Blaming us for something. Feedback is most helpful when people make it clear that this is how they see us. They make it clear that it is their view of us. It is their opinion. We listen to feedback when people relate to us and not just react to what we say or do. We listen to feedback when we feel the other person understands us. When this happens, we learn about ourselves. We become more aware of who and what we are.

When you enter this program of self-improvement and change, you are saying "give me feedback about me. Tell me about me so that I can change." But the feedback will be given to you in a non-blaming manner. You will not be told you're right or wrong. The feedback is given to you to help you become more aware of yourself.

*We listen to feedback when we feel the other person understands us.*

## Goal and Objectives of this Module:

What we do in this part of the program will be one of the most difficult things you have done. The challenge is for you to become more self-aware. To do this, we want you to engage in an honest and open sharing about yourself. We want you to take the risk of receiving feedback as to how people see and experience you. We want you to look at yourself and then to talk about yourself. We want you to be open to learning about yourself from hearing how others see you. To meet this goal, we will help you to:

◆ Learn communication skills that will help you talk about yourself and to self-disclose;

◆ Learn communication skills that will get others to talk with you about themselves;

◆ Learn some tools on how to write down and record your thoughts and life experiences;

◆ Learn communication skills that will get others to talk with you about themselves;

◆ Look more deeply at your AOD use and involvement in criminal conduct;

◆ Be open to receiving feedback on how staff and other persons in the program see you and then make up your mind whether that feedback fits you.

This module will be your first step in this program to really talk about your drug and alcohol use and your past criminal thinking and conduct. Later in the program, you will look more deeply at these areas of your life.

## NOTES:

_____

_____

_____

_____

_____

_____

_____

_____

_____

# NOTES:

# MODULE 4: SELF-DISCLOSURE AND RECEIVING FEEDBACK: PATHWAYS TO SELF-AWARENESS AND CHANGE

## Session ⑩ : Learning Communication Tools and Skills

### 1. Objectives of Session:

> ⮕ Understand verbal and nonverbal communication;
>
> ⮕ Learn the process and tools of self-directed communication, or talking about yourself, and receiving feedback from others so as to encourage and increase self-disclosure and then self-awareness;
>
> ⮕ Look at the basic tools of other-oriented communication or getting others to talk to you and to have others be open to receiving feedback from you.

### 2. What we will learn in this session:

a. **Two kinds of communication that, as humans, we use in relating to others. They are nonverbal and verbal.**

1) Nonverbal communication is "talking" without words. We show it through our face, how we move our body and our hands, and in the tone of our voice. In this way we tell people what we think and feel. What we show by our "talking" without words (nonverbal communication) often is not the same as our talking with words (verbal communication). If we are to have people understand us, we must say the same thing with words that we say without words.

Think about how you might show these emotions without words—nonverbally.

ANGER  FEAR  SHAME  JOY  LOVE  SURPRISE

2) Verbal communication is talking with words. When using words to communicate, we need to check out if the other person is understanding us. Keep in mind that people have different opinions. Those opinions are based on how each of us sees the world. Most often, these opinions are not right or wrong. They are opinions. Clear and honest verbal communications help other people understand us. Clear and honest verbal communication will help us better understand our own thoughts, feelings and behaviors. Then we can change those thoughts and behaviors that are hurting us and others.

**OPINIONS are different from FACTS.** We can solve problems if we stick to the facts and hear the opinions of others. Sometimes the same words have different meanings, like "music" or "food." Sometimes different words have the same meaning, like "young man," "boy" and "lad." Opinions and facts have different meanings—that's why it is sometimes hard to communicate clearly.

*Verbal and nonverbal communication should say the same thing.*

### b. Developing self-awareness through self-oriented communication and other-oriented communication:

There are two ways that we direct ourselves in communicating with others: self-oriented communication and other-oriented communication. Both are important if you want to understand and be understood. You need skills to do both.

1) **Self-oriented communication:** This is communication about you. It is made up of two kinds of communication: self-disclosure and receiving feedback.

**Self-disclosure** involves talking about yourself and not the other person. It is sharing with someone—your counselor, your group—how you see your past and your current feelings, thoughts and actions. It is using the "I" message in communication. Your message is: "This is how I see myself," "this is what has happened to me," "I feel," "I think." Self-disclosure does three things. *These are keys to change.*

- It tells you about yourself. It is "you talking to yourself." You are disclosing to yourself. Thus, you are making yourself more aware.

- It allows others to see who you are and allows others to give you honest feedback on how they see you.

- It helps others to self-disclose to you.

Use the word "I" and not "you" in this kind of communication. When we start with the word "you" we are talking about the other person, and not about our own feelings and thoughts. When we are mad at someone, or in conflict, we use the word "you." We want to blame, tell the other person what he or she should do or did. Practice talking with others using only the word "I" and not the word "you."

**Receiving feedback** involves listening to someone as to how they see you. Feedback is less threatening if the other person makes you feel that this is only his or her opinion and is not necessarily true. What you really say is "Tell me about me." We will look at what makes up good feedback statements as we look at other-oriented communication below.

When we receive feedback from others, it is important that we want them to tell us how they see us. As well, we want to *not be defensive,* for when we get defensive, we stop the other person from sharing their views and thoughts about us. When feelings and emotions are high between two people, this is not always possible. The feedback becomes blaming and people get defensive. If you want feedback, you will want to try not to get defensive.

Look at the picture below (Figure 9). This provides a picture of self-oriented communication. When we self-disclose, we increase self-awareness and we also allow others to give us feedback about ourselves which also makes us more self-aware. Talk to a person close to you about this picture. How does it fit you?

**Figure 9**
**The Path to Talking and Learning About Self**

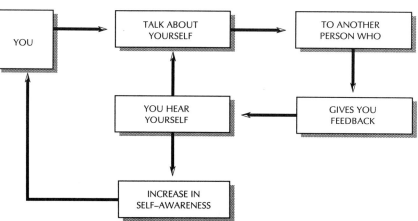

2) **Other-oriented communication:** This is getting people to talk to you and you share how you see them. You need two skills to do this:

- The open statement or open question skill: This encourages people to tell you about them. "Tell me how you feel." "How are you doing today?" Practice this each day.

- The feedback or reflective listening skill: "This is how I see you," or "I see you as upset." We call these reflective listening or active listening skills. We will focus more on this kind of communication in Module 9.

## Classroom or homework assignment:

a. Start talking with someone. Share a feeling about something. What are the other person's verbal and nonverbal responses to what you say? Now, write down:

1. Who was the person?_____

2. What was the feeling you shared? _____

_____

3. What did the other person say or do?_____

_____

_____

_____

4. What nonverbal behavior did the other person show?_____

_____

_____

b. Try to use only "I" messages for the coming week. Did you find yourself talking about the other person, and not about your feelings and thoughts about the other person? Did you find yourself using "you" messages more than the "I" messages?

c. Remember how many times you tried to defend yourself this week. Write down one time you tried to defend yourself. How could you have made it better by using the communication skills above?

_____

_____

_____

_____

_____

d. Read over material for Session 11.

# NOTES:

# Session ⑪ : Tools of Self-Disclosure: Autobiography, Thinking Reports, Journaling and Participating in the Reflection Group

## 1. Objectives of Session:

> ⮕ Review thought distortions or thinking errors;
>
> ⮕ Learn to use the autobiography, journals and thinking reports. These tools help us to be more aware of our thoughts, feelings, attitudes and beliefs.

## 2. What we will learn and experience in this session:

### a. Errors in thinking:

When we use errors in thinking or twisted thinking, our thinking is automatic. These are thoughts that we have in similar situations, like when you see your boss coming toward you and wonder if you are in trouble—again. Sometimes we use these thoughts, even though they are not based on fact. This may help us get through a hard time. This kind of thinking helps us deal with stress and problems. But sometimes our thinking errors cause us big problems. Once again, go back over Work Sheet 4 in Session 9 of Module 3.

### b. Our tools for directing change:

There are three important parts to our mental life: memories, mental responding to the here-and-now, and our dreams. It is through our *memories* that we construct our history—our autobiography. But memories come from the fabric of every-day experiences. So our memories will be set or determined by how we choose to live each day. We control our memories by how we choose to live. Yet, things happen to us beyond our control. But we always have a choice of how we handle what happens to us. So how we choose to handle what happens to us also will determine our memories.

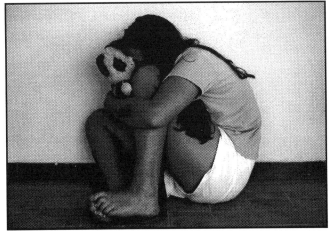

*Things happen to us beyond our control, but we choose how we handle what happens to us.*

Our journaling and thinking reports will capture our *mental responding to the here-and-now*. Three important parts of our mental responding to the here-and-now are thinking, feeling and speaking. These three help us to reason and learn. Reasoning and learning help us to organize our here-and-now. They are the glue that holds our mental life together.

Dreaming, setting goals, planning and hoping are the maps of living. But we make that map possible if we know where we have been (memory) and where we are now (mental responding to the here-and-now). Our journal and thinking reports help us keep track of our dreams.

#### 1) Your Autobiography:

We will write our autobiography over the next four weeks. This represents our history. It describes our roots and our past experiences. A tree stands on its roots and trunk. That is its history. We cannot stand in the present in any meaningful way without memory—without our history.

Not all of our history and our roots are pleasant. But it is important that we look at both the unpleasant and the pleasant, the negative parts as well as the positive parts of our history. This is why it is not easy to write your autobiography. But it is important in your effort for self-correction and change.

If you have already written your autobiography, you do not have to do it over. Read it again. But, as a result of our program thus far, you may have remembered some parts of your history that you did not recall when you first wrote your autobiography. You may find that parts of the autobiography we now want you to write were not part of the one you have already written. Then you are asked to add those parts to your own autobiography.

Here is the outline that we want you to follow:

   a) Describe the family you grew up in;

   b) Describe your childhood from first memories through your teen years;

   c) Describe your adult years including your education, jobs, marriage(s) and interests;

   d) Then, write a history of your criminal conduct, beginning with your first offense;

   e) Write a history of your AOD use beginning with your first use of alcohol or other drugs;

   f) Describe what brought you into this program.

**2) Your Journal:**

You will use your journal to write down your thoughts, feelings and actions on a daily or weekly basis. You might write on a particular day: "I had a good day at work." This will help us look at how we think and feel over time. It is helpful to include the following in each journal entry you make: the situation, your feelings and your thoughts and what you did in that situation. Did you handle it well? How would you have done it differently? It is important that you use your journal as a friend: "someone to talk to."

**3) Your Thinking Reports:**

A thinking report will help you to pay attention to your thoughts and actions. The first step in making changes in our lives is learning to pay attention to our own thinking. What are the things we say to ourselves? What is it that we feel moment to moment?

Here are the basic parts of the thinking report:

   • **Event:** Describe in a few words the situation; Be factual and describe what you see (or be objective): Do not write thoughts or feelings;

   • **Thoughts:** What thoughts do you remember? You do not have to explain or blame or condemn or make excuses;

   • **Feelings**: Make a list of all the feelings you had: Nervous, angry, irritated;

   • **Attitudes and Beliefs:** What attitudes and beliefs are related to this event?

   • **Outcome:** What was your action and behavior that came from this event and the thoughts, feelings, beliefs and attitudes that went into the whole event?

c. **You will receive two notebooks, one for your autobiography and one for your journal and thinking reports.**

a. Start your autobiography;

b. Write each evening one sentence as to how the day went for you. Record two thoughts and two feelings;

c. Journal project assignment: Describe past drinking patterns that have led to a drinking problem;

d. Do one thinking report about an event that happened during the week. Use the form in the workbook;

e. Read over material for Session 12.

## NOTES:

_____

_____

_____

_____

_____

_____

_____

_____

_____

_____

_____

# NOTES:

## Session ⑫ : Deeper Sharing: Your Deep Emotions and Your AOD Use

### 1. Objectives of Session:

We now will now start to take a deeper look at our past use of drugs and alcohol and our past criminal conduct. We will:

> ⯈ Share some deep emotion that you have been holding on to for some time;
>
> ⯈ Share your thinking report around your past drinking;
>
> ⯈ Retake the tests you took when you were first referred to this program or when you first entered the program:
> 1) The Drug Use Questionnaire (DAST-20);
> 2) The Alcohol Use Questionnaire;
> 3) The Adult Substance Use Survey (ASUS).
>
> ⯈ Compare your scores on these instruments now with those taken before you entered the program.

### 2. What we will do and learn in this session:

#### a. Introduction to session:

We have come to the point in our program where we will *begin* to take an honest look at who we are and what has happened in our emotional life, our history of AOD use and abuse and our history of criminal conduct. This will not be easy. We hold on dearly to a certain view of ourselves. This often causes us to use thinking errors and it often causes us not to clearly address our past behaviors. But now you have prepared yourself for this moment. Now you have met the challenge to improve and change. You would not be in this program now had you not met that challenge in a mature and adult manner.

#### b. Sharing a deep emotion:

During this session, you will be asked to look at a deep emotion that you have carried with you for some time. That might be a hurt, a disappointment, a feeling of being betrayed, or a deep resentment toward someone who has hurt you. Write a few lines about that emotion now.

*We look deeply at who we are and what has happened.*

_____

_____

_____

_____

_____

_____

_____

c. **A look at your alcohol and other drug use history and problems:**

Now you are asked to look more honestly than ever at your past AOD use and problems. In this session, you will retake the tests you took when being selected for this program. Your counselor will help you score the tests and make your profile. Then you will compare your test results with those from the first time you took the tests. After you score your tests, write down the scores in Work Sheet 5 below. Then you will be asked to write down in Work Sheet 6 as many specific negative or problem episodes as you can remember which resulted from your use of alcohol or other drugs.

d. **How does the deep emotion you shared relate to your alcohol or other drug use? What are your thoughts?**

_____

_____

_____

_____

_____

## Classroom or homework tasks:

a. Journal project: On three different occasions this week, write one word to describe a situation or event you experienced this week. Then, write one thought and one feeling related to that situation.

b. Do a thinking report to identify the event, thoughts, beliefs, feelings and results of one criminal offense you were involved in in the past.

c. Continue to work on your autobiography.

d. Read material for Session 13. Complete columns 1 through 4 on Work Sheet 8 in the next session (Session 13).

# WORK SHEET 5

## YOUR TEST SCORES

| TEST | 1ST SCORE | 2ND SCORE | HOW ARE THE SCORES DIFFERENT? |
|------|-----------|-----------|-------------------------------|
| DAST | | | |
| ADS | | | |
| ASUS–INVOLVE | | | |
| ASUS–DISRUPT | | | |
| ASUS–MOOD | | | |
| ASUS–SOCIAL | | | |

# WORK SHEET 6

## RECORDING PROBLEM EPISODES COMING FROM AOD USE

| DATE | DESCRIBE THE PROBLEM OR NEGATIVE EPISODE |
|------|------------------------------------------|
|      |                                          |
|      |                                          |
|      |                                          |
|      |                                          |
|      |                                          |
|      |                                          |
|      |                                          |
|      |                                          |
|      |                                          |
|      |                                          |
|      |                                          |
|      |                                          |
|      |                                          |
|      |                                          |
|      |                                          |
|      |                                          |
|      |                                          |
|      |                                          |
|      |                                          |

# NOTES:

## Session ⓭ : Deeper Sharing: Your History of Criminal Conduct

### 1. Objectives of Session:

> ➧ Increase your awareness of past criminal conduct and offenses by logging all past arrests and convictions;
>
> ➧ Relate this logging of offenses with your recorded legal history;
>
> ➧ Review the thinking report homework that dealt with one past offense;
>
> ➧ Develop an understanding of how your AOD use was related to your past criminal offenses.

### 2. What we will do in this session:

a. **Introduction to session:**

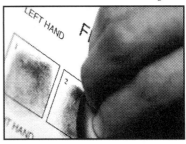

*We look at how our criminal past is related to alcohol or drug use.*

We all want to feel that we are good people who want to do good. Even persons with a long history of criminal offenses have a hard time seeing and accepting their past criminal conduct. Most offenders are aware of their past criminal history, but many have not taken a clear and honest look at that history. Many offenders have not really looked at how their criminal past related to their AOD use. This is what we want to do in this session. Be as honest as you can in doing this session's exercises.

b. **Now complete the ten items in the Level of Service Inventory** in Work Sheet 7 in your workbook below. Is your score different from the one the criminal justice worker gave you when you first took it?

c. **Review your "History of Criminal Conduct Log:"** Do Work Sheet 8. Now, go over what you have written. Review this log in class. You completed only the first four columns:

1) The arrest date;

2) Type of charge;

3) Date convicted if applicable;

4) Date of probation or parole;

5) Time served.

d. **Now compare your recorded legal history with your list of offenses in the Criminal Conduct Log you just completed.**

e. **Do last Column of Work Sheet 8.** Write "No" if alcohol or other drugs (AOD) were not involved. Write (B) if you used AOD before the offense; write (D) if you used AOD during the offense; write (A) if you used AOD after the offense. If all three apply, write BDA.

### Classroom or homework activities:

a. Do a thinking report on one event or time when the use of alcohol or other drugs led to a criminal offense. Remember, you wrote down the situation, thoughts, feelings, attitudes and beliefs and the outcome. The outcome is important. Use your Journal notebook;

b. Using only a few words, record in your journal a time in the past when you were not honest about your substance abuse and/or criminal behavior. In one sentence, now write an honest response.

c. Continue working on your autobiography.

# WORK SHEET 7

## CRIMINAL HISTORY PART OF THE LEVEL OF SERVICE INVENTORY

Check if any apply to you. Then total your score at the end.

_____1. Any prior convictions as an adult? Total number_____?

_____2. Two or more prior convictions?

_____3. Three or more prior convictions?

_____4. Three or more present offenses. Total number_____?

_____5. Arrested under age 16?

_____6. Ever incarcerated upon conviction?

_____7. Escape history—institutions?

_____8. Ever punished for institutional misconduct? Total _____?

_____9. Charge laid or probation/parole suspended during prior community supervision?

_____10. Official record of assault or violence?

TOTAL SCORE (ADD UP NUMBER OF CHECKS) _____.

YOUR SCORE ON THE LSI WHEN YOU FIRST CAME INTO THE PROGRAM _____.

# WORK SHEET 8

## CRIMINAL CONDUCT LOG WORK CHART

| Arrest Date | Name or Type of Charge | Convicted | Probation | Time Served | Relationship with AOD |
|---|---|---|---|---|---|
|  |  |  |  |  |  |
|  |  |  |  |  |  |
|  |  |  |  |  |  |
|  |  |  |  |  |  |
|  |  |  |  |  |  |
|  |  |  |  |  |  |
|  |  |  |  |  |  |
|  |  |  |  |  |  |
|  |  |  |  |  |  |

For the last column, use the following:

Put (B) if you drank or used other drugs before the offense.

Put (D) if you drank or used other drugs during the offense.

Put (A) if you drank or used drugs after the offense.

Put BDA if you drank or used drugs before, during and after the offense.

# NOTES:

# MODULE 5

## Preventing Relapse and Recidivism:
## Identifying High-Risk Situations

# MODULE 5: PREVENTING RELAPSE AND RECIDIVISM: IDENTIFYING HIGH-RISK SITUATIONS

We often think of relapse as going back to drinking or to the use of other drugs. Likewise, we often think of recidivism as going back to committing criminal acts. The purpose of Module 5 is to give you a different view of relapse and recidivism so as to help you avoid going back to AOD use and abuse and to criminal behavior.

Relapse into AOD use and abuse is a gradual process of erosion. The first steps in that erosion process occur when you place yourself in situations that have involved AOD use and abuse in the past. These are called *high-risk situations*. Often, either before or while you are in those situations, you let yourself become involved in thoughts about AOD use. This is called *high-risk thinking*. Thus, you begin to relapse before you begin using substances. Either the high-risk situation or the high risk thinking or both may be prevented through the use of mental and action skills. This is what much of this program is about—learning those skills. But the high-risk situation or high-risk thinking may result in a lapse. A lapse is when you begin to use substances, but you check your use before it leads to a full relapse. A full relapse is when you once again become involved in a pattern of substance use which leads to abuse. Again, a purpose of this program is to help you use the mental and action skills that prevent relapse.

*You will learn the mental and action skills to prevent relapse and recidivism.*

You can think of many relapse high-risk situations or instances of high-risk thinking. Spending time at the bar with friends and drinking soft drinks may be such a situation. Reacting to stressful situations by thinking "just one drink would calm me" is high-risk thinking.

Recidivism back into criminal conduct is also a gradual erosion process. It begins long before a crime is committed. This process is much the same as that of relapse into AOD use patterns. The process begins when you place yourself into situations which lead to criminal behavior; or when you become involved in criminal and deviant thinking. Beginning to hang around peers who are actively involved in criminal behavior is a high-risk situation. Thinking about robbing or stealing with the thought "I can get away with it just this time" is high-risk thinking. Full recidivism, or the actual involvement in a criminal act, always follows placing yourself in high-risk situations or high-risk thinking. With recidivism, you must check yourself at the points when you are in a high-risk situation or when you find yourself involved in criminal thinking. Full recidivism leads to legal results which will be followed by legal punishment. Again, the purpose of this program is to learn the mental and action skills to prevent full recidivism.

The goal of Module 5 is to learn to identify high-risk situations or high-risk thinking related to relapse and recidivism. We will look at the process and cycles of relapse and recidivism. We will look at some of the warning signs of relapse and recidivism.

# Session ⑭ : Relapse and Recidivism Prevention I: Identifying High-Risk Situations and Understanding Relapse and Recidivism

## 1. Objectives of Session:

> ➠ Develop the skills to identify warning signs for criminal behavior;
>
> ➠ Develop the skills to identify warning signs for substance abuse;
>
> ➠ Increase your understanding of the relationships between AOD abuse and crime.

## 2. Session Content:

### a. Defining high-risk (HR) situations for Relapse (AOD use) and Recidivism (criminal conduct):

High-risk (HR) situations for AOD use are usually those situations that have led to AOD use and abuse in the past. They are situations that make you think or feel you need to use alcohol or other drugs. For example, conflict with your significant partner that produces undue stress may lead to the feeling of needing to drink. A high-risk situation is also one which increases the urge, craving and desire for alcohol. Having a romantic evening with your significant partner may lead to the desire or urge to drink. A high-risk situation may be defined as any circumstance or situation that is a threat to your sense that you cannot cope without the use of drugs. You begin relapse when you expose yourself to these high-risk situations, even though you have not yet used substances. Episodes of relapse often occur after you are in a stressful situation that you are unprepared to deal with.

High-risk situations for recidivism are any situations that lead up to being involved in criminal behavior. A high-risk situation is one that makes you think or feel you need to be involved in criminal actions. It is a situation that increases your impulse or desire to commit a crime. It is any situation that suggests you cannot go on without engaging in criminal conduct. One clear high-risk situation is hanging out with peers actively involved in criminal behavior. Another is allowing yourself to be in a situation which, in the past, has involved violence or assaultive acting out.

### b. Defining high-risk thinking for AOD abuse and criminal conduct:

High-risk thinking for AOD use and abuse involves those thought habits or automatic thinking patterns that lead to the use of substances. These thought habits could be set off by involvement in HR situations, or HR thinking could lead you into high-risk circumstances. Such thoughts as "I need a drink, I've had a tough day," or "I might just as well get high, no one gives a damn," are examples of automatic high-risk thinking habits. Such thinking often takes place when you feel threatened, cheated, or not treated fairly. High-risk thinking also may be hooked in with cravings and desire for using substances.

HR thinking for engaging in criminal conduct is those thought habits and automatic thoughts that lead to committing criminal acts. Again, these high-risk thought habits usually take place before you engage in criminal activities. They could be set off by involvement in HR situations or could lead you into high-risk situations. Intense thoughts of being *treated badly, deserving more than what I'm getting,* or thinking about committing a crime are examples of high-risk criminal conduct thinking.

### c. Defining relapse and recidivism:

Relapse begins to occur when you put yourself in situations that have led to AOD use and abuse in the past. Relapse is also defined as engaging in thought habits or automatic thoughts about using substances as an option to dealing with high-risk situations. The early stage of relapse is when you engage in AOD use but have not gone back to a pattern of AOD abuse.

85

A full relapse is when you return to a prior pattern of use which has led to AOD problems and abuse.

Recidivism begins to occur when you start to engage in high-risk thought habits that lead to criminal conduct. It also occurs when you start to engage in actions or put yourself in situations which, in the past, have led to criminal activities. Thus, recidivism does not necessarily mean you have committed another crime. Full recidivism does mean just that.

### d. Relapse/Recidivism Prevention:

We will use RP to mean both relapse and recidivism prevention. Remember, relapse refers to the condition of lapsing back into thought habits or action habits that lead to AOD use. Recidivism refers to lapsing back to the thinking and acting that leads to criminal conduct.

### e. A look at triggers for Relapse/Recidivism (RR):

One way to think about a relapse is when you feel you do not have the power or strength to deal with a feeling or problem that you face. If drinking or taking drugs changes the way you act, think and feel, you need to find out what the situations are in which you are most likely to use, and what you are thinking and feeling at the time. By understanding everything you can about these high-risk situations and high-risk thinking, you can figure out what kinds of things trigger involvement in AOD use and abuse or involvement in criminal conduct. Then you can test out other ways that you can deal with these high-risk situations without becoming weakened once again by the many problems associated with AOD abuse and criminal conduct. What are your triggers for relapse/recidivism (RR)? Here are some that may fit you:

1) **Conflict with another person;**

2) **Social or peer pressure or hanging out with criminal peers;**

3) **An unpleasant feeling: stress, depression, intense anger;**

4) **A change in self-image** from being an abstainer to again being a user; change from the image of living a straight, crime-free life to one who does criminal acts.

Use the Relapse/Recidivism (RR) Log in Work Sheet 9. Take each of the four high-risk situations described above and in Work Sheet 9 and write down a specific situation that applies to you. Then write your thoughts and feelings and either your positive (coping) or negative (relapse/recidivism) thinking and behavior. Then use Work Sheet 10 to write down how you coped with each of those specific situations that applied to you.

### f. Relapse/Recidivism (RR) calendar:

What has been your RR history? Relapse prevention begins to take place when you fully understand your own RR history. You can understand this pattern by using the RR Calendar in Work Sheet 11. This will help you understand your AOD and criminal RR pattern. You will gain insight into how your AOD and legal problems are related. Write in the dates of your first serious attempts to stop AOD abuse and criminal behaviors. Use a straight line to indicate periods of sober and non-criminal behavior. Use a wavy line to indicate periods of relapse or recidivism. When you come to the next session, describe the series of events that led to AOD relapse and crime.

## Review of classroom or homework activities for the coming week:

a. Do the Relapse/Recidivism Log in Work Sheet 9;

b. Write a short description in Work Sheet 10 or discuss in group how you have coped or now cope with these four situations described in Work Sheet 9.

c. Complete the Relapse/Recidivism Calendar.

# WORK SHEET 9

## RELASPE/RECIDIVISM LOG

Below are four situations that are often seen as high-risk situations which can lead to relapse or recidivism. Write in specific situations that apply to you. Then write down your thoughts and feelings. What was the action you took? Discuss the positive and negative outcomes. Describe at least one situation in each of the categories.

| TRIGGERS | THOUGHTS/ FEELINGS | BEHAVIOR + − |
|---|---|---|
| 1) Conflict with another person: | | |
| 2) Social or peer pressure: | | |
| 3) An unpleasant feeling: | | |
| 4) A change in self-image: | | |

# WORK SHEET 10

## COPING SKILLS

Write a short description of how you have coped or now cope with the situations outlined in Work Sheet 9. Write a statement for each of the four situations.

1) Conflict with another person.
2) Social or peer pressure.
3) An unpleasant feeling.
4) A change in self-image.

# WORK SHEET 11

## THE RELAPSE/RECIDIVISM CALENDAR (adapted from Gorski, 1993)

Use this exercise to examine your AOD and criminal relapses. You will gain insight into how your AOD and legal problems are related. Write in the dates of your first serious attempts to stop AOD abuse and criminal behaviors. Use a straight line to indicate periods of sober and responsible behavior. Use a wavy line to indicate periods of relapse or recidivism. When you come to the next session, describe the series of events that led to AOD relapse and to criminal involvement.

| YEAR | JAN | FEB | MAR | APR | MAY | JUN | JUL | AUG | SEP | OCT | NOV | DEC |
|------|-----|-----|-----|-----|-----|-----|-----|-----|-----|-----|-----|-----|
| AOD | | | | | | | | | | | | |
| CRIME | | | | | | | | | | | | |

| YEAR | JAN | FEB | MAR | APR | MAY | JUN | JUL | AUG | SEP | OCT | NOV | DEC |
|------|-----|-----|-----|-----|-----|-----|-----|-----|-----|-----|-----|-----|
| AOD | | | | | | | | | | | | |
| CRIME | | | | | | | | | | | | |

| YEAR | JAN | FEB | MAR | APR | MAY | JUN | JUL | AUG | SEP | OCT | NOV | DEC |
|------|-----|-----|-----|-----|-----|-----|-----|-----|-----|-----|-----|-----|
| AOD | | | | | | | | | | | | |
| CRIME | | | | | | | | | | | | |

# NOTES:

## Session ⑮ : Relapse and Recidivism Prevention II: Learning the Cognitive-Behavioral Map for AOD Abuse and Criminal Conduct

### 1. Objectives of Session:

> ➠ Understand the idea of relapse/recidivism (RR) erosion;
>
> ➠ Understand the inside-the-mind and outside events that lead to RR;
>
> ➠ Identify the mental and action skills to avoid RR by recognizing the thoughts, feelings, and attitudes that trigger AOD relapse and CC recidivism.

### 2. Session Content and Process:

#### a. The RR erosion:

RR is a process of erosion. Soil erosion is a gradual wearing away of the topsoil that has the power to produce rich and healthy crops. It is often hidden and difficult to see. It takes place over a long period of time. The same is true in the process of relapse and recidivism. There is a gradual wearing away of the rich resources of the mind. It is gradual and may take place over long periods of time. Sometimes, it takes a year or two before this gradual wearing away leads to a full relapse (relapse into the full behavior of AOD use or crime) even though the RR episode may appear to be the result of an impulsive act (spur of the moment). Figure 10 gives us a picture of this erosion process.

## Figure 10: The Relapse Process
(adapted from Daley and Marlatt, 1992)

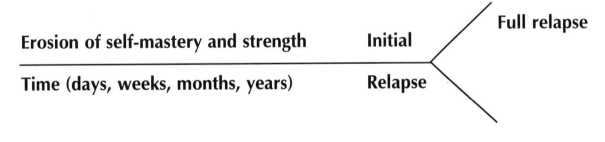

Adapted with permission of the authors of Relapse Prevention: Cognitive and Behavioral Interventions, D.C. Daley & G.A. Marlat (p. 537). In J.H. Lowinson, P. Ruiz, & R.B. Millman (Eds.), *Substance Abuse: A Comprehensive Textbook* (2nd ed., p. 537). Williams & Wilkins.

#### b. Understanding the RR Process: The RR Steps:

Relapse and recidivism (RR) occurs in steps. Again, you can be in RR before you use a substance or before you commit a crime. Figure 11 describes these steps:

### *High-Risk Situation and High-Risk Thinking*

Any situation that threatens your sense of control, thereby increasing the risk for RR.

### *Self-Efficacy or Self-Mastery*

Your judgment about how well you cope with stressful or difficult situations. This is based on whether or not you have succeeded or failed in similar situations, how others judge or influence you, and your emotional state.

### Expected Outcome

This is what you expect the outcome to be. You may expect a drug to have a particular desired effect (e.g., makes you feel good). However, "expected effects" may be quite different from "real effects." When the prospect of AOD use is hooked in with a positive outcome of AOD use, the probability of relapse skyrockets. Or, you feel that the crime you are thinking you are going to do will make you feel more powerful, successful or important.

### Rule Violation Effect

This is your reaction resulting from a fall from complete abstinence or some deviation from an absolute rule (e.g., *never go into a bar*). You have been seeing yourself as *clean and sober.* Then you use (drugs) or plan a crime. That view of yourself as *clean and sober* must change. You are now getting in touch with a part of your old self. So what are you? *Clean and sober* or *user and offender?* You now are experiencing inner conflict. To solve this conflict, you are likely to return to your old view of yourself—*substance abusing offender.* The strength of this rule violation will depend on 1) how much conflict and guilt you feel due to your RR and 2) how much you blame your personal weaknesses for the cause of the RR behavior.

### Self-Attribution or Self-Credit

This type of thinking is most important when you find yourself taking part in RR behavior. If you believe that the initial RR is due to your personal "weakness," then you may be setting yourself up for continuing the relapse/recidivism process. This is because you believe you have lost total control or it is beyond your control. If you credit strength to yourself by stopping at the point of initial relapse (engaging in thinking or action which leads to drinking or actual drinking) or stopping at initial recidivism (engaging in obsessive CC thinking) then it is unlikely that you will go into a full relapse/recidivism.

c. **RR erosion warnings and signs:**

You become weakened to relapse or to going back into thinking and beliefs that lead to criminal conduct when you find yourself in high-risk situations or into high-risk thinking. But more important, it is how you deal with the HR situation. When you engage in thinking and acting which helps you cope a HR situations, you will feel a sense of inner power (increased self-mastery) and you will avoid full relapse (AOD use) and full recidivism (criminal conduct). If your thinking and actions are weak, you will feel a loss of power and feel weak (decreased self-efficacy) but you might expect a positive outcome from the effect of the substance or committing a crime. You have thus relapsed; you feel the rule violation effect, plus the positive effects of the substance. This increases the possibility of full relapse and recidivism. Let us now return to our example of soil erosion. The farmer has learned to prevent erosion with proper care of the land. He builds up terraces or rows of soil which are barriers to the water wearing away the topsoil. Crops are planted around the hills and not up and down so that the rains do not wash away the soil. There is the continual adding of soil food or fertilizer to refresh and build up the soil. The same is true with our lives. We need to build good mental and action defenses against high-risk situations and thinking. These are mental skills that we can apply to our errors in thinking, and not placing ourselves in high-risk situations. We refresh ourselves with healthy friends and positive activities. And we are always aware of the RR warnings. Some of these are:

1) Changes in attitudes: from positive to negative;

2) Changes in thoughts: from self-confidence to weakness;

3) Changes in emotions and moods: from an up and hopeful mood to depressed mood, from a calm to an anxious mood.

4) Changes in actions: from activities not involving alcohol or other drugs to activities that are AOD involved.

# FIGURE 11
## Cognitive-Behavioral Model for Relapse and Recidivism

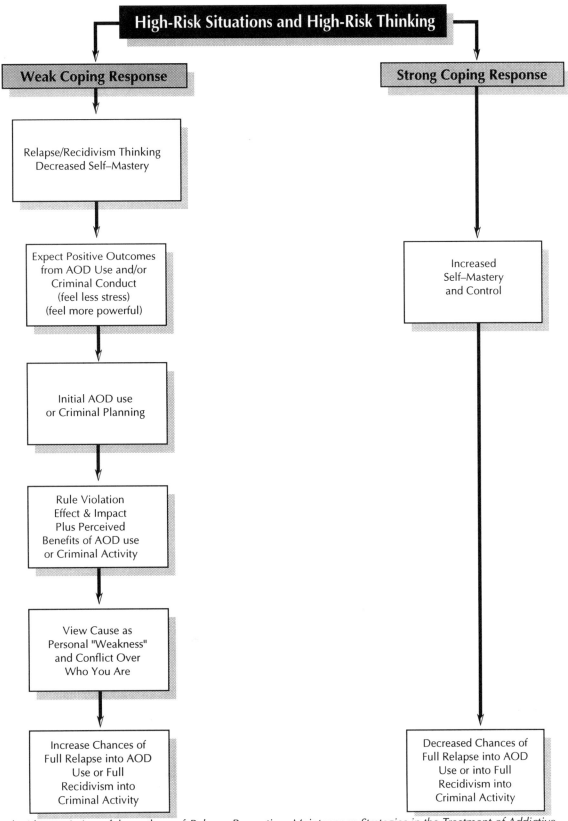

Adapted with permission of the authors of *Relapse Prevention: Maintenance Strategies in the Treatment of Addictive Behaviors*, (page 38) Edited by G.A. Marlatt and J.R. Gordon, The Guilford Press, 1985.

## Classroom or homework activities:

a. Take Figure 11 and see how this fits your past relapse experiences;

b. Write in your journal what high-risk situations you put yourself in this week and high-risk thoughts you had this week.

# NOTES:

# MODULE

# 6

## How Do People Change:

## Understanding the Process
## of Self-Improvement and Change

# MODULE 6: HOW DO PEOPLE CHANGE:
# UNDERSTANDING THE PROCESS OF SELF-IMPROVEMENT AND CHANGE

## Overview of Module 6

In our last Module, we learned that the first step to self-improvement, self-correction and change was to be more aware of what has caused us problems in the past, and what we need to change. We also learned that the pathway to self-awareness involves self-disclosure and sharing and being open to feedback from others as to what they think and feel about you.

Now we will decide whether we really want to change. We have spent a lot of time and energy looking at how thoughts and actions have caused problems for us and for people around us. Now we are faced with some important questions.

◆ Do we want to change?

◆ What do we want or need to change?

◆ Do we want to commit to change? Do we want to take action?

◆ Are you still wavering—still ambivalent about changing?

◆ Do you want to commit yourself to Phase II of this program?

For some of you, Phase II of this program is part of what you have to do for probation, parole or sentencing. If this is true, then we want you to take an honest look at how you might be fighting or resisting making Phase II work for you.

### Objectives for Module 6

The following objectives will help you to see whether you have taken or will take action to change:

◆ Understand what we go through when making change. This will mean we will review the thinking and behavioral cycles we learned in Module 3: Building the Knowledge Base;

◆ Spot thinking and behavioral targets of change that we want to make in our lives;

◆ Begin to learn some specific skills to work on the targets of change;

◆ Understand the barriers to self-improvement and change;

◆ Make a decision to commit to the full process of change and a commitment to Phase II of treatment.

*Take an honest look at how you can make Phase II of this program work for you.*

# Session 16: Reviewing the Process and Stages of Change and Selecting Targets for Change

## 1. Objectives of Session:

> ➠ Again look at the process of changing our mental world and our actions;
>
> ➠ Look at and understand the stages of change and identify what stage you are in;
>
> ➠ Learn the idea of selecting targets for change.

## 2. Session Content and Process:

### a. Introduction to Session:

You have worked hard to get to this point in your program. You have prepared yourself for change by becoming more aware of your past and your present problems. You have done this by taking great risks in sharing your personal feelings, thoughts and past actions. This sharing has brought you to a better understanding of the problems you have had with AOD use and your criminal and deviant conduct. These sessions helped prepare you for really committing yourself to change. Now you are ready to see where you are in giving yourself to making changes in your life.

### b. Review of the process of change:

Figure 12 provides a picture of this change process. This is similar to the diagram we saw in Session 5, "The Process of Learning and Change." This picture now puts in the actions of AOD abuse and criminal conduct. We can see that outside events and inside memories and feelings lead to our automatic thinking. These set loose certain attitudes, beliefs and emotions. *We can choose our thoughts and our beliefs*. These "inside-the-head workings" can lead to behavior or action. *We can choose our actions*. We know what the outcomes of our thoughts and actions will be. Review Figure 12 on the following page. How does it fit you? Fill in Work Sheets 12 and 13.

1) Work Sheet 12: Choose a past event that led to an AOD use episode. Fill in the bottom part of the cycle first. How would you change things? Fill in the coping behaviors to show how you would do it.

2) Work Sheet 13: Choose an event in the recent past that led to criminal conduct. Again, fill in both the top and bottom parts of the chart.

**You will do these during your classroom sessions.**

**Figure 12**

Pathways to Changing AOD and Criminal Conduct

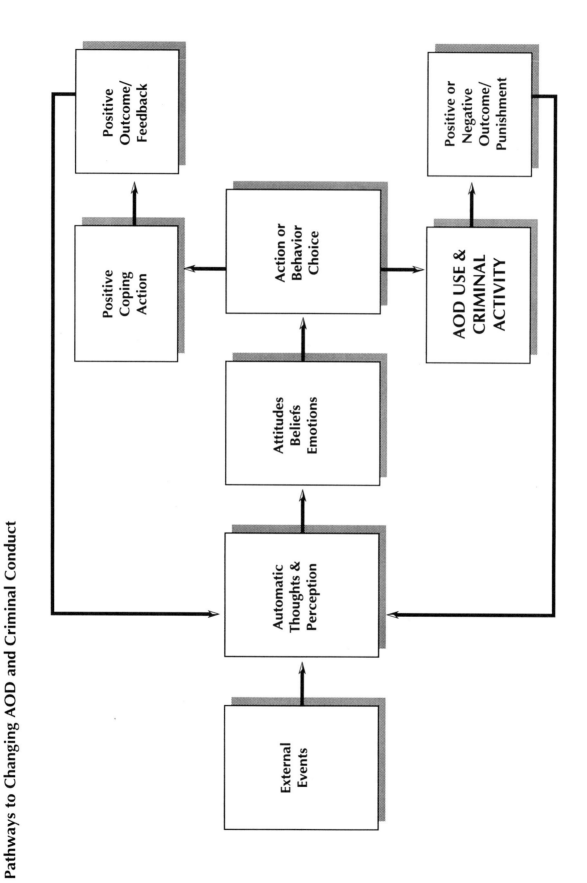

# WORK SHEET 12

## YOUR PATHWAYS TO ALCOHOL AND OTHER DRUG USE

Choose a past event that led to alcohol or other drug use. Fill in each of the squares as to what happened to you.

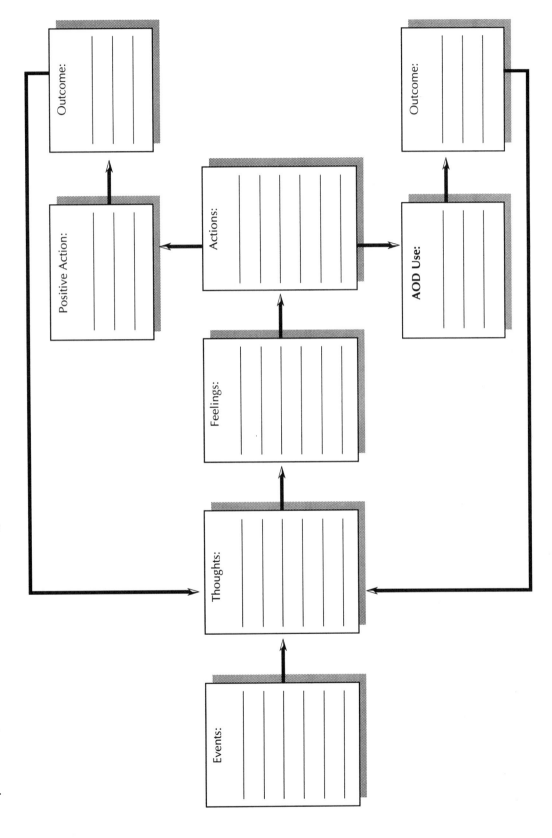

# WORK SHEET 13

## YOUR PATHWAYS TO CRIMINAL CONDUCT

Choose a past event that led to criminal conduct. Fill in each of the squares as to what happened to you.

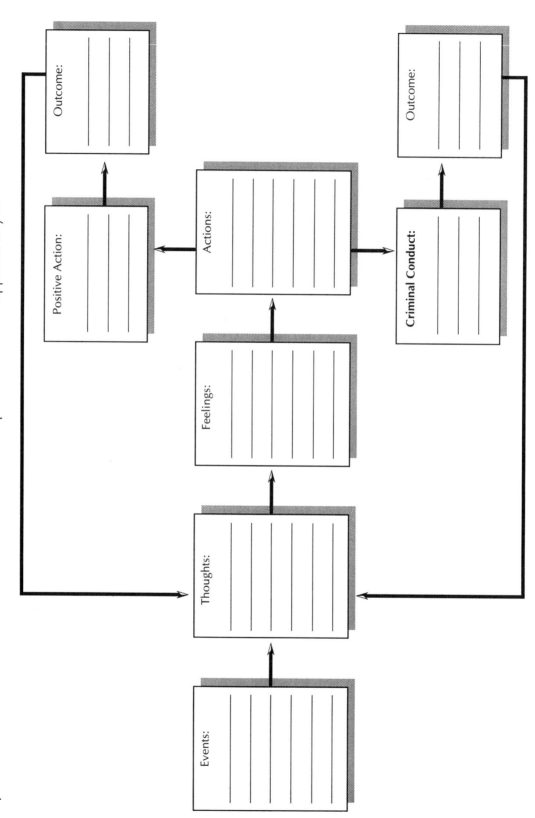

### c. The Stages of Change—Where are you?

As you have already learned, there are three phases to this program: *Challenge to Change, Commitment to Change* and *Taking Ownership of Change.* These phases are built around what we know to be stages that people go through when making changes. It is important for you to know where you are at this time. Have you been challenged to give serious thought to change? Have you begun to do some changing? What is your commitment to making change? Are you determined yet you have not really taken action? Let us look again at these phases of change, so that you can see where you are.

1) **Challenge to change:** If you are in this stage, you have begun to meet the challenge to give thought to change and to look seriously at yourself to see where and what changes need to be made. You are open to getting information about yourself and your problems. If you are in the early phase of this stage, you are building self-awareness. If you are in the latter part of this stage then you are taking greater risks in disclosing your problems and talking about yourself. You have met the challenge when you are willing to commit to continued and even more intense treatment and a desire to learn the skills to be free of AOD use problems and avoid criminal conduct. The key words here are thinking or *being thoughtful;* being *self-aware;* being aware of *areas needing change; self-disclosing; and being willing to commit* to further help.

2) **Commitment to change:** If you have made a commitment to change, you are now open to disclose or talk about your problems, to talk openly about what changes need to be made. You are making efforts to change your thoughts, attitudes and beliefs. You have been able to go a definite period of time AOD free. You feel less desire to drink or use other drugs. You find yourself changing your thinking when you start thinking about getting involved in criminal conduct. You replace drug use activities with alternative activities. You catch yourself thinking about using drugs but replace those thoughts. You have made a promise and pledge to change. You are now more involved in learning the skills of thinking and acting which keep you away from criminal activity and AOD use. You practice those skills. If you are in the early part of this phase, you have been able to correct your thinking and actions which lead to criminal behavior and AOD use. If you are in the latter part of this stage, you have been able to demonstrate control over involvement in criminal conduct (CC) and AOD use problems.

3) **Taking Ownership of Change:** When you reach this stage, you are making changes because you want to and not because others—the court, family, probation officer, counselor—want you to. You have been able to go a long time free of AOD problems and free from criminal conduct thinking. You have clearly replaced your criminogenic needs and the need to use alcohol or other drugs. You feel strong in your abstinence from drugs and criminal involvement. You are not nagged and bugged by thoughts of doing crimes. You may relapse into AOD use thinking or CC thinking but you prevent relapse back into the action part of the relapse cycle. You are in the program because you want to be not because you have to be.

*You replace drug use activities with alternative activities.*

101

Classroom Exercise: Where are you in each of these stages of change for AOD use and criminal conduct? Use Work Sheet 14 for AOD abuse. Use Work Sheet 15 for your criminal thinking and conduct. Shade in the profiles. Your counselor is doing the same. Compare yours with his/hers. Are they different?

d. **Your targets for change:**

We have learned that the first step in change is to become more aware of the thinking and actions that cause our problems. The most important person we disclose to is ourselves. It is ourselves that we want to be most honest with. The next step to change is to decide what you want to change. These are things you think or do that cause you problems in your life. We will call them *target thoughts* and *target actions*. Target thoughts are specific thoughts or thought patterns that lead to problem behavior. What is important is that you can change these without having to change a behavior. You don't have to wait for a behavior to come along.

You can spot the target thoughts or behaviors for change. Others may help you spot them. But, only you can make the choice. No one else can do it. Although many people may have told you about what you should be doing, only you can say: "I'm going to make my life different."

**Here are the steps to change a target behavior:**

1) First pick the thought or behavior;

2) What are the attitudes and beliefs behind the thought or the thinking behind the behavior?

3) Think how you would like to think or how you would like to act and behave—set goals; GOALS. **This is new.** Stop and think. If we are going to act differently than we did, what would we want the new behavior to be? Think how it would be to behave in a different way. You may feel uncomfortable about changing and that's o.k. New goals require a gradual change—give yourself time to make the change. Once you have set a goal, live up to it.

4) Pick a thinking or action method (intervention) you will use to change the thought or behavior. This will be a very important part of Phase II. But we will introduce you to this in the next session.

5) CHANGE THE TARGET BEHAVIOR. This, too, is a project of Phase II, where you will learn the skills to reach goals you have set for yourself. If you really want to change, you will. Practice the method to replace or eliminate the old thought or behavior.

## Classroom or homework activities:

a. Write another part of your autobiography;

b. Do a thinking report involving a situation that could have led to criminal conduct or drug use. Bring this report to the next session;

c. Write one sentence each night in your journal as to a thought that bugged you or you carried around all day;

d. Pick one target thought or behavior you want to change. Don't do anything but pick the thought or behavior. Think about it all week, but do not try to change it. It could be a thought about wanting to drink. It could be a thought about "the world is not fair." It could be an angry thought toward your spouse or another family member;

e. Read material for next session.

# WORK SHEET 14

## SELF-RATING ON STAGES OF CHANGE FOR AOD USE ONLY

Rate yourself on each stage of change.

### CHALLENGE TO CHANGE

| KEY ELEMENTS IN STAGE | LOW | | | | MODERATE | | | HIGH | |
|---|---|---|---|---|---|---|---|---|---|
| Given thought to changing | 0 | 1 | 2 | 3 | 4 | 5 | 6 | 7 | 8 |
| Want information about self | 0 | 1 | 2 | 3 | 4 | 5 | 6 | 7 | 8 |
| Level of self-awareness | 0 | 1 | 2 | 3 | 4 | 5 | 6 | 7 | 8 |
| Commitment to more treatment | 0 | 1 | 2 | 3 | 4 | 5 | 6 | 7 | 8 |

### COMMITMENT TO CHANGE

| KEY ELEMENTS IN STAGE | LOW | | | | MODERATE | | | HIGH | |
|---|---|---|---|---|---|---|---|---|---|
| Pledge to change | 0 | 1 | 2 | 3 | 4 | 5 | 6 | 7 | 8 |
| Open to self-disclosure | 0 | 1 | 2 | 3 | 4 | 5 | 6 | 7 | 8 |
| Efforts to change attitudes | 0 | 1 | 2 | 3 | 4 | 5 | 6 | 7 | 8 |
| Efforts to change thoughts | 0 | 1 | 2 | 3 | 4 | 5 | 6 | 7 | 8 |
| Use relapse prevention skills | 0 | 1 | 2 | 3 | 4 | 5 | 6 | 7 | 8 |
| AOD thought-free for long period | 0 | 1 | 2 | 3 | 4 | 5 | 6 | 7 | 8 |
| Corrected relapse thinking | 0 | 1 | 2 | 3 | 4 | 5 | 6 | 7 | 8 |
| Learned skills to avoid AOD thought | 0 | 1 | 2 | 3 | 4 | 5 | 6 | 7 | 8 |

### TAKING OWNERSHIP OF CHANGE

| KEY ELEMENTS IN STAGE | LOW | | | | MODERATE | | | HIGH | |
|---|---|---|---|---|---|---|---|---|---|
| In program because want to be | 0 | 1 | 2 | 3 | 4 | 5 | 6 | 7 | 8 |
| No desire for AOD involvement | 0 | 1 | 2 | 3 | 4 | 5 | 6 | 7 | 8 |
| Long time free of AOD thinking | 0 | 1 | 2 | 3 | 4 | 5 | 6 | 7 | 8 |
| Replace need for AOD use | 0 | 1 | 2 | 3 | 4 | 5 | 6 | 7 | 8 |

# WORK SHEET 15
## SELF-RATING ON STAGES OF CHANGE FOR CRIMINAL THINKING AND CRIMINAL CONDUCT ONLY

Rate yourself on each stage of change.

| CHALLENGE TO CHANGE | | | | | | | | | |
|---|---|---|---|---|---|---|---|---|---|
| KEY ELEMENTS IN STAGE | LOW | | | MODERATE | | | HIGH | | |
| Given thought to changing | 0 | 1 | 2 | 3 | 4 | 5 | 6 | 7 | 8 |
| Want information about self | 0 | 1 | 2 | 3 | 4 | 5 | 6 | 7 | 8 |
| Level of self-awareness | 0 | 1 | 2 | 3 | 4 | 5 | 6 | 7 | 8 |
| Commitment to more treatment | 0 | 1 | 2 | 3 | 4 | 5 | 6 | 7 | 8 |

| COMMITMENT TO CHANGE | | | | | | | | | |
|---|---|---|---|---|---|---|---|---|---|
| KEY ELEMENTS IN STAGE | LOW | | | MODERATE | | | HIGH | | |
| Pledge to change | 0 | 1 | 2 | 3 | 4 | 5 | 6 | 7 | 8 |
| Open to self-disclosure | 0 | 1 | 2 | 3 | 4 | 5 | 6 | 7 | 8 |
| Efforts to change attitudes | 0 | 1 | 2 | 3 | 4 | 5 | 6 | 7 | 8 |
| Efforts to change thoughts | 0 | 1 | 2 | 3 | 4 | 5 | 6 | 7 | 8 |
| Use recidivism prevention skills | 0 | 1 | 2 | 3 | 4 | 5 | 6 | 7 | 8 |
| CC thought-free for long period | 0 | 1 | 2 | 3 | 4 | 5 | 6 | 7 | 8 |
| Corrected recidivism thinking | 0 | 1 | 2 | 3 | 4 | 5 | 6 | 7 | 8 |
| Learned skills to avoid CC thought | 0 | 1 | 2 | 3 | 4 | 5 | 6 | 7 | 8 |

| TAKING OWNERSHIP OF CHANGE | | | | | | | | | |
|---|---|---|---|---|---|---|---|---|---|
| KEY ELEMENTS IN STAGE | LOW | | | MODERATE | | | HIGH | | |
| In program because want to be | 0 | 1 | 2 | 3 | 4 | 5 | 6 | 7 | 8 |
| No desire for CC involvement | 0 | 1 | 2 | 3 | 4 | 5 | 6 | 7 | 8 |
| Long time free of CC thinking | 0 | 1 | 2 | 3 | 4 | 5 | 6 | 7 | 8 |
| Replace need for CC | 0 | 1 | 2 | 3 | 4 | 5 | 6 | 7 | 8 |

## Session ⑰ : Ways to Change and Barriers to Change

### 1. Objectives of Session:

> ➠ Begin to learn some specific methods or techniques for changing target thoughts or actions;
>
> ➠ Spot the barriers that keep us from changing.

### 2. What we will do and learn in this session:

a. **Some thoughts for this session:**

Last session we learned to identify change targets. These change targets can be beliefs, thoughts, attitudes or actions. When we pick thinking targets, we don't have to wait for the behavior to change. We change our thoughts.

1) **Example:** We find ourselves thinking about something that makes us angry—such as paying for something that we felt was not worth it. We think about being cheated. We can let that thought "eat us up" and eventually lead to "cheating someone else to get back" or we can change that thought, if it is a thought that we continue to dwell on.

2) **Example:** We find ourselves thinking about getting together with friends and "getting high." We can change that thought before we actually get high. This is the power of the mind. But even more powerful is the use of certain skills or methods to change target thoughts or behavior. One focus for this session will be to just look at a few of these techniques or methods to change our target thoughts or actions.

In all that we have done, it would seem easy to change. But remember the word **ambivalence**: This means we waver back and forth about change. As we have talked about before, we want to keep ourselves the way we are even though we want to change. We have mixed feelings about changing. We even put up roadblocks to change. We call these barriers. We will look at these barriers in this session.

Write down three thoughts that you have put up as roadblocks or barriers to change:

_____

_____

_____

b. **Beginning to learn some ways to change thinking and doing:**

1) **"Self-Talk."** This is teaching ourselves. We talk to ourselves. Here are some "self-talk" methods.

   a) **Thought stopping:** I want to stop my target behavior of being distrustful. If I find myself thinking, "I can't trust this stranger," I can stop this automatic thinking by saying, "I'm feeling distrustful, I'm not going to think this way." I may still feel slightly distrustful, but I have interrupted my automatic thinking and made myself think new thoughts.

   b) **Thinking "Responsibility" and "Their Position":** What if I were in THEIR POSITION? What are they thinking? RESPECT the other person as a human being. Think of THE PERSON YOU WANT TO BE. "Responsibility" and "Their Position" are cures for antisocial behavior and criminal conduct. "Responsibility" makes us take the blame for our own behavior; "Their Position" makes us place ourselves in the other's position.

c) **Planting a positive thought:** When you find yourself into negative thinking, replace a negative thought with a positive thought. Do it every time it happens. If you dwell on negative thoughts they will lead to negative behavior. Train yourself to have POSITIVE THOUGHTS toward others. As you change your negative thinking patterns or thought-habits, you are training yourself to have different and more positive thoughts toward people with whom you normally have problems.

d) **Countering or going against a thought:** The idea here is that when you argue against an error in thinking or a thought that doesn't make sense, and you do it every time, that thought becomes weaker. A counter can be one statement: "That's stupid." "Not true." Sometimes the counter is a coping statement: "I can do it." Or it can be a joking statement: "It's terrible to make mistakes." Babe Ruth hit 714 home runs but struck out 1,330 times."

2) **Shifting the view (perceptual shifting):** This is a method of changing our mental sets or views. It is based on how we see things inside and outside ourselves. Getting caught up in destructive and damaging ideas, beliefs and thoughts will often lead us into AOD use and abuse and/or criminal conduct. These often are errors of how we see the world—or our beliefs. But if we can change our view, or shift our view, we can often see the other side of the belief or thought. The brain changes what it brings in. It can shift what it sees. Look at Figure 13. Depending how the brain "views" the picture, you see an old woman or a young woman.

**Figure 13: Old or Young Woman**

*What we perceive is often due to our expectations. When looking at this famous ambiguous figure, do you see a young woman or an old woman?*

Over a long period of time, you may have held on to the belief *I deserve more than what I'm getting. I've been cheated.* This continued view of yourself and the world will only lead to going out and getting what you feel you have coming. It leads to criminal thinking and acting.

3) **Exaggerate or overstate the thought:** When Victor Frankl (1960), a famous psychiatrist, was in a German concentration camp, he found people wanting to give up. He would say "Go ahead and give up. See if I care. Do it right now. Give up." He found that in almost every case, this forced the person back to reality and doing just the opposite. You can do this to yourself. When you find yourself worrying about something in an irrational way (a way that doesn't make sense), you can say, "OK, I'm going to worry about this for the next ten hours. I'll show you how much I can worry about this." When we do this, it forces us to look at the error in our thinking or the irrational belief. It is like "typing the error" to realize you make the error and then you correct it.

4) **Conditioning: Making our thoughts weaker or stronger:** You can reward the positive thoughts. You can make your destructive or negative thoughts weaker. For example, if you think about drinking, then think about all of the bad things that happened when you drank in the past. When you think about replacing drinking with a positive activity, think about the rewards that come from the positive activity. When you do not drink but want to, reward yourself. Buy yourself something.

5) **Logical (sensible) study—going to court with your thought:** This technique involves you fighting your errors in thinking or your nonsense or irrational thoughts with logic or sensible thinking. You want to go out to drink. You have a thought about stealing something. Think: How much sense does this make? In the long run, is it logical? Three simple steps to this technique of going to court with your thought: State your thought; get your evidence; make your verdict. This gives you time to think it through.

*Learning to relax will help us regain control.*

6) **Relaxation skills:** When we are under stress and tense, we are more likely to let our automatic thoughts or thought habits take over. We get tired, fatigued. The fatigue and stress reduces our mental control. We are more likely to let our thought habits and our behavior habits take over. Learning to relax will help us regain control; it will give us control. In class, you will learn several relaxation skills and your counselor will guide you through these skills and help you learn them. These include:

- Muscle relaxation: learning to tense and then relax your muscles one at a time;

- Imagining calm scenes: learning to put yourself in a very calm and relaxing place such as near the ocean or by a mountain stream;

- Mentally relaxing parts of your body: Closing your eyes and saying to yourself—"my arms are heavy and relaxed; my forehead is cool";

- Deep breathing: This is a powerful relaxation skill that you can do at any time. You take in your breath deeply and let it out; we do this almost naturally when we give a sigh of relief.

Now, you can start to use these techniques. Feel their power to help you change your thinking and doing.

c. **Let us look at some roadblocks we put up to change:**

We can put up many barriers to change. We put these barriers up because it is too uncomfortable to change or just too much of a burden. Sometimes it involves just not coming to the session. Sometimes it involves just *getting tired of pleasing people* and *throwing in the towel*. Sometimes we see other things as more important than involving ourselves in the change process. Most often, however, it involves thinking barriers—which are often automatic thoughts or just errors in our thinking.

**Here are some thinking and behaving roadblocks we put up as barriers to change. How do these fit you?**

1) "Everyone thinks the way I do";

2) "I've got to be honest, this is what I really believe";

3) "There are no alternatives";

4) "My thoughts and feelings don't need changing in this situation because I'm right";

5) Building yourself up to put down the ideas of change;

6) Being silent in group;

7) Not listening or attending;

8) Stating "I've tried that and it didn't work";

9) Thinking "I've always done it that way";

10) Attacking others.

d. **Make the effort—it's worth it:**

What happens if we change one thing in our thinking and behavior that keeps us out of trouble? We find that this makes life better. Then we look for another thing to change to make it better. When you do this, you are "practicing change" and, with practice, we overcome one of the greatest roadblocks to change: NOT MAKING THE EFFORT. To avoid this barrier, be honest with yourself. If you are not really trying to change, admit it. You are not going to change.

We may find that feeling good about what we are doing and doing what most of the world finds "right" pays off. It is better than any payoff we found when we were abusing drugs and doing criminal activities.

## Classroom or homework activities:

a. Finish your autobiography and bring it to the next session;

b. Try out the techniques and methods this week. Record in your journal the date and the event or circumstance when you did put one of these to work. Feel the power of these techniques. They put you in control;

c. Write in your journal the strongest feeling you had this week. Just write the feeling down; nothing else;

d. Thinking Report: Recall a situation when being with your friends caused you to stray away from changing one of your target behaviors. Maybe the target behavior was to not be around people who use drugs. But you are with your friends who are using. Remember the parts of your thinking report:

SITUATION:

THOUGHTS:

FEELINGS:

ATTITUDES AND BELIEFS ABOUT THE SITUATION:

THE OUTCOME OF THE SITUATION OR EVENT:

e. Think seriously this week about the program you have been in. Be prepared to evaluate and share your commitment to change;

f. Read over material for next session.

# NOTES:

_____

_____

_____

_____

_____

_____

# Session 18 : Looking Forward: Making a Commitment to Change

## 1. Objective of Session

> ➥ Look at the progress you made in the program;
>
> ➥ Spot the important changes you have made;
>
> ➥ Receive feedback from other members of the group as to their perception of your change and progress;
>
> ➥ Receive feedback from the counselor and group members;
>
> ➥ Make a decision around commitment to change and involvement in Phase II.

## 2. Some thoughts for this session:

You have now come to a fork in the road in your treatment journey. You have experienced a lot; you have learned a lot; you have worked hard; you have grown and matured. Now you will need to address this question:

DO I WANT TO COMMIT MYSELF TO THE ACTION PHASE OF TREATMENT?

You may be saying: "I've taken action. I've done my changing. I'm OK." What barriers are you putting up to not continuing into Phase II?

Some of you may have to continue because that is the condition of probation, parole or your sentencing. Even if this is the case, we want you to express your feelings and opinions honestly and openly. We want you to take an honest look at how you might be fighting or resisting making Phase II work for you.

## Classroom or homework assignments:

a. First you will be asked to complete the Adult Self-Assessment Questionnaire again. We will then score that and compare your profile now with the one you had when you first started the program;

b. Review your homework and your autobiography. You will be asked to share one important piece of that autobiography;

c. As you come to this session, think about:

1) How are you feeling now about the program?

2) What have you gotten out of the program?

3) Where do you see yourself now as to your stage of change?

4) Do you now want to commit yourself to change?

# NOTES:

# PHASE II

## COMMITMENT TO CHANGE
### INTRODUCTION AND OVERVIEW

*You can live a happy, successful life.*

# PHASE II:
# COMMITMENT TO CHANGE

You have decided to enter Phase II of this program. Phase II will involve 22 two and a half hour sessions over a period of five and one-half months—or one session a week. Because you are now in Phase II, you have made a commitment or promise to change in the area of AOD abuse and criminal conduct. You developed trust and harmony with staff and other clients during Phase I. You showed that you were inspired to change.

During Phase I, you gained knowledge and facts about alcohol and drug abuse and the cycles of abuse. You learned about criminal conduct and the cycles of criminal behavior. You learned about the part that thoughts, beliefs and attitudes play in controlling behavior and action. You learned the rules of how thoughts and behavior are strengthened and reinforced. You also learned important ways to prevent thoughts about crime and drug use from turning into actual criminal behavior or drug use itself.

Change begins with self-awareness. But self-awareness depends on self-disclosure and getting feedback from others about yourself. In Phase I you took many risks to talk about yourself and your problems. You opened yourself up to have others tell you how they saw you. You learned and practiced basic communication skills to help you in self-disclosure and to receive and give feedback. You focused on spotting your thinking errors and distortions. You spent time learning about relapse and recidivism prevention. In order to help you become more aware of yourself, you wrote your autobiography, wrote in a journal and wrote thinking reports.

Finally, we brought Phase I to a close by helping you to make the methods of change work for you. You learned to spot thinking and behavioral targets that you could work on to change. You learned to spot and overcome the barriers to change.

Phase II will involve following through with your commitment or promise to change—to change your thinking which leads to drug abuse and to criminal conduct. You are committing to learning new thoughts and actions to replace those that led to AOD abuse and criminal conduct. You now will do a more in-depth evaluation of your past AOD problems and criminal conduct. You will gain a better understanding of your own ways of thinking and doing which have gotten you into trouble in the past. You will look at other problems in your life. These will give you targets for change. These will help you to develop a *Master Assessment Plan* (MAP) to guide you on the pathway for change. Your MAP will be your guide as you go through basic skill development sessions to give you the skills and tools for self-correction and change. These programs are set up to help you prevent relapse (into drug use) and recidivism (into criminal thinking and acting). As we learned in Module 5, we call this RP— relapse/recidivism prevention.

But this program is more than just helping you to avoid substance use and abuse and more than just helping you to avoid criminal thinking and acting. We want you to set a goal of living a happy, successful life. We feel strongly that you can do this.

## Here are our Goals and Objectives for Phase II:

◆ Through more intensive self-disclosure and feedback, you will develop a deeper understanding of your thinking and behavior in the following areas:

◆ Criminal conduct;

◆ AOD use and abuse;

◆ How AOD abuse and criminal conduct hook together to strengthen each other;

◆ How patterns of thinking, feeling and perceiving lead to criminal conduct and AOD abuse;

◆ Your own specific life problems;

◆ Strengthening drug-free living and positive social and community involvement by building basic life skills.

## What is expected of you in Phase II:

◆ Learning and skill development:

1) Complete the in-depth assessment;

2) Complete all Basic Skills for Self-Improvement and Change sessions;

3) Show specific changes in AOD and criminal conduct thinking and behavior patterns;

◆ Participation Expectations:

1) Complete all homework and classroom assignments;

2) Be on time for sessions;

3) Work in harmony with staff and other clients;

4) Be self-directed;

5) Work with other clients in completing the tasks of Phase II;

6) Complete thinking reports and work in your journal;

7) Take part fully in the sessions for Basic Skills for Self-Improvement and Change.

# NOTES:

_____

_____

_____

_____

_____

# NOTES:

# MODULE 7

## Introduction to Phase II:
## Developing Commitment to Change

# MODULE 7: INTRODUCTION TO PHASE II: DEVELOPING A COMMITMENT TO CHANGE

## Overview of Module 7

This Module is an introduction to Phase II. You may be taking Modules 7 and 8 in a small group. When you finish, you may be placed in a larger group which is going through Module 9. You are in Module 7 because you have decided to go on to Phase II. This is a big decision for you. It is a large commitment. You are to be commended on your decision.

**Goals and Objectives for Module 7:**

The overall goal for this module is to introduce you to Phase II, Commitment to Change. Phase I challenged you to change by offering opportunities to change. In Phase II, you are expected to take clear action to change. This is the greater test of your commitment to change. Our goals and objectives for this module will be to:

◆ Review and recall what you achieved in Phase I and look at the major issues you addressed in that Phase;

◆ Recognize your own readiness to change;

◆ Learn the basic steps of problem solving and practice problem solving;

◆ Learn to choose different ways to think and act and then practice these alternatives;

◆ Understand that real change is based on a freedom of choice;

◆ Bring your most significant other into program involvement.

**Structure for Modules 7 and 8:**

Module 7 will be two weeks long. This will be followed by Module 8 which is also two weeks long. All sessions in Phase II will be held weekly, and they will be from two to two and a half hours long, with the exception of Module 8 which will require two, 3-hour sessions for doing an in-depth assessment of yourself.

# NOTES:

_____

_____

_____

_____

_____

_____

## Session ⑲ : Recognizing Readiness to Change: Problem Solving and Doing Something Different—It's Your Choice

### 1. Objectives of Session:

What we want to achieve in this session is to recognize that change is not just "knuckling under." It is giving yourself power to make things different and better in the long run. There are four objectives of this session:

> ➠ Look at the progress and change you made in Phase I and look at your commitment to Phase II;
>
> ➠ Recognize your willingness and readiness to change in Phase II;
>
> ➠ Learn problem solving skills and have you look at the idea of finding new choices or alternatives to your thinking and behavior;
>
> ➠ Become aware that change comes from within, that it is of free choice, and that you give yourself the power to change.

### 2. Session Content:

#### a. **How do you know you are ready to change?**

Real change comes from within. It is just not "knuckling under." It is giving yourself the power to make things different and better in the long run. But how do you really recognize that you are ready to change?

Here are some points that may help you to be aware that you are ready to make change:

- You are open to people telling you about your drug use and your past criminal actions;
- You see that you have a problem with AOD use;
- You see that you have a problem with criminal conduct;
- You talk about wanting to make things different and to change;
- You hear yourself say that you can change.

Even more important, if you have made some change, then you are saying "I'm ready to change." Here are some changes you may have made to tell you that you want to commit or promise to change.

- You stop resisting and raising objections;
- You ask fewer questions and talk more about yourself;
- You are more settled and more at peace;
- You hear your self-talk saying "I guess I need to do something about my drug use." "If I wanted to kick this, what could I do?" Or, you tell yourself you have changed—"I stopped for about two weeks."

You do need to know that you will get discouraged. Every day, problems will come up to make you feel: "Is it worth it?" This is part of everyday life. If you have not learned the skills of dealing with everyday problems—which is what we will be learning in this Phase of the program—then you will fall back into the old habits of thinking about AOD use or fall back into criminal thinking. Learning these basic skills for self-improvement and change is important. That is why we will spend some time to learn the skill of problem solving and begin to learn to replace old thoughts and actions with new thoughts and actions. If you are willing to problem solve, you are saying that you do want to change.

117

b. **Learning problem solving:**

A problem is an action, situation, or circumstance that causes you difficulty. The difficulty might boil down to not getting your way in a situation, not being sure what is expected, conflict with another person over how things should be done, a difference between your goal and the goal of someone close, or trying to find someone or something. Usually, there is a goal attached to a problem.

When we are faced with problems, we may have physical symptoms such as our heart beats fast, we sweat, we cry, or we get angry. Most problems involve other people. Some problems are serious, others are easy to solve. Sometimes we identify that we have a problem but are not able to clearly figure out what the problem is. This often leads to being anxious and uneasy until we can clearly identify the problem or the situation causing the problem.

A problem may only be in our thinking. That is the best place where we can solve our problem. We solve it in our head before it takes place in our actions.

**THE SIMPLE STEPS OF PROBLEM SOLVING:**

1) **Identify** the problem situation;

2) **What is my goal?** What would I like to see as the solution to the problem? What do I want the outcome to be?

3) **What are the various solutions** to the problem? What is in my power to do? What action should I take or can I take? Are there different solutions? Get information you need to make the best choice;

4) **What are the obstacles** that get in the way of solving the problem?

5) **Make a choice and start the action;**

6) **Study the outcome** of your choice. What was the result? Was it in my best interest? Could I have done something different? What will I do next time?

**Example:** John would like to go out with his friend Cliff tonight, but Cliff always drinks. That means he will drink if they go out together. When he goes out and drinks with Cliff, he usually puts himself at risk of getting into trouble. *Apply the steps above to this example.*

c. **Learning to apply different choices:**

An alternative or "different choice" plan allows you to think in many different directions. You have learned to do one kind of thing in a certain situation. Change that choice. It is in your power. Think of a problem situation where you can replace the old choice with a new one. What are the steps of applying this "different choice" method? Here are the simple steps of applying different choices or alternatives:

1) **LEARN TO BE AWARE YOU ARE MAKING A DECISION—A CHOICE: STOP AND THINK.** Don't rush into a solution. When you can make a decision, you have a choice. Practice this. Even in the simple things. "I can decide to go to the grocery store first or the hardware store." This leaves you with a choice. It is your freedom. You look at the alternatives;

2) **GET INFORMATION—TAKE YOUR TIME.** Details are important. Brainstorm, thinking of all the possible answers. Ask yourself: "What do I still need to know?" "What else might be contributing to the situation?" "What is another way I can think of this?" "How can I figure out what might happen? What are the possible outcomes?"

3) **MAKE YOUR DECISION—YOUR CHOICE.**

4) **LOOK AT THE OUTCOME—THE RESULTS.** Did it save time to go to the grocery store first? Replay the tape. What would be different had you gone to the hardware store first?

Thus—always think—I have a decision to make. Make your choice. Process the outcome.

### d. Are you blocking change? Are you resisting?

*You can problem solve...find alternatives.*

You have a lifetime of habits, attitudes and beliefs. You may even argue against yourself about making change. Will you continue to do things as you always have? You have a choice. You can problem solve. You can find alternatives. If you are too invested in these old patterns of thinking and acting, you may fight changing. No one can force you. But if you don't change, what will be the results? If you do, what will be the long-term result?

If you find yourself fighting being in the program, you are blocking. You can do several things inside your head. Hold a debate with yourself. Go ahead and argue. But after you do that, then just echo or reflect back what you heard inside. "I don't want to be in this program." "But I don't want to go back to breaking the law and ending up in jail." "No, I want to be free. I have a choice."

### e. Review of Thinking Reports and Journals:

These will be important tools in problem solving, looking at different choices and in seeing the outcome of your actions. Now we see the Thinking Report and Journals in a new light. When we look at the outcome now, we know we had a choice—we made a decision in that event.

Remember the basic parts of the Thinking Report:

1) **Event:** Describe the situation;

2) What were your **thoughts** about and during the event? What were the automatic thoughts?

3) What were your **feelings** before, during, after the event?

4) What were your **attitudes** and **beliefs**? Were these long-held beliefs?

5) What was the **outcome** of the event? Did your decision or choice make a difference?

Remember the basic parts of writing in the journal around a target thought or behavior:

1) Describe the situation around the target thought or action;

2) Write down your feelings and thoughts;

3) Look at your patterns and cycles of thinking and acting;

4) What thoughts did you change? What action did you take to correct or change the situation?

## Homework assignments:

a. Apply the problem solving steps to a problem that you had this week. Use Work Sheet 16;

b. Do a thinking report around the problem: Events, thoughts, feelings, beliefs, outcome. Do this in your journal.

# WORK SHEET 16

## PROBLEM SOLVING EXERCISE

Choose a problem to solve or one you did solve. Fill in the blanks around the problem.

1. Identify the problem.

_____

_____

_____

2. What is my goal?

_____

_____

_____

3. What are the different solutions to the problem?

_____

_____

_____

4. What are the obstacles? What's getting in the way of solving the problem?

_____

_____

_____

5. Make a choice. Choose a solution and start your action.

_____

_____

_____

6. What was the outcome of your choice or solution? Did it meet your goals? Could you have done something different?

_____

_____

_____

# Session **20** : Involving Significant Others

## 1. Objectives of Session:

➠ Have your significant other(s) get acquainted with the program and begin to feel comfortable about being involved in the future;

➠ Provide a positive and supportive place for you to talk and communicate about what your involvement has been in the program;

➠ Give your significant other(s) a chance to talk about the effect your use of drugs and involvement in criminal conduct have had on your relationship and your family;

➠ Give your significant other(s) and yourself a chance to share your goals and expectations for the relationship.

## 2. Session Content:
### a. **Our need for closeness and our need for separateness:**

A famous psychologist by the name of Abraham Maslow concluded that people have five basic needs. These are:

1) **Physical needs:** needs for that which sustains life such as food, air, sleep, elimination and water;

2) **Safety need:** needs for protection from danger and threat;

3) **Social needs:** needs for friendship, acceptance and love;

4) **Esteem needs:** needs for self-esteem or to have self-confidence, self-respect; need for esteem from others, to be recognized, be important, appreciated;

5) **Self-Actualization needs:** need to fulfill your talents, or bring out from within you your best.

This list tells us that we have two important needs in relationship to people around us. We have a need to be loved, to be in a relationship, to be close to people. But we have a need to be ourselves, to be an individual, to be separate and to fulfill the best within us. How do we balance these two needs? We do this by respecting both of these needs in ourselves and in others: to put effort into keeping healthy relationships; to keep and maintain our selves as separate human beings. We need to give to relationships; we need to give to ourselves.

The three diagrams in Figure 14 on the next page indicate how we might see the relationship between the need for closeness and the need for separateness. Circles Set One shows a situation where there is no individuality in the relationship; it is all relationship. The person cannot go fishing, read the paper, or do anything separate without the relationship trying to control the person. Circles Set Two shows no relationship, and the individual's energy is directed only at the self. Circles Set Three shows a good balance; there is separateness of the individual; and there is closeness and relationship. As we involve our significant others in our program, it is important that we keep this balance in mind. We will look closer at our relationships in one of our later sessions.

*We have a need to be loved and to be ourselves.*

**Figure 14**

**Relationship Balance Between Closeness and Separateness**

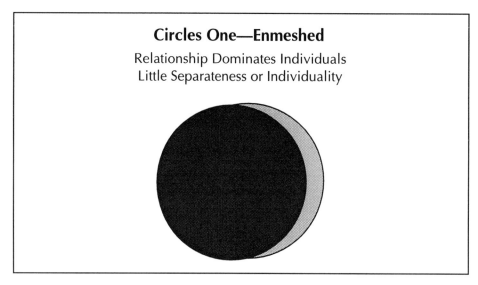

### Circles One—Enmeshed

Relationship Dominates Individuals
Little Separateness or Individuality

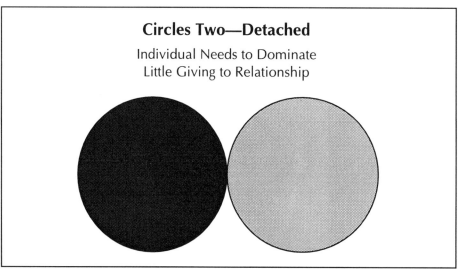

### Circles Two—Detached

Individual Needs to Dominate
Little Giving to Relationship

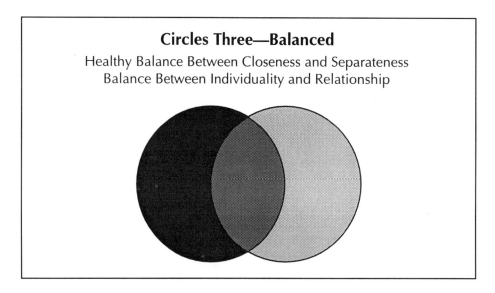

### Circles Three—Balanced

Healthy Balance Between Closeness and Separateness
Balance Between Individuality and Relationship

b. **Your significant other(s) may have opportunity to be involved in the program in these ways:**

1. To join a Significant Others Support Group;

2. Depending on the outcome of our in-depth assessment to be done in the next Module, you and significant others may be asked to join a Multiple Family Problem Solving Reflections Group. This group will be directed at solving problems. It is not set up to be a therapy group. You can be in that group with your significant other(s) as long as you want or until you feel you have addressed and solved the problems you may have between and among you;

3. More in-depth family or conjoint (with spouse or significant other) counseling;

4. Your significant other(s) will be asked to join us in two of our Basic Skills for Self-Improvement and Change sessions.

## Classroom or homework assignments:

a. Present the thinking report that you did for homework this week in your reflection group with your significant other(s);

b. Write down in your journal a problem that you would like help with now. Then answer these questions: Who might help you with this problem? What would you want this person to do that would be helpful? How can you ask this person for help? What do you think you should say to get help with your problem? Pick a good time to ask this person for help and do it. What was the outcome? Describe what happened in your journal;

c. Using Work Sheet 17, list the problems you have under the specific areas on the Work Sheet. This will prepare you for the next session.

# NOTES:

_____

_____

_____

_____

_____

_____

_____

_____

# WORK SHEET 17

## LIST OF PROBLEMS TO WORK ON

List problems that you need to work on for each of the focus areas:

A. Problems you have carried over from childhood and youth:

1. _____

2. _____

3. _____

4. _____

5. _____

6. _____

B. Problems with alcohol and other drug use and abuse:

1. _____

2. _____

3. _____

4. _____

5. _____

6. _____

C. Problems with criminal thinking and antisocial acting:

1. _____

2. _____

3. _____

4. _____

5. _____

6. _____

D. Thinking and feeling patterns and errors:

1. _____

2. _____

3. _____

4. _____

5. _____

6. _____

E. Current life situation problems:

Employment and job problems:

1. _____

2. _____

3. _____

Living situation and accommodations:

1. _____

2. _____

3. _____

Social and relationship problems:

1. _____

2. _____

3. _____

Marital and family issues and problems:

1. _____

2. _____

3. _____

Physical health problems:

1. _____

2. _____

3. _____

Psychological and emotional problems:

1. _____

2. _____

3. _____

## NOTES:

_____

_____

_____

_____

_____

_____

_____

_____

_____

_____

_____

**MODULE 8**

**In-Depth Assessment:**

**Looking at the Areas of Need and Change**

# MODULE 8: IN-DEPTH ASSESSMENT: LOOKING AT THE AREAS OF NEED AND CHANGE

## Overview of Module 8

In Phase I you were given a chance to talk about and disclose your present and past problems in the area of alcohol and other drug abuse. You also talked about your past involvement in criminal conduct. The main reason for this was to help increase your self-awareness in these problem areas. As we have learned, self-awareness is one of the first steps toward change.

The purpose of this part of the program, Module 8, is to have you take a closer look at your past and present problems and situation. We are calling this the In-Depth Study and Assessment of Yourself. You will be asked to complete several tests. These tests, along with the ones you have already taken, will be used to build what we will call a *Master Profile*. From this profile, we will build a *Master Assessment Plan* (MAP). This MAP will be the guide for your involvement in the rest of the program. It will be your guide as you enter the programs for developing and enhancing Basic Skills for Self-Improvement and Change in Module 9. Your MAP will also help you to determine if you need some further services beyond this program.

**Goals and Objectives for Module 8:**

◆ To do a study of the following areas:

1. Your patterns of AOD use and abuse;

2. Your criminal conduct and risk factors;

3. Your thinking and feeling patterns;

4. Your life situation problems and conditions.

◆ From these areas of study, to identify or define your specific targets of change;

◆ To develop your *Master Assessment Plan* (MAP).

**Time and Presentation Structure for Module 8**

Two 3-hour sessions will be used for this Module. Most work will be done within the sessions. You will do a lot of the work alone or with the help of your counselor. You may be asked to spend some individual time with your counselor as you put together your *Master Profile* and your *Master Assessment Plan*. You will be asked to share some of your findings with the group, but only what you feel comfortable sharing.

# Session ㉑: The In-Depth Assessment: Getting the Information to Plot the Master Profile

## 1. Objectives of Session:

> ⇒ Complete and score the self-administered test which will provide an in-depth look at your problems associated with AOD use, criminal conduct and other life-situation problems;
>
> ⇒ Complete the List of Problems to Work On, Work Sheet 17, which was your homework this past week.

## 2. Session Content:

### a. Introduction to Session:

At this point in our program, it is important for you to develop a plan or MAP for change. Up to this time, you have shared a lot about yourself. Much of the information you shared has been about the general areas of your AOD use and your involvement in criminal conduct. In the next two sessions, you will take a closer look at these two areas. We call this an in-depth study and assessment. You will have a chance to tell us more about how you see yourself doing in a number of other areas. We will want to see if there are specific problem areas and conditions that you need to work on and change. This information will help you get the most out of the Basic Skills for Self-Improvement and Change sessions and your individual treatment plan.

Self-improvement and change can best take place when you, your counselor and your peers in the program work together as partners. Thus, this in-depth assessment will be done together with your counselor, and in some ways, with the peers in your group. But this "closer look" and in-depth evaluation is for you—it is to benefit you.

### b. The Assessment Window:

We now know that we learn about ourselves through sharing and disclosing and through the feedback we get from others. Self-disclosure and feedback are two very important ways that we communicate with others. There are several areas of information about ourselves that are communicated. There are things we know about ourselves that others do not know. This is the *Hidden Area*. There are things that others see about us that we don't see. That is the *Blind Area*. There are things about ourselves we do not know and others do not know. This is the *Unknown Area*. Then there are things about ourselves that we see and know and that other people see and know. This is called the *Free Area* or the "open area." Our goal of assessment is to increase that "open area."

The Johari Window in Figure 15 gives us a picture of these areas of information. This is a way of looking at and understanding the self. The goal of this module is to make the *Free Area* larger and to shrink the *Blind* and *Hidden* areas. This will be done through tests and surveys that allow you to report more about yourself. You will also do this through getting feedback from others. From all of this, you will put together what we will call a *Master Profile* (MP). This MP will become the guide for making up a *Master Assessment Plan* (MAP). *The Master Profile* will help you to organize and put together all of this information about yourself. From the *Master Profile* you will develop the *Master Assessment Plan*.

# Figure 15

*The Assessment Framework or Picture: The Johari Window*

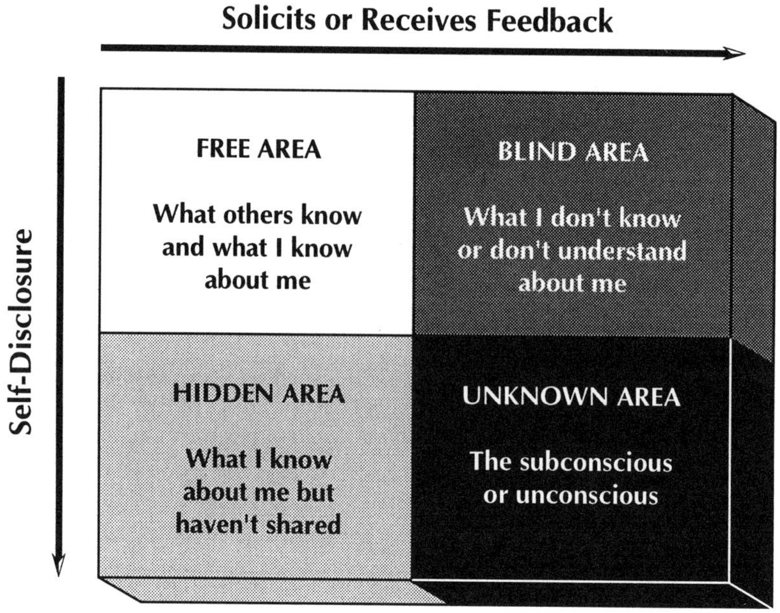

**Solicits or Receives Feedback**

| | FREE AREA | BLIND AREA |
|---|---|---|
| **Self-Disclosure** | What others know and what I know about me | What I don't know or don't understand about me |
| | HIDDEN AREA | UNKNOWN AREA |
| | What I know about me but haven't shared | The subconscious or unconscious |

c. **The areas of our In-depth Study and Assessment:**

Our in-depth study of ourselves will involve looking at several important areas of our life in order to understand our thought and behavior habits and to identify problems that have developed from these habits and patterns. We began to prepare for this self-study through our work on the List of Problems to Work On (Work Sheet 17) which was part of this week's homework. We will now complete that work sheet in class. Here is an outline of the important areas of our life that we will address:

1) Alcohol and Other Drug Use and Abuse:

- Drugs of choice;
- Styles of use;
- Benefits of using alcohol and other drugs;
- Type of problems from use;
- Readiness for help;
- Degree of problems from use.

2) Criminal and Antisocial Thinking and Conduct:

- Degree of involvement in criminal conduct;
- Type of involvement (property offenses, person offenses, etc.);
- Antisocial attitudes and thinking and criminogenic needs.

3) Thinking and Feeling Patterns:

- Victim stance: Blame projection;
- Narrow or restricted thinking;
- Personalizing—feeling victimized;
- Superior or grandiose thinking;
- Self-centered (narcissistic) thinking;
- Self-defeating thinking (depressed, put self down);
- Antisocial and irresponsible thinking.

4). Background Problems and Adjustment:

- Adolescent AOD use;
- Delinquency;
- Family problems;
- School problems.

5) Current Life-Situation Problems:

- Employment and job productivity;
- Residential stability;
- Social-interpersonal;
- Marital-family relationship adjustment;
- Health;
- Psychological-emotional.

6) Interest and Readiness for Treatment:

- Awareness of AOD/CC problems;
- Acknowledge need for help;
- Willingness to accept help;
- Other perception of my need for help;
- Taken action to change.

7) Stage of Change:

- Challenged to change;
- Commitment to change;
- Taking ownership of change.

## Classroom exercises and assignments—Preparing for the next Session:

a. Complete Problem Focus Work Sheet 17 that you did for homework;

b. Complete the following instruments:

Life Situation Questionnaire;
Mood Appraisal Questionnaire;

c. Score the following instruments taken at admissions and construct profiles;

Alcohol Use Inventory (AUI);
Drug Use Self Report (DUSR);

d. Use the Johari Window as a basis for talking about what you learned from the various tests and profiles you completed. Discuss your alcohol and drug use patterns in group. Share what you learned from completing the List of Problems to Work On, Work Sheet 17.

e. For next session, you will use all of the following tests and information in developing your *Master Profile* and your *Master Assessment Plan*. Look over the results of these tests and work sheets:

1) The tests that you took before you entered this program and which you took again in Session 12 and 13.

- Level of Service Inventory;
- Alcohol Use Questionnaire (ADS);
- Drug Use Questionnaire (DAST);
- Adult Substance Use Survey (ASUS);

2) The tests you took at admission to this program:

- Alcohol Use Inventory (AUI);
- Drug Use Self Report (DUSR).

3) The tests you took in this session:

- Mood Appraisal Questionaire;
- Life situation Questionaire.

4) The list of Problems to Work On (Work Sheet 17)

## NOTES:

_____

_____

_____

_____

_____

_____

_____

_____

_____

_____

_____

_____

_____

# Session 22: Targets of Change and the Master Assessment Plan (MAP)

## 1. Objectives of Session:

> ➧ Complete the Master Profile (MP) using all of the tests outlined in Session 21 and the List of Problems to Work On (Work Sheet 17);
>
> ➧ Develop a Master Assessment Plan (MAP).

## 2 Session Content and Exercises:

a. **Introduction:**

You have given information about yourself in the tests and questionnaires you completed and in the information you gave through the homework you did on the List of Problems to Work on Work Sheet. You have looked at the results of these tests. Now we will make a *Master Profile (MP)*. From the MP you will make a *Master Assessment Plan*. This plan or MAP will be a guide for you during the next five months of this program. Your MAP will change as you add new information about yourself.

b. **Exercise 1:** Develop the *Master Profile (MP)*. This is provided in Work Sheet 18. Complete the first part of the MP, the Alcohol and Other Drug Use Assessment. Use the results from the Alcohol Use Inventory (AUI) and the Drug Use Self Report (DUSR) or other instruments in the AOD abuse area that you completed. Complete the other parts of the MP, using information from profiles from the other tests you completed. Your counselor will help you in this process.

c. **Exercise 2:** From the MP, complete the *Master Assessment Plan*. Use Work Sheet 19, the "Master Assessment Plan." This will involve identifying a specific problem area, what changes in thinking and action need to be made and then the specific treatment activity that might be helpful in correcting and changing the problem. Identify as many problems as you want for each of the four main areas. Your counselor will give you examples on how to complete your MAP.

d. **Share what you found in your Reflection Group.**

### Classroom or homework assignments:

a. Classroom Assignment: Complete the *Master Profile and Master Assessment Plan*. Look it over carefully. Is it accurate?

b. Take the one problem in the MAP that you feel is most important. Discuss it with someone you trust and feel close to. Get that person's ideas.

## NOTES:

_____

_____

_____

_____

_____

# WORK SHEET 18: MASTER PROFILE (MP)

## I. Alcohol and Other Drug Use Assessment

| | Area of Assessment | Low | | | | Moderate | | | | High | |
|---|---|---|---|---|---|---|---|---|---|---|---|
| **Drug Choice** | Alcohol Involvement | 1 | 2 | 3 | 4 | 5 | 6 | 7 | 8 | 9 | 10 |
| | Marijuana Involvement | 1 | 2 | 3 | 4 | 5 | 6 | 7 | 8 | 9 | 10 |
| | Cocaine Involvement | 1 | 2 | 3 | 4 | 5 | 6 | 7 | 8 | 9 | 10 |
| | Amphetamine Involvement | 1 | 2 | 3 | 4 | 5 | 6 | 7 | 8 | 9 | 10 |
| | Other Drug Involvement | 1 | 2 | 3 | 4 | 5 | 6 | 7 | 8 | 9 | 10 |
| | Poly Drug User | 1 | 2 | 3 | 4 | 5 | 6 | 7 | 8 | 9 | 10 |

| | Area of Assessment | Low | | | | Moderate | | | | High | |
|---|---|---|---|---|---|---|---|---|---|---|---|
| **Style** | Convivial or Gregarious | 1 | 2 | 3 | 4 | 5 | 6 | 7 | 8 | 9 | 10 |
| | Sustained & Continuous | 1 | 2 | 3 | 4 | 5 | 6 | 7 | 8 | 9 | 10 |
| | Compulsive & Obsessive | 1 | 2 | 3 | 4 | 5 | 6 | 7 | 8 | 9 | 10 |

| | Area of Assessment | Low | | | | Moderate | | | | High | |
|---|---|---|---|---|---|---|---|---|---|---|---|
| **Benefits** | Cope with Social Discomfort | 1 | 2 | 3 | 4 | 5 | 6 | 7 | 8 | 9 | 10 |
| | Cope with Emotional Discomfort | 1 | 2 | 3 | 4 | 5 | 6 | 7 | 8 | 9 | 10 |
| | Cope with Relationships | 1 | 2 | 3 | 4 | 5 | 6 | 7 | 8 | 9 | 10 |
| | Cope with Physical Distress | 1 | 2 | 3 | 4 | 5 | 6 | 7 | 8 | 9 | 10 |

| | Area of Assessment | Low | | | | Moderate | | | | High | |
|---|---|---|---|---|---|---|---|---|---|---|---|
| **Results** | Behavioral Control Loss | 1 | 2 | 3 | 4 | 5 | 6 | 7 | 8 | 9 | 10 |
| | Emotional Disruption | 1 | 2 | 3 | 4 | 5 | 6 | 7 | 8 | 9 | 10 |
| | Physical Disruption | 1 | 2 | 3 | 4 | 5 | 6 | 7 | 8 | 9 | 10 |
| | Social Irresponsibility | 1 | 2 | 3 | 4 | 5 | 6 | 7 | 8 | 9 | 10 |
| | Overall Disruption | 1 | 2 | 3 | 4 | 5 | 6 | 7 | 8 | 9 | 10 |

| | Area of Assessment | Low | | | | Moderate | | | | High | |
|---|---|---|---|---|---|---|---|---|---|---|---|
| **Ready** | AOD Problem Awareness | 1 | 2 | 3 | 4 | 5 | 6 | 7 | 8 | 9 | 10 |
| | Treatment Receptiveness | 1 | 2 | 3 | 4 | 5 | 6 | 7 | 8 | 9 | 10 |
| | Motivation to Change | 1 | 2 | 3 | 4 | 5 | 6 | 7 | 8 | 9 | 10 |

# WORK SHEET 18: MASTER PROFILE (continued)

## II. Criminal and Antisocial Thinking and Conduct

| | Area of Assessment | Level of Problem Severity | | | | | | | | | |
|---|---|---|---|---|---|---|---|---|---|---|---|
| | | **Low** | | | | **Moderate** | | | | **High** | |
| **Conduct** | Property Offenses I | 1 | 2 | 3 | 4 | 5 | 6 | 7 | 8 | 9 | 10 |
| | Property Offenses II | 1 | 2 | 3 | 4 | 5 | 6 | 7 | 8 | 9 | 10 |
| | Person Offenses I | 1 | 2 | 3 | 4 | 5 | 6 | 7 | 8 | 9 | 10 |
| | Person Offenses II | 1 | 2 | 3 | 4 | 5 | 6 | 7 | 8 | 9 | 10 |
| | Motor Vehicle—Non AOD | 1 | 2 | 3 | 4 | 5 | 6 | 7 | 8 | 9 | 10 |
| | Motor Vehicle—AOD Involved | 1 | 2 | 3 | 4 | 5 | 6 | 7 | 8 | 9 | 10 |

| | Area of Assessment | Level of Problem Severity | | | | | | | | | |
|---|---|---|---|---|---|---|---|---|---|---|---|
| | | **Low** | | | | **Moderate** | | | | **High** | |
| **Criminal Thinking** | Antisocial Peers & Models | 1 | 2 | 3 | 4 | 5 | 6 | 7 | 8 | 9 | 10 |
| | Impulsive Thinking/Acting | 1 | 2 | 3 | 4 | 5 | 6 | 7 | 8 | 9 | 10 |
| | Self-Centered Thinking | 1 | 2 | 3 | 4 | 5 | 6 | 7 | 8 | 9 | 10 |
| | Criminal Thinking/Thoughts | 1 | 2 | 3 | 4 | 5 | 6 | 7 | 8 | 9 | 10 |
| | Need for Family Attachment | 1 | 2 | 3 | 4 | 5 | 6 | 7 | 8 | 9 | 10 |
| | Social/Interpersonal Skills | 1 | 2 | 3 | 4 | 5 | 6 | 7 | 8 | 9 | 10 |
| | Problem Solving/Self-Management | 1 | 2 | 3 | 4 | 5 | 6 | 7 | 8 | 9 | 10 |
| | Angry/Aggressive Attitude | 1 | 2 | 3 | 4 | 5 | 6 | 7 | 8 | 9 | 10 |
| | Rebellious/Anti-Authority | 1 | 2 | 3 | 4 | 5 | 6 | 7 | 8 | 9 | 10 |

## III. Assessment of Thinking and Feeling Patterns

| | Area of Assessment | Level of Problem Severity | | | | | | | | | |
|---|---|---|---|---|---|---|---|---|---|---|---|
| | | **Low** | | | | **Moderate** | | | | **High** | |
| **Thinking** | Blame, Victim Stance | 1 | 2 | 3 | 4 | 5 | 6 | 7 | 8 | 9 | 10 |
| | Narrow-Restricted Thinking | 1 | 2 | 3 | 4 | 5 | 6 | 7 | 8 | 9 | 10 |
| | Personalizing Responses | 1 | 2 | 3 | 4 | 5 | 6 | 7 | 8 | 9 | 10 |
| | Superior/Grandiose Thinking | 1 | 2 | 3 | 4 | 5 | 6 | 7 | 8 | 9 | 10 |
| | Self-Defeating Thinking | 1 | 2 | 3 | 4 | 5 | 6 | 7 | 8 | 9 | 10 |
| | Irresponsible Thinking | 1 | 2 | 3 | 4 | 5 | 6 | 7 | 8 | 9 | 10 |
| | Self-Centered Thinking | 1 | 2 | 3 | 4 | 5 | 6 | 7 | 8 | 9 | 10 |

## IV. Background Problems of Childhood Development

| | Area of Assessment | Level of Problem Severity | | | | | | | | | |
|---|---|---|---|---|---|---|---|---|---|---|---|
| | | | **Low** | | | **Moderate** | | | | **High** | |
| **Ready** | AOD Use Adolescence | 1 | 2 | 3 | 4 | 5 | 6 | 7 | 8 | 9 | 10 |
| | Delinquency | 1 | 2 | 3 | 4 | 5 | 6 | 7 | 8 | 9 | 10 |
| | Family Problems | 1 | 2 | 3 | 4 | 5 | 6 | 7 | 8 | 9 | 10 |
| | Cope with Physical Distress | 1 | 2 | 3 | 4 | 5 | 6 | 7 | 8 | 9 | 10 |

## V. Current Life Situation Problems

| | Area of Assessment | | **Low** | | | **Moderate** | | | | **High** | |
|---|---|---|---|---|---|---|---|---|---|---|---|
| **Current Stage** | Job and Employment Problems | 1 | 2 | 3 | 4 | 5 | 6 | 7 | 8 | 9 | 10 |
| | Residential Instability | 1 | 2 | 3 | 4 | 5 | 6 | 7 | 8 | 9 | 10 |
| | Social/Interpersonal Problems | 1 | 2 | 3 | 4 | 5 | 6 | 7 | 8 | 9 | 10 |
| | Marital/Family Problems | 1 | 2 | 3 | 4 | 5 | 6 | 7 | 8 | 9 | 10 |
| | Health and Physical Problems | 1 | 2 | 3 | 4 | 5 | 6 | 7 | 8 | 9 | 10 |
| | Emotional/Psychological | 1 | 2 | 3 | 4 | 5 | 6 | 7 | 8 | 9 | 10 |

## VI. Motivation and Readiness for Treatment

| | Rate Each Area Separately | | **Low** | | | **Moderate** | | | | **High** | |
|---|---|---|---|---|---|---|---|---|---|---|---|
| **Readiness** | Awareness of AOD/CC Problem | 1 | 2 | 3 | 4 | 5 | 6 | 7 | 8 | 9 | 10 |
| | Acknowledgment of Need for Help | 1 | 2 | 3 | 4 | 5 | 6 | 7 | 8 | 9 | 10 |
| | Willingness to Accept Help | 1 | 2 | 3 | 4 | 5 | 6 | 7 | 8 | 9 | 10 |
| | Other's Perception of Need | 1 | 2 | 3 | 4 | 5 | 6 | 7 | 8 | 9 | 10 |
| | Other's Perception of Need | 1 | 2 | 3 | 4 | 5 | 6 | 7 | 8 | 9 | 10 |
| | Has Taken Action to Change | 1 | 2 | 3 | 4 | 5 | 6 | 7 | 8 | 9 | 10 |

## VII. Stage of Change

| | Rate Each Stage Separately | | **Low** | | | **Moderate** | | | | **High** | |
|---|---|---|---|---|---|---|---|---|---|---|---|
| **Stage** | Challenge to Change | 1 | 2 | 3 | 4 | 5 | 6 | 7 | 8 | 9 | 10 |
| | Commitment to Change | 1 | 2 | 3 | 4 | 5 | 6 | 7 | 8 | 9 | 10 |
| | Ownership of Change | 1 | 2 | 3 | 4 | 5 | 6 | 7 | 8 | 9 | 10 |

# WORK SHEET 19
## MASTER ASSESSMENT PLAN (MAP)

I. Alcohol and Other Drug Use Problem Areas

| Problem Area & Description | Changes Needed in Thought & Action | Programs & Resources to Be Used to Make Changes | Date Worked On |
|---|---|---|---|
| | | | |
| | | | |
| | | | |
| | | | |
| | | | |
| | | | |
| | | | |

# WORK SHEET 19
## MASTER ASSESSMENT PLAN (continued)

II. Criminal and Antisocial Thinking and Conduct

| Problem Area & Description | Changes Needed in Thought & Action | Programs & Resources to Be Used to Make Changes | Date Worked On |
|---|---|---|---|
| | | | |
| | | | |
| | | | |
| | | | |
| | | | |
| | | | |

# WORK SHEET 19
## MASTER ASSESSMENT PLAN (continued)

III. Thinking and Feeling Patterns

| Problem Area & Description | Changes Needed in Thought & Action | Programs & Resources to Be Used to Make Changes | Date Worked On |
|---|---|---|---|
|  |  |  |  |
|  |  |  |  |
|  |  |  |  |
|  |  |  |  |
|  |  |  |  |
|  |  |  |  |
|  |  |  |  |

# WORK SHEET 19
## MASTER ASSESSMENT PLAN (continued)

IV. Current Life Situation Problems

| Problem Area & Description | Changes Needed in Thought & Action | Programs & Resources to Be Used to Make Changes | Date Worked On |
|---|---|---|---|
|  |  |  |  |
|  |  |  |  |
|  |  |  |  |
|  |  |  |  |
|  |  |  |  |
|  |  |  |  |

# MODULE 9

# Strengthening Basic Skills for Self-Improvement and Change:

# Acting on the Commitment to Change

# MODULE 9: STRENGTHENING BASIC SKILLS FOR SELF-IMPROVEMENT AND CHANGE: ACTING ON THE COMMITMENT TO CHANGE

## Overview of Module 9

We now are going into the most important part of this program. This is another test for your commitment to change. You have really done well up to this point. You have given a great amount of time and energy to this program. You have made some very important changes. Now we are going to focus on learning skills that we can apply to critical areas of change.

These special focus programs will be directed at building or strengthening the skills needed to relate to ourselves, to others and to society in effective and healthy ways. We will look at how you can build values and develop the kind of critical reasoning and thinking that will help you live a drug-free life. We will look at developing the kind of prosocial skills and moral reasoning that will help you to live a crime-free life. For those who have already developed these skills, it will be a matter of building upon that foundation and strengthening those skills you already have.

**Objectives for Module**

Our overall goal for Module 9 is to help you learn the skills to put your commitment to change into action. These skills will give you the self-confidence and mastery to bring about changes in your life and to strengthen positive thoughts about yourself and how you relate to others and your community. Here are our specific aims of this Module:

➠ Learn the following coping and communication skills in order to manage your social world and your relationship:

  ◆ Communicate and express your feelings, thoughts and beliefs to others and help others to do the same;

  ◆ Begin and strengthen meaningful relationships with others;

  ◆ Effectively handle social and intimate interpersonal relationships and expectations (e.g, marriage, intimate partner relationships; social involvement);

  ◆ Be assertive in relationship to others;

  ◆ Prevent aggression and violence;

  ◆ Learn to practice empathy;

➠ To manage and cope with your mental world, you will learn:

  ◆ Skills to effectively manage attitudes, beliefs and errors in thinking which lead to AOD and CC;

  ◆ Skills of problem solving.

➠ To manage and cope with the cravings, urges and need to engage in AOD use and criminal activities, you will learn:

  ◆ To identify high-risk situations for AOD use and criminal conduct;

  ◆ To identify and understand AOD cravings and urges;

  ◆ AOD refusal skills;

  ◆ CC refusal skills.

⫸ To develop positive responses and skills in social responsibility:

◆ Strengthen driving attitudes and patterns.

◆ Increase job and economic productivity.

◆ Understand the meaning of values and moral development and to apply the skills of moral responsibility to community living.

### How this Module will be set up

Module 9 will run for 18 weeks. Sessions will be two and a half hours in length to include breaks. At certain break-points in this module, new participants may enter the program. We will try to get to know these new folks as they enter the program. Make them welcome.

# NOTES:

_____

_____

_____

_____

_____

_____

_____

_____

_____

_____

_____

_____

# NOTES:

# Session ㉓: Coping and Social Skills Training: Basic Communication Skills— Active Sharing and Active Listening

## 1. Objectives of Session:

> ▥➡ Review and practice the basic skills of self-directed communication: Active sharing;
>
> ▥➡ Review and practice the basic skills of other-oriented communication: Active listening.

## 2. Session Content and Process:

a. **THIS SESSION WILL REVIEW AND PRACTICE THE COMMUNICATION SKILLS WE LEARNED IN SESSION 10. THERE IS POWER IN COMMUNICATION. IT IS THE POWER OF TALKING AND THE POWER OF LISTENING.**

b. **Communication is a two-way street:**

1) Active sharing;

2) Active listening.

Self-disclosure is accomplished through the use of active sharing skills. This is self-directed communication. But communication is a two-way street. Other-directed communication is just as important. We accomplish this through active listening.

c. **Active sharing:**

There are two key skills that make for successful active sharing or self-directed communication.

1) The first key skill: *Telling the other person about you—using the "I" message.* This is talk about you. There are four basic parts to this communication:

- I feel;

- I need;

- I think;

- I do or I act.

The most unselfish thing you can do is to start a sentence off with *"I."* Why? Because when you use the word "I" you share yourself. Sharing yourself is unselfish. Active sharing is about you, not about the other person. It's not bragging. It's just being honest about yourself. Most important, you hear yourself through yourself.

2) The second key skill to active sharing: *Listening to feedback from others about you.* You hear yourself through others. This is hard to do. But you give people permission to do this. When people talk about you, it should be on the basis that you give them permission. The key to receiving feedback is to not get defensive. When we get defensive—or push away and ward off—with someone who gives us feedback, then we stop that person from giving us feedback. If the feedback is critical or negative, we often get openly defensive. But even when the feedback is a compliment or positive, we still tend to push that feedback away. We will look at the skill of receiving compliments in a later session.

d. **Active listening:**

1) There are the two key skills in other-directed communication or active listening communication:

- Invite the person to share by using OPEN STATEMENTS OR QUESTIONS: "How are you today?" "Tell me more about your accident." Avoid "Do you?" questions. Those are closed questions. Closed statements get a "yes" or "no" answer.

- Reflect back what you hear the other person saying. "I hear you saying you are upset." "You seem to feel happy today."

2) Bypass your thinking filters, choosing an "open channel" to listen:

Our "thinking filters" are the screens that we run through what other people say. These thinking filters are our beliefs, our attitudes and our values. We don't have to give up these beliefs and attitudes to listen. We can have an open "listening channel." We can then make our response come from that channel and not our "thinking filters."

When we run what we see and hear through our "thinking filter," we may twist and distort what we are hearing. It is easy to run it through our own "filter"—which are our beliefs and our attitudes and our values.

3) "Listening" to body talk. Here is some body talk that we can listen to and learn from:

POSTURE

FACIAL EXPRESSION

TONE OF VOICE

PERSONAL SPACE

HAND, FACE AND FOOT GESTURES

*Look at the person and pay attention to what is being said.*

4) Here are some points for good active listening:

- Look at the person you are talking with; establish eye contact;

- Watch the person's body language: facial expression, gestures, tone of voice;

- Pay attention to what is being said; try to understand. If you don't understand, ask open questions;

- When you do understand, nod your head to encourage the speaker;

- Reflect back what you hear; mirror back what you hear; this tells the other person you hear them;

- Use some ACTIVE SHARING skills. Share with the other person who you are and what you feel and think.

## Classroom or homework activities:

a. For the first few days of this coming week, practice only ACTIVE SHARING. Use "I messages," not "you messages." Talk about you. Don't talk about the other person;

b. For the rest of the week, practice invitations to talk and reflect. Reflect at the end of each day as to how successful you were;

c. Do the homework or classroom exercises in the Workbook, Work Sheets 20 and 21 on the following pages.

# WORK SHEET 20

## HOMEWORK FOR ACTIVE SHARING

Take one situation you were involved in when you were practicing active sharing.

1. Describe the situation.

_____

_____

_____

_____

_____

2. Who was involved?

_____

_____

_____

_____

3. What specific active sharing skills did you use?

_____

_____

_____

_____

4. How did they work? Did the other person listen? Did the other person get defensive?

_____

_____

_____

_____

# WORK SHEET 21

## ACTIVE LISTENING

Use one of the options below.

Option 1: Start and continue a conversation with someone you know. Pay attention to the skills that have been discussed during this session.

Option 2. Watch a conversation between two other people, paying attention to the skills that have been discussed during this session.

1. Describe the situation.

_____

_____

_____

2. Who was involved? Do you know the relationship between the people?

_____

_____

_____

3. What specific active sharing listening skills did you use?

_____

_____

_____

4. How did they work? Did the other person talk more? Did they get defensive?

_____

_____

_____

5. What were the verbal cues that encouraged additional conversation?

_____

_____

_____

# Session ㉔ : Coping and Social Skills Training: Basic Communication Skills—Starting Conversations

## 1. Objectives of Session:

We will now begin to build our coping skills and our social and relationship skills on the communication foundation of active sharing and active listening. Here is what we want to learn and practice in this session:

> ➠ Review the skills of active sharing and active listening;
>
> ➠ Learn and practice the skill of starting a conversation;
>
> ➠ Develop the ability to communicate in unfamiliar situations.

## 2. Session Content and Process:

In Session 10 (Module 4), we learned about verbal and non-verbal communication. In our last session, we also learned about self-oriented communication skills and other-oriented communication skills. Now we will take what we have learned from those sessions and look at one important area of communicating: Starting conversations.

a. Remember two important parts of self-oriented communication:

   1) Self-disclosure: talk about yourself; use the "I" message and not the "you" message;

   2) Receiving feedback: be open to have people tell you about how they see you.

b. Remember the two important parts of other-oriented communication:

   1) Using open statements or questions to get people to tell you about them: "How are you feeling?" "Tell me about your fishing trip."

   2) Using feedback or reflective statements—acting as a mirror for others—to have the other person feel that you are listening to them. We call this "reflective listening."

c. When starting a conversation, keep these things in mind:

   • You don't have to have an "important" topic. Small talk is OK;

   • You don't have to do all the talking—conversation is a two-way process;

   • It's OK to talk about yourself;

   • Guidelines for a good first conversation— listen and observe;

   • What are people around you interested in?

   • Speak up;

   • Use open ended questions;

   • Conversations can be long or short— they should be fun for both parties;

   • End the conversation gracefully.

*Be open to have people tell you about how they see you.*

d. Remember: There is power in communication. There is power in talk. You will feel power when you put these skills to work.

a. Practice starting a conversation. Use skills learned above. Remember who, where and what you shared, how the other person responded, verbal and non-verbal communications used;

b. Do a thinking report on starting conversations. Use your journal to do this. Use one of these options:

Option 1. Describe a situation in which you were meeting someone who you were nervous about meeting. Do a thinking report;

Option 2. Do a thinking report on the conversation you had for homework.

Remember the parts of the thinking reports:

SITUATION;

THOUGHTS;

FEELINGS;

ATTITUDES AND BELIEFS ABOUT THE SITUATION;

OUTCOME OR WHAT HAPPENED.

# NOTES:

_____

_____

_____

_____

_____

_____

_____

_____

_____

_____

_____

## Session ㉕: Coping and Social Skills Training: Basic Communication Skills —Compliments

### 1. Objectives of Session:

We will continue to build our communication foundation. Here is what we want to do in this session:

> ⮕ Learn the skills involved in giving sincere compliments;
>
> ⮕ Learn to accept compliments in a gracious and appropriate manner.

### 2. Session Content and Process:

Feeling good about yourself and about how others feel about you are important as we learn to develop thoughts and actions that lead away from substance abuse and criminal behavior. Giving and receiving compliments are two ways to feel good about yourself. This involves learning and practicing two skills:

1) Learning to accept praise and compliments from others;

2) Giving sincere compliments and praise to others.

    a. **Receiving compliments** is based on the second key skill of self-directed communication—being open and listening to feedback from others about you. Remember that we shut down the feedback we get from others when we get defensive or push away the feedback. We sometimes do this when we receive compliments. Maybe the compliment is embarrassing. Maybe receiving a compliment means that we take ownership for our positive behaviors. Maybe we don't want to be that responsible since this will mean that we have to take responsibility for our negative behaviors. To own a compliment will also mean that we may have to take ownership of a criticism or of a correction of our behavior. Or, we may push away a compliment because we don't think a lot of ourselves. If we have poor self-esteem, we will push away compliments.

*Take time to listen to praise.*

    HERE ARE SOME TIPS ON RECEIVING COMPLIMENTS:

- Take time to listen to the praise;

- Do not deny their praise. Be gracious. Let them know it makes you feel good;

- Use clear words to respond back to the praise;

- Even though you may not agree, let them know you like what they said and that you appreciate it.

    b. **Giving compliments** is based on other-directed communication or active listening. Compliments are effective when you know about the other person. We get to know the other person when we use open statements and open questions. The actual giving of a compliment involves using the reflection skill. A compliment is reflecting back what you see as positive about the other person.

HERE ARE SOME TIPS ON GIVING COMPLIMENTS:

- Make the compliment sincere and real;

- What is the point you want to recognize?

- Be brief with your praise;

- Be specific. What is the action you want to compliment? Rather than saying "You're a good guy," it is better to be specific as to why you think the person is a "good guy." "It was good of you to give me a ride home."

- State the compliment in terms of your feelings and not just the facts as you see them. Not only "it was good of you to take me home," but also "I felt good to know you offered to give me a ride home." This helps the other person feel that the compliment is sincere and really comes from you and not from them. People don't like to compliment themselves;

- Be sensitive to the other person's personality when you give compliments. Some people get embarrassed if they are complimented with others around. If the person is shy, he or she might feel better if you gave praise when no one is around.

- Listen to the person's response to your praise.

## Classroom and homework activities:

a. Complete Work Sheets 22 and 23.

b. Read over Session 26 for next week.

c. Focus on receiving and giving compliments during this coming week. Remember: to receive compliments, you have to receive feedback from others; to give compliments, you have to use active listening skills.

d. Look at your drinking styles and patterns in your Master Profile. Did you rate yourself high on the drinking benefits scales in Part I of the profile? Would the communication skills you learned in the last three sessions help you better express yourself or feel more comfortable in social settings or to feel more socially comfortable? Would it be easier for you to handle those situations now without alcohol or other drugs? Look at the rest of your profile. In what areas did you rate yourself high? Will the skills you learned in the last three sessions help you handle your problems in those areas in which you rated yourself high?

# NOTES:

_____

_____

_____

_____

_____

# WORK SHEET 22

## PRACTICE COMPLIMENT GIVING

### Practice giving a compliment and then use this work sheet to write down what happened:

Think of a close friend or family member who may not know how much you appreciate her/him. Before the next group meeting, make a point of complimenting that person.

1. Describe what happened.

_____

_____

2. What kind of compliment did you give?

_____

_____

3. What were the specific compliments you gave?

_____

_____

4. What feelings did you express when giving the compliments?

_____

_____

5. How did the person receive the compliment?

_____

_____

6. How did you feel about praising or complimenting someone?

_____

_____

# WORK SHEET 23

## RECEIVING A COMPLIMENT

**Pay attention this week to words of praise or a compliment that someone gives you. Then use the following points to see how you handled the compliment.**

1. What was the compliment or praise that the person gave you?

_____

_____

2. What was your specific action or behavior that the person praised or complimented?

_____

_____

3. What were the specific words you said in response to the compliment or praise?

_____

_____

4. How did you feel about the praise or compliment?

_____

_____

5. Did you listen carefully to the praise or compliment?

_____

_____

6. How did you express your thanks for the compliment?

_____

_____

7. Did you deserve the praise or compliment?

_____

_____

## Session 26: Recognizing and Being Aware of Negative Thoughts and Negative Thinking

### 1. Objectives of Session:

> ▶ Review the "Pathways to Changing AOD and Criminal Conduct" model (see Figure 12 in Session 16, Module 6.
>
> ▶ Recognize negative thought patterns.
>
> ▶ Recognize how negative thought patterns contribute to problem behaviors.

### 2. Session Content and Process:

a. **Introduction to session:**

Remember: **THE WAY WE THINK CONTROLS HOW WE FEEL AND ACT.** Negative thinking can become a way of life. It leads to negative and angry behavior. It may be difficult not to think negatively.

Negative thoughts lead to negative emotions which then lead us to tension. The escape may be to use drugs or to engage in criminal conduct. Sometimes we can have a overall negative feeling about the world. "The world sucks!" When we believe that long enough, we then believe that the world doesn't deserve anything positive. It makes it easier to "take what you want," regardless of how it might hurt people.

Negative thinking can lead to negative feelings about oneself including reduced self-respect, anger and depression.

When we change our negative thoughts, we experience power. The power comes in using certain techniques to manage and control negative thinking. There is "power in positive thinking." The power is really ourselves becoming more skilled. We learned that this gives us greater self-mastery or what we call self-efficacy.

*When we change our negative thoughts we experience power.*

b. **Recognizing negative thoughts and thinking:**

Before we can change negative thoughts and the pattern of negative thoughts—negative thinking—we have to learn to recognize them. They can be errors in thinking. Here are some errors in thinking that represent negative thoughts:

1) EXPECTING THE WORST: The worst always happens—you can count on bad results: "I know it won't work out."

2) SELF PUT-DOWNS: "I'm no good."

3) JUMPING TO CONCLUSIONS: "I'm going to get fired."

4) CATASTROPHIZING: "I know something terrible is going to happen."

6) SELF-BLAME: "I deserve it."

7) MAGNIFYING: "No matter what may happen, it couldn't be worse."

8) NEGATIVE VIEW OF WORLD: "The world sucks."

**Exercise:** Using Work Sheet 24, in column 1, list 10 negative thoughts that you get into. Then, in column 2, label these thoughts using the list above or the list of errors in thinking in Session 9 of Module 3 (page 62).

c. **The major steps necessary to change negative thinking are:**

1) Notice the negative thinking.

2) Replace the negative thoughts or thinking. We will learn more about this next session.

d. **The ABC method for understanding rational or wise thinking:**

A famous psychologist, Dr. Albert Ellis, has given us what he calls the ABC method of rational (wise or logical) thinking which also helps us understand how negative thoughts lead to negative feelings and behavior. This ABC method is much like the model we presented in Figure 12 to help us understand the pathways to changing AOD use and criminal conduct. **A** stands for the antecedent or the event (the forerunner) which precedes and leads to **B** or our beliefs and thoughts. The beliefs or thoughts then lead to **C** or what Dr. Ellis calls the consequences which are our feelings and actions.

As we have learned in our other sessions, the **A** or events can lead to automatic thoughts or beliefs. Often, these thoughts are not wise; they are irrational or crazy and unsound. Such thoughts or beliefs can lead to automatic behavior or action habits. Dr. Ellis makes it clear that we can make choices to either use an irrational (crazy, unsound, silly) thought or a rational thought. By choosing a rational or sensible thought, we will then be on the path to take rational or sensible action. It is our choice. We have the power to change the automatic thoughts which are irrational or which are errors in thinking, to rational thoughts. We may not be in control of the **A**, but we are in control of the **B** and the **C**. Here is the ABC method as suggested.

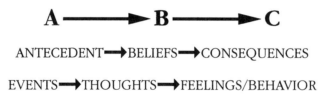

$$A \longrightarrow B \longrightarrow C$$

ANTECEDENT→BELIEFS→CONSEQUENCES

EVENTS→THOUGHTS→FEELINGS/BEHAVIOR

## Classroom or homework tasks:

a. Make a list of some of your automatic negative thoughts by doing Work Sheet 24 below.

b. Compare Ellis's ABC method with the model outlined to you in Figure 12. How are they the same?

c. Then, use the ABC rational thinking model above and do the exercise in Work Sheet 25.

d. Do a thinking report in your journal around a situation where negative thoughts led you to emotions and feelings which then led to using substances, getting drunk or getting high. Remember the five parts of the thinking report:

SITUATION

THOUGHTS

FEELINGS

ATTITUDES AND BELIEFS ABOUT SITUATION

OUTCOME OF THE EVENT.

e. Review your MP and MAP in the areas of criminal and antisocial thinking and conduct. Identify the specific areas of your profile where you need to change and specific problems in your MAP that relate to criminal thinking and conduct.

# WORK SHEET 24

## NEGATIVE THOUGHTS AND THINKING ERRORS

| List of Negative Thoughts | What Kind of Error in Thinking |
|---|---|
| | |
| | |
| | |
| | |
| | |
| | |
| | |
| | |
| | |
| | |

# WORK SHEET 25

## USING THE ABC RATIONAL THINKING APPROACH

Sometimes it seems the behaviors triggered by an event happen so fast that we don't have time to think. It may be easier to describe your reaction to the event before you describe the thoughts you had. Even if you don't remember your exact thoughts, you should be able to think of the things you probably said to yourself. Look mainly at the negative thoughts. Using the ABC rational thinking approach described above, do the following:

1. Describe an EVENT or the **ANTECEDENT (A)** that seemed to make you want to drink or use drugs.

_____

_____

_____

_____

2. List as many of the things or **BELIEFS (B)** that you might have been thinking that would help explain why the event upset you so much. Show which of these thoughts are negative thoughts. Do these fit a pattern of negative thoughts or negative thinking?

_____

_____

_____

_____

3. Describe the **CONSEQUENCES (C)** or your feelings or behaviors in response to the event.

_____

_____

_____

_____

# Session ㉗ : Managing and Changing Negative Thoughts

## 1. Objectives of Session:

We will now focus on how to manage or stop our negative thoughts and replace them with more positive ones. Here is what we want to achieve this session:

> ➡ Identify the specific negative thoughts that lead to AOD use and abuse;
>
> ➡ Put to practice some of the tools we learned in Phase I which can be used to handle the mental processes that lead to alcohol and other drug (AOD) use and abuse and criminal conduct (CC);
>
> ➡ Understand and own the notion that you are in control of your behavior, and that you choose to act in a positive or negative manner.

## 2. Session Content and Process:

### a. **You are in control:**

People and events in your life can lead to bad results if you allow them to do so. But remember, you are in control of everything you think or say to yourself. "People don't upset you; you allow them to upset you." In all situations, you have a choice of responses, as we have seen in Figure 12, page 98. You may say "I am justified in what I did to hurt others." Or you may say "I had no choice, they made me do it." This is not so. You always have a choice of your thoughts and actions.

### b. **What are the negative thoughts that have led you to AOD use and/or criminal conduct?**

**Exercise:** Use Work Sheet 26: List negative thoughts that have led you to AOD use or criminal conduct.

### c. **Practice changing negative thinking:**

1) Here are two ways you can do this:

   a) **Thought stopping:** Allow yourself to think a negative thought. Then STOP the thought right away. Be aware of your negative thought first. Then tell yourself to STOP the thought. Choose one target negative thought. (e.g., "nothing works out.") Every time that happens: **BE AWARE! STOP THE THOUGHT!**

   b) **Positive thought planting:** Pick a target negative thought. Every time you have that thought, replace it with a positive thought: **NEGATIVE THOUGHT! REPLACE WITH POSITIVE.**

2) Use the ABC method to handle negative thoughts: Pick a situation (A). Then identify the irrational or negative thought or belief (B). What were the feelings that came from the thought (C)? Now, replace the negative thought or belief B with a positive thought or belief B (replacement). Now, what are the new feelings or behaviors that come from the thought replacement?

A ➡ B (replacement) ➡ C (new feelings)

EVENT ➡ NEW THOUGHT ➡ NEW FEELING

d. **Positive Thought Arming:**

This is arming yourself with positive thoughts. It's having the thought and action there ready to use. It's like knowing where the light switch is before you enter a dark room. You don't stumble around. You go right to the switch. Use Work Sheet 27 to make a list of positive thoughts to arm yourself with. Here are some examples:

1) REMEMBERING GOOD THINGS: What are the good things in life, the things you do well, the people whom you care about?

2) STATEMENTS OF HOPE: Make positive self statements, "I can manage this situation"; "This may be hard, but I am strong enough to do this."

3) SELF-REWARDS: When you have done something well, reward yourself with positive self-talk. "I came close to using, but I found another way to cope. I did a really good job controlling myself." This is a key to change. Reward yourself when you have made the change. The idea of self-reward will come up again.

e. **It's a lot about Self-Talk:**

A lot of what we are doing is self-talk. It is talking to yourself. When you replace a negative thought with a positive thought, you are telling yourself to do this. This is self-talk. Self-talk is powerful. But it can also be negative and irrational. Our goal is to replace negative self-talk with positive self-talk. We will continue to use self-talk as a tool for change.

*Remember good things, the things you do well, the people who care about you.*

## Classroom or homework activities:

a. Practice Thought Stopping and Planting Positive Thoughts. Do Work Sheet 28;

b. Thinking Report: FREEDOM OF CHOICE. Think of a time when you thought "I have no choice" but to do something you shouldn't. Do a thinking report on the situation.

# NOTES:

# WORK SHEET 26

## NEGATIVE THOUGHTS THAT LEAD TO AOD USE AND CRIMINAL CONDUCT

| Negative Thoughts That Lead to AOD Abuse | Negative Thoughts That Lead to Criminal Behavior/Conduct |
|---|---|
|  |  |
|  |  |
|  |  |
|  |  |
|  |  |
|  |  |
|  |  |
|  |  |
|  |  |
|  |  |

# WORK SHEET 27

## POSITIVE THOUGHT ARMING

Make a list of positive thoughts that you can use. This is arming yourself with positive thoughts. They are there ready to use. Repeat these thoughts to yourself. Use self-talk in practicing these positive thoughts. Each time this week you get into a negative thought, pull out one of these positive thoughts on your list.

1. _____

2. _____

3. _____

4. _____

5. _____

6. _____

7. _____

8. _____

9. _____

10. _____

# WORK SHEET 28

## PRACTICING THOUGHT STOPPING

Practice thought stopping following the steps we learned using the planting positive thought method. Do two situations. Write down the situation. Then spot the negative thoughts. Then replace your negative thoughts with positive thoughts.

SITUATION 1:

_____

_____

NEGATIVE THOUGHT

_____

_____

STOP!
POSITIVE THOUGHT

_____

_____

SITUATION 2:

_____

_____

NEGATIVE THOUGHT

_____

_____

STOP!
POSITIVE THOUGHT

_____

_____

# NOTES:

# Session 28 : Errors in Logic and Thinking

## 1. Objectives of Session:

➡️ Understand how certain thinking patterns (thought-habits) and the attitudes and beliefs that go along with them can cause the action-habits that get us into trouble;

➡️ Recognize distorted thinking patterns (thought-habits) and begin to change those thinking habits.

## 2. Session Content and Process:

### a. Introduction to session:

Our attitudes, beliefs and thinking patterns have not always served us well in the past. They have gotten us into trouble with the law. They have been barriers to change. However, we know they are very difficult to change. Our goal is to change the ideas that have gotten us into trouble and replace those with correct or rewarding ideas. We want to replace them with beliefs that can lead us to the most satisfying lifestyle possible.

### b. Here are some common thought patterns or thought-habits that lead us to errors in thinking and become barriers to change. Remember, these are automatic thoughts:

1) *"I had no choice:"* After having reviewed our thinking reports from last session, we should be convinced that "I had no choice" is rarely a true statement, but it is one of the most commonly used excuses to do something wrong.

2) *"Everyone thinks the way I do."* The fact is, there is no subject on which everyone agrees. It is a great comfort to the person who steals to believe that everyone would steal if they weren't afraid of getting caught.

3) *"I'm right in this situation and my thoughts don't need changing."* Sometimes being right or wrong is not the issue, but stubborn refusal to think differently may mean getting into trouble. There is no issue in the world where there isn't another way of thinking about it. Don't let stubbornness be a barrier to change.

### c. Beliefs and errors in thinking that get us into trouble:

1) Errors in thinking are distortions that we make as a matter of habit. They become so automatic that we accept them even if we have no facts to support what we think.

2) Table 4 gives you a list of common distortions that get people in trouble with the law. These are the same as those you worked on in Session 9 of Module 3. In Work Sheet 4, you checked how those errors of thinking applied to you. Now we have put a name on them. Go back to your Work Sheet 4 (page 62) in Session 9 and choose one error you checked that you use a lot or use all of the time. Now find that error in thinking in Table 4 below. Try to remember the name that is now given to that error in thinking. Use self-talk in reviewing this. For example, take the error "can't trust anybody." We are calling that CAN'T TRUST. Now think of a situation where you thought that way. Now use self-talk. *"Can't Trust anybody. CAN'T TRUST."* Now counter that. *"That's not true. I can trust some people. I trust I'm going to get paid for each day I work at my job."* Think of someone you do trust. Use self-talk. *"I do trust..."*

3) Exercise: Use the Thought change skill "Shifting the view." Take the error in thinking SCREWED: *"I feel I've been screwed."* You may have had this view a long time. This may be the basis of your anger. Shift the view. Use some statements that change that view of people. Try this one: *"There have been some people who have helped me and not 'screwed' me."*

a. Complete Work Sheet 29.

b. Work on recognizing errors in thinking this week and then use the change skill "Shifting the View" to change your beliefs and thoughts. Use self-talk in taking ownership of using an error in thinking and in shifting the view from that error. For example, when you find yourself blaming others, say: "VICTIM STANCE. I'm using VICTIM STANCE. I'm blaming my boss for this. But that's not true. I'm responsible for not doing a good job. I'll take the responsibility."

c. Look at Part III of your Master Profile. How did you rate yourself on the seven thinking errors on the profile? Now, find those errors in thinking in Table 4 that are like the thinking errors in your Master Profile. Was this a problem area on your MAP?

# NOTES:

_____

_____

_____

_____

_____

_____

_____

_____

_____

_____

_____

_____

_____

# Table 4

## Common Thinking Distortions or Errors in Thinking

| List of Errors in Thinking in Session 9, Work Sheet 4: |
|---|

1) POWER THRUST—Put people down; dominate over others;

2) CLOSED CHANNEL—Seeing things only your way;

3) VICTIM STANCE—Blaming others;

4) PRIDE—Feeling superior to others;

5) DON'T CARE—Lack of concern as to how others are affected;

6) CAN'T TRUST—Can't trust anybody;

7) WON'T MEET OBLIGATIONS—Refuse something you don't want to do;

8) WANT IT NOW—Want what you want now and won't settle for less;

9) STEALING—Take what you want from others;

10) DON'T NEED ANYBODY—Refuse to lean on anyone;

11) PROCRASTINATE—Put off things to tomorrow;

12) DON'T HAVE TO—I don't have to do that;

13) STUBBORN—Won't change your ideas;

14) RIGID THINKING—Think in black or white terms; has to be one way or the other;

15) CASTASTROPHIZING—Mountains out of molehills; blowing things out of proportion;

16) FEEL PICKED ON—feel singled out and picked on;

17) THEY DESERVE IT—People have it coming; people deserve to get ripped off;

18) SCREWED—Feeling that you are being screwed over; mistreated;

19) SELECTIVE HEARING—Tune out what you hear people say if it doesn't fit your thinking;

20) WON'T GIVE—Demand from others but won't give;

21) CRIMINAL THINKING—Think about criminal things; doing crimes;

22) LYING—lying is almost automatic for you;

| Additional List of Errors and Their Names: |
|---|

1) ANGER—Rage that makes you illogical and irrational;

2) LONER—Feeling separated, isolated and different from others;

3) REFUSAL—Feeling that you don't have to do that;

4) FAIR DESSERTS—I deserve more than what I'm getting; I've been cheated;

5) THEY DESERVE IT—People have it coming;

6) NO EMPATHY—Can't put yourself in another person's position;

7) FAILURE TO CONSIDER HARM TO OTHERS—lack of concern about how others are affected by you;

8) SEE SELF AS GOOD—In spite of having harmed others;

9) NO EFFORT—Won't exert energy to achieve a goal; do what comes easy;

10) CONCRETE THOUGHTS—Won't change your ideas;

11) FICKLE—Change your mind or goals all the time;

12) SEXUAL POWER—using sex as a way to increase your self-image;

13) ZERO STATE—Feeling of no value; worthy of nothing.

# WORK SHEET 29

## THINKING DISTORTIONS

Pick two thinking distortions from Table 4 that you use a lot of the time or all of the time. Or, pick any other thinking distortions that you use a lot and which are not listed in Table 4. Put the number from Table 4 in the blank spaces. Describe how you used each error. Did it get you into trouble? How?

**1. DISTORTION NO. _____:**

Describe the situation.

_____

_____

How did you use it?

_____

_____

Did it get you into trouble? How?

_____

_____

**2. DISTORTION NO. _____:**

Describe the situation.

_____

_____

How did you use it?

_____

_____

Did it get you into trouble? How?

_____

_____

## Session ㉙ : Errors in Thinking and the Entitlement Trap

### 1. Objectives of Session:

➠ Recall our objectives from last session. These were: 1) understand how thinking errors lead to problem behaviors; 2) identify our own thinking distortions and begin to change them;

➠ Understand and change the "entitlement trap" belief.

### 2. Session Content and Process:

a. **Discuss the work you did for last week's session on your two most often used errors in thinking:** What are your two most often used thinking errors? How do these errors or distortions get you into trouble? What do these errors in thinking do for you? Does the group seem to agree on the way you see each distortion?

- **Now, what thoughts did you replace those errors with?**

- **How did the mental change skill "Shifting the View" work for you?**

b. **The "Entitlement trap":**

Many substance abusing offenders use this as a way to excuse or explain their criminal and substance abusing behavior. Because of past problems and hurts—which you feel were beyond your control—you may feel you were the victim. You may feel you were punished, deprived, badly treated. This merely makes you feel you have something coming. You may feel "entitled" to whatever you can get. Here is a story told by an SAO who committed crimes because he felt he had something coming:

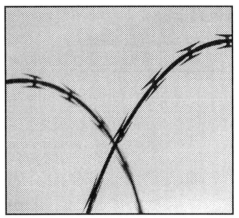

*How do thinking errors or distortions get you in trouble?*

"I had a rough childhood. I was abused by my alcoholic dad. We didn't have money. He sometimes told us to steal if we needed something. He beat up my mom. But she really had a hard time caring for us. She'd always protect him. I got high when I was nine. It was a way out of hell. Then stealing became fun. Then it became the way I "earned" my living. I needed some big cash. I got drunk. Stuck up the liquor store. Got away with it. I told myself 'I deserved it.' The second time went easy. Got caught the third time. Guess I was relieved. No more running. But I still feel I got something coming."

c. **Use the cognitive change skill "Countering" (see Module 6, Session 17, page 105) to change the entitlement trap thinking.**

**Exercise:** Think of a thought that falls into the "entitlement trap" class. Now, counter that thought. Argue against it hard. Now, share with the group how that felt.

d. **Practice changing the thoughts about the entitlement trap belief by using the three cognitive change skills you learned in Session 17 and that you have been using:**

1) **Thought stopping;**

2) **Planting positive thought (if you have watered and fertilized these thoughts, they should be growing well);**

3) **Strong countering.**

a. Do Work Sheet 30 on the "Entitlement Trap."

b. Do a thinking report called ALTERNATIVES in class:

Think of a situation in which you were tempted to perform a crime but decided against it. Do a thinking report on the situation. Remember the parts to the thinking report:

SITUATION;

THOUGHTS;

FEELINGS;

ATTITUDES AND BELIEFS ABOUT THE SITUATION;

WHAT WAS THE OUTCOME.

c. Look closely at yourself this week as to how you use entitlement traps. Write in your journal at least two entitlement trap thoughts you had during the week;

d. Use countering all week. Work hard at it.

# NOTES:

_____

_____

_____

_____

_____

_____

_____

_____

_____

_____

_____

# WORK SHEET 30

## THE ENTITLEMENT TRAP

Describe a situation in which you did something wrong because you felt like you had the right to do it. Then answer these questions:

1. How did you justify the act?

_____

_____

_____

_____

2. Did you get away with it or were you caught?

_____

_____

_____

_____

3. Knowing what you know now, would you do it again? Why or why not?

_____

_____

_____

_____

_____

# NOTES:

## Session ③⓪ : Recognizing High-Risk Situations for AOD Use and CC and Refusal Training

### 1. Objectives of Session:

➠ Review the important points in Module 5, Sessions 14 and 15—Relapse and Recidivism Prevention;

➠ Learn and practice refusal skills to cope with these high-risk situations.

➠ Identify situations that are high-risk for AOD use or CC involvement and which make refusal of AOD and CC involvement difficult.

### 2. Session Content and Process:

#### a. Review and recall our relapse-recidivism work:

In Module 5, Session 14 (page 85), we spent a lot of time learning to spot the high-risk (HR) situations that lead to relapse and recidivism. **Recall these ideas:**

1) **High-risk situations** are those situations that have led you to AOD use and abuse in the past or that have led up to your being involved in criminal behavior in the past. They are situations in which you think or feel you need to use alcohol or other drugs. They are situations in which you think or feel you need to be involved in criminal conduct;

2) **High-risk thinking** involves those thought habits or automatic thinking patterns that lead to the use of substances or involvement in criminal behavior or that place you in high-risk situations that lead to the use of substances or involvement in criminal behavior;

3) **Relapse** begins when you engage in high-risk thinking or high-risk situations that have led to AOD use and abuse in the past. It starts when you take part in thought habits or automatic thoughts about using substances as another way to deal with high-risk situations;

4) **Recidivism** begins when you start high-risk thinking or start to take part in high-risk thought habits that lead to criminal conduct. It also starts when you take part in actions or put yourself in high-risk situations which, in the past, have led to criminal activities.

#### b. Learning and practicing the Refusal Skills:

Refusing to take part in the opportunity to use drugs or to engage in criminal behavior will require that you are not only committed to "refusing," but that you have learned and practiced the skills of refusal. It will also require that you are very aware of the high-risk thinking and situations you can get involved in.

Here are some keys to these REFUSAL SKILLS:

- Saying "no" without hesitation and in a firm, clear voice;

- Looking at the person directly will make it clear that you do not want to relapse;

- Don't feel guilty for refusing. You won't hurt anyone by saying "NO." You could hurt yourself by saying "yes."

- Choose another action: take a ride, go for a walk, go to a movie;

- Ask the person to change their behavior of asking or putting pressure on you. A friend will hear your message;

*Choose another action: take a ride, go for a walk, go to a movie.*

- Tell the person what you have to lose by saying yes;

- After you say "no," change the subject. Don't debate with the other person. That means you are wavering; you are debating with yourself;

- Don't make excuses. An excuse means you won't now, but you might later.

**Now practice these skills in class by role-playing with a classmate.**

c. **Identifying high-risk situations for AOD use and situations in which refusal will be difficult:**

Learning the skills of refusal will also mean that you know the situations in which you put to work the REFUSAL SKILLS.

**Exercise:** Let's try to identify situations that you think will place you at high risk for AOD use problems or becoming involved in criminal conduct. These should also be situations that will make it difficult for you to say "NO" to AOD use or criminal behavior. Make your list, using Work Sheet 31. Then check whether it applies to AOD use, CC, or both. If you know what to expect, it may be easier to hold your own. Then share your list with the group.

## Classroom or homework activities:

a. Practice refusal skills this week. Role-play with a friend or family member;

b. Complete Work Sheet 31 in Workbook, listing high-risk situations where it is difficult to refuse AOD use and involvement in criminal conduct (CC);

c. Use Work Sheet 32 and recall 3 occasions in the past where different people have offered you alcohol or other drugs and you accepted. Imagine that you can repeat the scene and say no. How would you do this?

d. Do a thinking report on REFUSAL SKILLS:

Think of a time when someone wanted you to commit a crime and you didn't do what they asked. Do a thinking report on the situation.

SITUATION;

THOUGHTS;

FEELINGS;

ATTITUDES;

OUTCOME.

e. Again, look at your Master Profile. How did this session on refusal skills help you to handle problems that your profile might show? For example, if you rated yourself high on Antisocial Peers and Models, did this session help you to handle the pressures from those peers to take part in drinking or criminal behavior? You might be the kind of drinker who likes to drink with friends. Did this session help you to refuse the offer from your friends to have a few drinks?

# WORK SHEET 31

## LIST OF HIGH-RISK—DIFFICULT REFUSAL SITUATIONS

List all situations. Then check if they apply to AOD use, criminal conduct or both. These situations are both high risk to relapsing into AOD use or going back to criminal conduct. They are also difficult situations to say "NO" in.

| High-Risk—Difficult to Refuse Situation | Fits AOD Use and Abuse | Fits Criminal Conduct |
|---|---|---|
| | | |
| | | |
| | | |
| | | |
| | | |
| | | |
| | | |
| | | |
| | | |

# WORK SHEET 32

## REFUSAL SKILLS

Recall 3 occasions in the past where different people have offered you alcohol or other drugs and you accepted. Imagine that you can repeat the scene and say no. How would you do this?

**1. Situation No 1:**

Describe the situation.

_____

Who was the person?

_____

How would you say no at this time?

_____

**2. Situation No 2:**

Describe the situation.

_____

Who was the person?

_____

How would you say no at this time?

_____

**3. Situation No 3:**

Describe the situation.

_____

Who was the person?

_____

How would you say no at this time?

_____

# Session ③ : Managing Cravings and Urges About CC and AOD Use

## 1. Objectives of Session:

> ⇒ Learn and practice how to insulate or avoid things around you that are high-risk for you to crave the use of drugs or have a desire to take part in criminal conduct;
>
> ⇒ Develop the skills to cope with cravings and urges when you cannot avoid occasions where they are likely to be triggered.

## 2. Session Content and Process:

### a. Introduction to session:

You will have cravings—or the wanting or desire to use drugs. Expect this. You may have a desire to commit a criminal act and get by with it. Cravings are uncomfortable, but they do not necessarily mean something is going wrong. Actually, they will last only a short time. But the problem is, they will begin to move into urges. A *craving* is a desire or wanting to use drugs or commit a crime. An *urge* is moving toward fulfilling the craving. An urge means you have even started to use or commit a crime.

Cravings may be triggered by some event that happens to you. These events are high-risk situations: being around friends who use; going to a party where there is alcohol or other drugs; a high-stress situation; talking with an old partner in crime. But the craving may trigger an urge. Urges may cause physical symptoms such as a feeling of nervousness or tightness in the stomach. Urges may cause psychological symptoms such as bringing on positive memories of being high or socializing over a drink. Urges also tend to peak quickly and then drop off. But the best way to stop an urge is to stop the craving. If you have an urge, you have to stop the action and response that goes with the urge. Craving is mental; the urge becomes more physical and there is action toward fulfilling the craving.

### b. Common but high-risk situations that trigger cravings and urges:

1) Being around substances;

2) Seeing other people using;

3) Being with people who use or are involved in criminal conduct;

4) Certain emotions, including fatigue, stress, self-doubt, nostalgia, anger, frustration, excitement or accomplishment.

### c. Here are some ways to cope with cravings and urges:

1) Finding another activity that will distract you from the craving or urge;

2) Talking to family or friends about the cravings or urges;

3) "Toughing it out" or "urge surfing" and getting control of the craving by bearing the discomfort. It will go away with time. Here is how you do it:

- Pay attention to how you experience the craving. What are your thoughts and feelings about the craving? Is it in your stomach?

*Craving is mental; the urge is more physical and there is action toward fulfilling the craving.*

177

- Is it still a craving? Or is it now an urge? If you feel it in your body and you are now taking action to fulfill the craving — like going to the liquor store or calling an old buddy you used to do crimes with—it is an urge. Remember: cravings are mental; urges have body senses and move you to action.

- When you feel the craving go to an urge, focus on your body where you feel the urge. "Talk down" the urge with self-talk. "Turn the corner" and go to talk to a non-using friend instead of continuing to the liquor store. The urge will go away faster than you think. But you have to *TURN THE CORNER*.

4) Remember the bad things that can happen if you start using or if you commit a crime. Think about the rewards of being drug-free or having positive behavior in the community—or what we call *prosocial action*. With the help of your counselor and group, make two lists:

- Make a list of bad things that have happened to you because of your AOD use—pain, ending up in jail, losing money—and because of your criminal conduct;

- Make a list of the positive things that come with sobriety (non-using) and prosocial or positive community acting.

5) Stop and Think:

- What do you have to lose by using substances?

- What do you have to lose by doing a crime?

- Now do Work Sheet 33.

d. **Practice managing a craving or urge using the cognitive change skills:**

1) Choose an episode of craving. What are the thoughts behind the craving?

2) Use thought stopping and countering. Try "shifting the view." How do these work?

3) What was the self-talk you used in managing the craving?

4) Were you managing a craving or an urge? It is much harder to deal with the urge. Try to stop the craving before it moves to an urge.

## Classroom or homework activities:

a. Do the "Loss of Joys and Pleasures" Work Sheet 33;

b. Use Work Sheet 34—Dealing with Cravings. This is an important work sheet. The plan you make up for this exercise can help you deal with cravings and urges you may get down the road.

c. Thinking Report—Dealing with cravings:

Recall the last time you had an urge to use or drink and were able to keep yourself from doing it. Write a thinking report on what happened. Here are the parts of the thinking report:

SITUATION;

THOUGHTS;

FEELINGS;

ATTITUDES AND BELIEFS ABOUT THE SITUATION;

OUTCOME.

# WORK SHEET 33

## LOSS OF JOYS AND PLEASURES

What are your joys and pleasures and would you lose them if you committed another crime or relapse back into full AOD use?

| List ten pleasures and joys that you have in your life. Make these your top pleasures and joys. | Would you lose them if you reoffended or relapsed? | |
|---|---|---|
| | yes | no |
| | | |
| | | |
| | | |
| | | |
| | | |
| | | |
| | | |
| | | |
| | | |
| | | |

# WORK SHEET 34

## DEALING WITH CRAVINGS

Make up a plan to deal with an episode of craving. Pick two or three of the strategies suggested in class and detail how you would use them when you feel tempted to lapse.

1. List your craving or urge.

_____

_____

_____

_____

2. What activities would you choose to distract you?

_____

_____

_____

_____

3. Who might you call for help?

_____

_____

_____

_____

4. What mental skills did you use? THOUGHT STOPPING? SHIFTING THE VIEW?

_____

_____

_____

_____

# Session ③②: Assertiveness Skills Development

## 1. Objectives of Session:

> ⯈ Learn four ways that people handle conflict and how they try to get their needs met;
>
> ⯈ Learn and practice the skills of being assertive.

## 2. Session Content and Process:

### a. Review of homework for last session:

In this session we will first look at the thinking report you did for last session in which you were successful in avoiding cravings or the urge to drink or use other drugs, or return to criminal conduct. In the situation you reported, were there other people trying to encourage you to use? Who were they, and what did you say to refuse? In this session, we will look at ways to be more assertive which will help us in those high-risk situations involving pressures from others to commit a crime or relapse into full AOD use.

### b. Three old ways to deal with conflict or solve problems that, in the long run, don't work at getting your needs met:

1) Avoid the problem or be passive: *FLIGHT*. The person who avoids problems:

  - Gives up his or her rights when there is any conflict with what someone else wants;

  - Doesn't get what he or she wants at her or his own expense;

2) Attack others or get aggressive: *FIGHT*.

  - The aggressive person protects her/his own rights but gets what he or she wants at the expense of others;

  - With the aggressive person, others pay.

3) Be passive-aggressive: *FAKE*.

  - FAKE falls between avoiding and being aggressive;

  - Person is not direct in approaching problems;

  - Fails to express needs in a way that other people can respond to them;

  - Passive aggressive people don't get what they want at the expense of themselves and others;

None of these give a positive result. None of these get your needs met in healthy ways. All three methods drive people away. When this happens, we will often use drugs or engage in criminal behavior to get our needs met. Engaging in criminal behavior is both passive-aggressive and aggressive behavior.

### c. What is the healthy choice?

How does the person resolve this? By learning the skills of assertiveness or being FAIR. The assertive person does not compromise his or her rights. But, the assertive person does not get something at the expense of others. Many of our problems come from trying to get our needs met. Learning to be assertive attempts to get your needs met but not by making others pay for it.

d. **What do we do to be assertive? Here are 10 key ways to be assertive:**

1) Recognize your rights in a situation without trespassing on the rights of others;

2) Know how to clearly state your opinions and what it is you want from others;

3) Consider the needs of others as you get your own needs met;

4) Be flexible and give, yet at the same time continue to make your position clear;

5) Avoid blaming; avoid using "you";

6) State how you feel and think; use "I" messages;

7) Have your goals clearly in mind. Know what you want;

8) Become part of the solution and not part of the problem;

9) Once you make a decision, stick with what you have decided. Don't relive or continually rehash "what might have been";

10) Confront the issues head on. Attack the problem and not the person.

e. **Apply what you have learned to this situation:**

You want to take a Friday afternoon off so that you can attend your son's football game. It is very important to you. You are out of vacation time. You have two days of sick time. The football game is two weeks away. Work is busy and the boss is not giving time away easily.

1) Give a statement to illustrate each of these four ways to handle the problem:

- Avoiding—FLIGHT;

- Aggressive—FIGHT;

- Passive-aggressive—FAKE;

- Assertiveness—FAIR.

2) Now, apply the 10 keys to being assertive to this situation. Come up with several assertive statements you can use with the boss.

## Review of homework for the coming week:

a. Before the next session, choose two situations in which you have an opportunity to be assertive and report on them. These may be simple instances in your everyday life. Use Work Sheet 35.

b. Thinking Report:

Think of a recent time when you were frustrated with a situation and needed it to be resolved. Do a thinking report on what happened. Remember the parts of the thinking report:

SITUATION;

THOUGHTS;

FEELINGS;

ATTITUDES AND BELIEFS ABOUT THE SITUATION;

OUTCOME.

# WORK SHEET 35

## PRACTICING ASSERTIVENESS SKILLS

Choose two situations in which you have an opportunity to be assertive and report on them. These may be simple instances in your everyday life.

**SITUATION #1. Describe the circumstances.**

_____

_____

_____

What did you do/say?

_____

_____

What was the outcome?

_____

_____

**SITUATION #2. Describe the circumstances.**

_____

_____

_____

What did you do/say?

_____

_____

What was the outcome?

_____

_____

_____

# NOTES:

# Session 33 : Deeper Problem Solving

## 1. Objectives of Session:

> ➠ Review the basic steps of problem solving;
>
> ➠ Learn some bigger steps to problem solving;
>
> ➠ Learn to consider different solutions to problems;
>
> ➠ Learn how to cooperate and to look for solutions for the good of everyone.

## 2. Session Content and Process:

### a. We haven't been good problem solvers:

Substance abusers and people with a history of criminal conduct have not been good problem solvers. Problems are part of life. They happen every day. They can come up in social situations, and in our own thoughts, attitudes and beliefs. Often, we problem solve on the spur of the moment (impulsively). We often fail to see different solutions. We often don't get the facts. We tend to keep our attention on the person we are problem solving with rather than the problem. One way we have learned to solve problems is to use drugs or commit a crime. Good problem solving skills will keep us from going back to drugs (relapsing) or criminal conduct (recidivism).

### b. Review the basic steps of problem solving which we learned in Session 19, Module 7:

### c. Here are some bigger steps to good problem solving:

*We haven't been good problem solvers.*

1) **Study the problem:** Identify the problem! What is it you want? Can you say what your goal is? What is keeping you from reaching your goal? What do you need to change?

2) **Do we have all the facts?** What other information would be good to have? Get more facts.

3) **Have you been here before?** If so, what did you do that time? The solution may have to be changed a little, but if it was successful in the past, it may be a good place to begin.

4) **Consider alternatives**—different solutions: How do other people see it? Can the person think of how the problem might look to the other person involved?

5) **Brainstorm:** Come up with all the ways to solve the problem (alternatives) you can think of—they don't have to be good solutions, just ideas.

6) **Consider the consequences:** Choose several of the suggested alternatives and consider what the positive and negative outcomes would be if they were used. Look at the long- and short-term results.

7) **Choose the best solution:**

8) **Work the solution:** Try it. Be open minded. Make it work. If it doesn't, start over.

9) **Study the results** or the outcome.

10) **Try the solution again** with another problem.

d. **How do we know we have a problem?**

Pay attention to your body and behavior. Do you feel signs of indigestion, anxiety, or depression? Are you not doing your work as well as usual, or not acting as you would like with your family? Are you not getting along with other people or do they seem to avoid you? If you are feeling uncomfortable about a situation, you probably have a problem.

e. **Make your problem solving solution focused. Here are the keys to this:**

1) Keep your attention on the problem and not the person;

2) Keep your attention on the needs and interests of people involved and not on the positions they take;

3) Don't argue about the positions people take;

4) Pick solutions for the gain of all, and not just for yourself.

## Review of homework for the coming week:

a. Complete Work Sheet 36—Problem Solving;

b. Thinking Report—PROBLEM SOLVING: Think back on a problem you have had in the past. What were the consequences of your solution? Do a thinking report on what happened. Use your journal. Remember: SITUATION, THOUGHTS, FEELINGS, BELIEFS, OUTCOME.

# NOTES:

_____

_____

_____

_____

_____

_____

_____

_____

_____

# WORK SHEET 36

## PROBLEM SOLVING

Pick a problem that you are now having. Go through the steps below. Use these simple steps for studying and coming up with solutions to this problem.

1. Identify or describe the problem.

_____

_____

2. What is your goal?

_____

_____

3. Give the key facts.

_____

_____

4. What are your alternatives? Brainstorm all of the possible solutions.

_____

_____

_____

5. What are the possible outcomes or consequences of these different solutions?

_____

_____

6. Choose the solution.

_____

_____

7. What do you think the outcome will be?

_____

_____

# NOTES:

## Session 34: Handling Feelings—Anger Management

### 1. Objectives of Session:

> ➠ Recognize angry thoughts and feelings;
>
> ➠ Understand that anger is usually caused by some problem, and that we need alternatives for successful problem solving;
>
> ➠ Learn the steps of handling anger;
>
> ➠ Become aware of the events that normally trigger anger and of the mental and physical signals you experience when angry.

### 2. Session Content and Process:

a. **Anger is a big part of your substance abuse and criminal conduct:**

Anger has been the basis of much of your substance abuse and criminal behavior. A criminal act is an angry act. Often, getting high or drunk is an angry act, since you know that the results may hurt others. Hurting others is an angry act. This is not an easy thing to be aware of. You may reject these statements. But give them some thought. Substance abuse behavior and criminal conduct are angry things to do. They strike out at others.

b. **What are some thoughts behind our anger?**

1) The beliefs and thoughts of being "shortchanged";

2) Feelings of not being treated fairly;

3) Feeling that you are a victim;

4) Feeling that your personal space has been tread upon or violated.

c. **Anger is set off by some problem:**

A big part of handling your anger is through problem solving. But remember: It's your thoughts that produce your emotions. Angry thoughts lead to angry feelings and actions. Anger is not *caused* by events, but by your thoughts in response to events.

d. **Basic steps to managing and controlling anger and other emotions:**

1) Be aware of your anger:

 • Be aware of your anger when you feel it. Use self-talk. Say to yourself, "I'm angry."

 • Be aware of what you are angry about and what are your angry thoughts. They're different. Use Work Sheet 37 to list what you are angry about and to list your angry thoughts. Are they different for you?

 • Pay attention to what goes on inside you when you get angry. You may feel your stomach churn, increased sweating, clenched fists, tight muscles, or any number of other sensations.

2) Know the difference between feeling angry and the results of being angry. Being angry might include aggression and violence. Anger is a powerful feeling. It is not good or bad. It is how we show or "act out" our anger that makes the difference. It can be destructive or constructive;

3) Destructive anger confuses people and leads to bad decision making. It makes us aggressive. This blocks communication. It gets people mad at us. It leaves you feeling helpless. It knocks down your feelings of self-worth.

4) Constructive anger expresses the emotions in such a way that you feel better afterward. It builds communication. People know you are angry and they listen. It can trigger problem solving. It helps you to be assertive.

5) When the anger builds, use some basic techniques to get self-control. Without self-control, you can't express your anger in constructive ways. You just get angry. These skills will help:

- Use self-talk: "CALM DOWN AND TRY TO STAY COOL."

- Take 5 deep breaths and exhale slowly, counting to 10, or counting backward from 20, leaving the situation.

6) Now, express your anger. Tell people you are angry. Don't just get angry. Don't act it out. Use the "I" message. "I'm feeling angry. I'm mad." You act out your anger when you blame others, when you use the "you message," when you yell, and when you turn against someone physically. There are two reasons for expressing anger:

*When your anger builds, use self-talk: "calm down and try to stay cool."*

- To get it off your chest;

- To communicate the thoughts that bring on the anger. If you yell, you don't communicate thoughts. They can't hear what you think.

7) After you express your anger:

- Again ask yourself "What am I angry about?" Was it rational? Did it make sense?

- Let the other person respond.

8) Study your anger and your angry thoughts after you have expressed your anger and you're over it. What am I really angry about? What were my thoughts? What are the positive things about this situation? Try to understand exactly what happened.

9) Move your anger into problem solving. Apply the problem solving skills learned in Sessions 19 and 33;

10) If you are successful, be proud and congratulate yourself. Reward yourself.

REMEMBER: CONSTRUCTIVE ANGER INVOLVES EXPRESSING YOUR ANGRY THOUGHTS, NOT JUST YOUR ANGRY FEELINGS.

"You're so angry I can't hear what you're thinking."

## Classroom and homework activities:

a. Using Work Sheet 37, list what makes you angry and list your angry thoughts;

b. Identifying triggers and symptoms of anger. Use Work Sheet 38;

c. Review next week's session;

d. Thinking Report—Self-Control: Think of a recent event in which you became angry but managed to control the emotion. Write a thinking report on that incident.

# WORK SHEET 37

## LOOKING AT YOUR ANGER AND ANGRY THOUGHTS

List what you are angry about and the angry thoughts that relate to what you are angry about.

| List What You Are Angry About | List Your Angry Thoughts |
|---|---|
|  |  |
|  |  |
|  |  |
|  |  |
|  |  |
|  |  |
|  |  |
|  |  |
|  |  |
|  |  |

# WORK SHEET 38

## IDENTIFYING TRIGGERS AND SYMPTOMS OF ANGER

Describe a situation in which you became angry and identify what triggered that anger. Describe what you felt during the episode.

**1. Describe the situation in which you got angry.**

_____

_____

_____

_____

**2. How did you handle it?**

What specifically made you angry in this situation?

_____

_____

_____

How did you handle the situation?

_____

_____

Describe your physical and emotional response.

_____

_____

_____

# Session 35 : Preventing Aggression and Violence

## 1. Objectives of Session:

> ➠ Understand the different types of aggression and violence and see which of these types you might fit;
>
> ➠ Become aware of the situations in which you are most likely to respond to arousal in an aggressive or violent manner;
>
> ➠ Learn and practice self-control skills to handle anger that leads to aggression and violence;
>
> ➠ Understand and identify three kinds of violence.

## 2. Session Content and Process:

   a. **This session is about self-control and keeping your freedom:**

Failure to control your anger will lead to aggressive behavior. That is a threat to your freedom. It's all about self-control. This is one of the most important skills for you to learn. Your success will depend on self-control.

   b. **Anger is an emotion or a feeling—aggression is a behavior:** Aggression is an action directed toward the goal of harming or injuring another living being. Aggression may be non-physical or physical:

1) **Non-physical aggression** is verbal and non-verbal behavior that abuses, injures or hurts someone emotionally or psychologically:

   • It can damage another person's sense of dignity and self;

   • It can lower another person's self-esteem;

   • It can be directed at a person's sexual well-being;

   • It can damage a person emotionally, creating lasting emotional injury (e.g., fear, anxiety, depression, hostility and anger);

   • It can cause another person to withdraw from others and feel threatened by any expression of anger;

   • It can be calculated or impulsive;

   • It can be controlled or it can be uncontrolled rage.

2) When aggression becomes *physical,* it is *VIOLENCE:* Violence does everything that non-physical aggression does but involves the person being physical. It causes physical harm and damage to things and people:

   • Violence can be directed toward objects involving smashing and breaking things but this violence is always person oriented; it is always about someone you know;

   • Violence can be directed at a person and can focus on the person's

   *position of strength or power:* this is when the victim has the strength or power to get in the way of the violent person's needs or goals and the violent person is initially weak;

   *position of weakness:* this is when the victim is weak and the violent person has to maintain a position of strength;

   *position of sex:* this is when the victim is a target of the violent person's distorted sexual needs and drives.

3) Sooner or later, non-physical aggression will end up in violence unless the aggression is controlled and dealt with in a positive manner;

4) Look at your own history of aggression and violence and be prepared to share how you see yourself in this arena.

c. **High-charged situations:**

Remember: events do not cause anger. It is our thoughts that come from the events that cause our anger. These thoughts that lead to anger are usually caused by some problem. These are high-charged situations. These are situations that bring angry thoughts. We can control much of our anger by controlling these thoughts. But we can also deal with much of our anger by not being involved in these high-charged situations. Use Work Sheet 39 in your Workbook to list situations for you that could lead to aggression. Then check the right column if these situations could lead to physical aggression or violence.

d. **Remember the clues that tell you when you are getting angry:**

- Feeling irritable, agitated, on edge, tense;

- Feeling your body change—your physical reaction to anger. These are inside clues;

- Losing your temper;

- Feeling impatient; feeling things are not going your way; feeling not in control.

- Being provoked or pushed by someone; maybe in a bar; maybe by your spouse; maybe by the boss;

- Thinking and feeling you are not being treated fairly.

*You learned how to arm yourself with positive thoughts.*

e. **Self-control is the key: How to manage anger and aggressive impulses and prevent violence:**

1) Use the relaxation skills;

2) Use self-talk. Hear your own voice calm yourself. Hear the angry thought. Use Thought Stopping;

3) Thought replacement: Replace the angry thoughts with positive thoughts. Remember in Session 27 you learned how to arm yourself with positive thoughts. Look at your list. Use one of those (page 162).

4) When you begin to feel the anger, problem solve:

- What are my angry thoughts?

- What is the problem that is bringing the thoughts?

- What is my goal?

- Choose an action? This action should replace the angry thoughts.

5) Remember that the other person may be angry too and not reasoning well. This may put you at harm.

f. **Practice self-control:**

1) With the help of your counselor and group, pick a scene that arouses anger for you. Imagine that scene. Now practice the relaxation techniques:

- Relax by taking slow, deep breaths;

- Inhale slowly, hold your breath, count to five, and then release your breath;

- Repeat your deep breathing exercise, releasing your breath slowly;

- Now clear your mind of all thoughts, and if a thought interrupts, tell yourself, "I AM RELAXED." REPEAT THIS EXERCISE.

2) Now, take another scene that brings up anger inside of you. This time use self-talk to address the feelings of anger and to develop control over the anger. Use thought stopping to do this. Use the other tools you have learned to manage your anger.

## Classroom or homework tasks:

a. Do Work Sheet 39 on high-charged situations.

b. Do Work Sheet 40 on Managing Aggression.

c. Review next week's session in Workbook.

d. No thinking report this week. Hooray!

e. For the past two sessions, we have been working on anger, aggression and violence. Look at your Master Profile. How did you rate yourself on the following scales:

- Results: Behavior Control Loss

- Conduct: Person Offenses I

- Conduct: Person Offenses II

- Criminal Thinking: Impulsive thinking and acting

- Criminal Thinking: Angry/aggressive attitude

- Rebellious and Anti-authority

If you rated yourself high on these scales, then you probably have problems with aggression, anger and even violence. How did the last two sessions help you with your anger? Also, look at the Profile to see if you rated yourself high on the Drug Benefits Scale: Cope with Emotional Discomfort and the Current Status Scale: Emotional and Psychological. Next session we will work on managing our emotional feelings of depression and guilt.

# NOTES:

_____

_____

_____

_____

# WORK SHEET 39

## MANAGING HIGH-CHARGED SITUATIONS

List high-charged situations that can lead you to anger or aggression. Then check if these can lead to violence.

| List high-charged situations that can lead to anger, angry thoughts and feelings or to aggressive behavior: | Check if could lead to violence |
|---|---|
|  |  |
|  |  |
|  |  |
|  |  |
|  |  |
|  |  |
|  |  |
|  |  |
|  |  |

# WORK SHEET 40

## MANAGING AGGRESSION

Give a situation in which you got angry this week or in the past that led to your being aggressive or even violent.

1. Situation:

_____

_____

_____

2. Who was involved?

_____

_____

_____

3. What self-talk statements did you use?

_____

_____

_____

4. Did the other person become angry? If he or she did become angry, how did you handle it?

_____

_____

_____

5. Did "self-talk" help you control your anger?

_____

_____

_____

# NOTES:

# Session 36: Managing Guilt, Anger and Depression: The Emotional Cycles of Rehabilitation

## 1. Objectives of Session:

> ➡ Learn skills to effectively manage negative thinking and the feeling states of anger, guilt and depression by changing the thoughts and behaviors that promote them;
>
> ➡ Become aware of the signs of the thinking and feeling states of depression, guilt and anger and take action to change their thinking patterns.
>
> ➡ Learn and apply the guilt-anger cycle.

## 2. Session Content and Process:

### a. The big three emotions: Anger, guilt and depression:

In the last two sessions, we spent a lot of time looking at how we can manage angry thoughts and feelings and how we can keep these thoughts and feelings from slipping into aggression and violence. Anger has many faces. One face of anger is how it becomes a part of guilt and depression. As we look at the emotions and moods of guilt and depression, we will also look at how anger becomes a part of these two companion emotions.

### b. How relapse is related to the three mood states:

Guilt, anger and depressive moods are common during the recovery and rehabilitation process. Strong feelings of guilt, anger and depression are high-risk emotions that, if not managed, can be considered to be the first stages of relapse or can lead to full relapse. But a full relapse can also lead to feelings of depression, guilt and anger. It becomes a vicious circle.

### c. The guilt-anger cycle:

Guilt, anger and depression are common with all folks. You are not special in having these feelings and thoughts. You are special in that your guilty, angry and depressive thoughts and feelings lead to drug use and criminal conduct. This is special. You must get a handle on these feelings if you want to keep your status of free choice.

When we grew up, we were often not allowed to be angry, feel guilty or get depressed. If we showed anger, we were told to *cool it* and so we did not learn to express it. If we felt overly guilty, someone would say, "It's OK, you don't have to feel bad about what you did." If we got depressed, we were told *cheer up*. It is no wonder that we never developed skills to deal with these moods and thoughts. But, we expressed these emotions through using drugs and through our criminal conduct. We used drugs to express these feelings, but when using drugs, we often did not control them. Thus, we began to experience the guilt-anger cycle. Here is how it works.

Because we did not learn healthy outlets for anger and hostility, we built them up inside. When we got high, we could let them go, but in destructive ways. We blew up, were irrational, or hurt others emotionally and even physically. After we sobered up, we would often have strong thoughts and feelings of guilt. This again keeps us from dealing with our anger. We feel too guilty. We again build up these feelings. They reach a peak, and when using drugs, we again let them out in hurtful ways. We start the cycle over. Figure 16 describes the cycle. How do we break the cycle? Let's look at some ways.

*When we got high, we blew up or hurt others emotionally or physically.*

d. **Managing the moods of guilt, anger and depression:**

Here are some ways that we can manage our moods of guilt, anger and depression:

1) Learn to become aware of having guilty, angry and depressed thoughts and feelings. Here is what we look for:

- First, *recognize the thoughts* of guilt, anger, depression. "I'm no good." "I let her down." "They deserve that." "What's the use?"

- *Notice when your mood changes.* Pay attention to your body. What are your posture and facial expressions?

- Are you *avoiding people and activities* that you used to enjoy? Do you have trouble concentrating or making decisions?

- Are you sitting around a lot, *doing nothing?*

- *Thinking and feeling hopeless;*

- *Not eating or overeating.*

**Exercise:** Use Work Sheet 41 and make a list of your thoughts of guilt, anger, depression.

**Exercise:** Retake the Beck Depression Inventory. Look over the answers. The inventory measures guilt, anger and depression. Retake the Mood Appraisal Scale. Discuss your results.

2) Deal directly with your angry, guilty and depressive thoughts and feelings;

3) Change guilt, anger and depression by doing these things: a) Be aware of your negative thoughts, b) Replace these thoughts with positive ones and c) Make these new positive thoughts part of your everyday life.

4) Use the skills you have learned. Review Module 6, Session 17 (page 105):

- Self-talk skills;

- Shifting your views;

- Relaxation skills.

e. **Be aware of your thoughts of guilt, anger and depression:**

Remember, the first step in handling your anger, guilt and depression is to be aware of your thoughts of anger, guilt or depression. They often are automatic thoughts. They lead us to negative thinking and uncontrolled feelings of anger, thoughts and depression. Here are some examples of these automatic thoughts:

*Magnifying*—Blowing negative events out of proportion. "This is the worst thing that could happen to me."

*Jumping to conclusions*—"I have a swollen gland. This must be cancer."

*Overgeneralizing*—"I always fail—I fail at everything I ever try."

*Self-blame*—"I'm no good." Blaming total self rather than specific behaviors that can be changed.

## Classroom and homework activities:

a. Do Work Sheet 41. Discuss it in group.

b. Thinking report—depression and guilt.

Think of a situation in which you felt depressed and/or guilty. Do a thinking report.

# Figure 16

## The Guilt-Anger Cycle

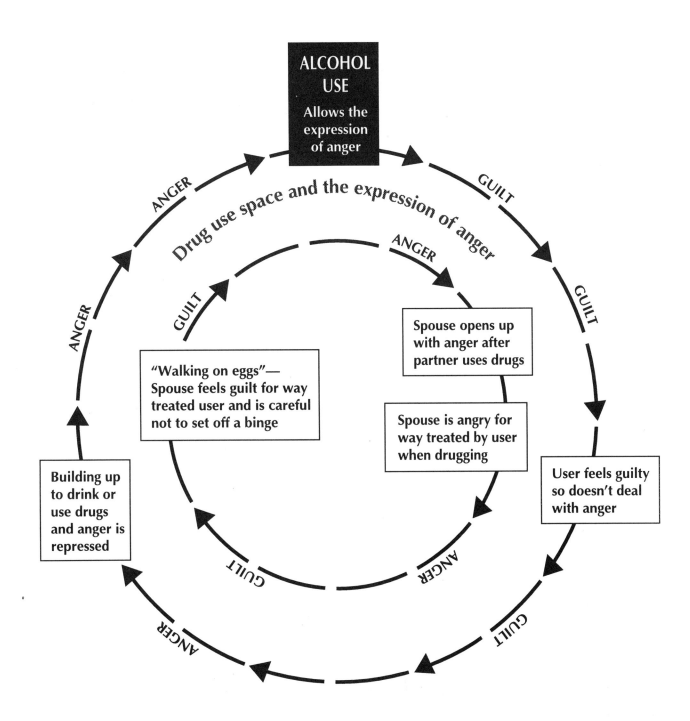

# WORK SHEET 41

## IDENTIFYING AND MANAGING YOUR ANGRY, GUILTY AND DEPRESSED THOUGHTS

List your angry, guilty and depressed thoughts. Then write in each box the skill you would use to deal with that thought. Example: Depressed thought: *"It's hopeless,"* Skill: self-talk, Example: *"There are ways that I can work things out."*

| List Your Angry Thoughts | List Your Guilty Thoughts | List Your Depressed Thoughts |
|---|---|---|
| **Angry Thought:**<br><br>**Skill:**<br><br>**Example:** | **Guilty Thought:**<br><br>**Skill:**<br><br>**Example:** | **Depressed Thought:**<br><br>**Skill:**<br><br>**Example:** |
| **Angry Thought:**<br><br>**Skill:**<br><br>**Example:** | **Guilty Thought:**<br><br>**Skill:**<br><br>**Example:** | **Depressed Thought:**<br><br>**Skill:**<br><br>**Example:** |
| **Angry Thought:**<br><br>**Skill:**<br><br>**Example:** | **Guilty Thought:**<br><br>**Skill:**<br><br>**Example:** | **Depressed Thought:**<br><br>**Skill:**<br><br>**Example:** |

# Session 37 : Developing and Keeping Intimate and Close Relationships

## 1. Objectives of Session:

> ➠ Help you see how important good communication is in intimate and close relationships;
>
> ➠ Help you to develop improved communication skills which will strengthen your intimacy and increase satisfaction from close relationships.

## 2. Session Content and Process:

### a. Background for this session:

In many of our sessions, we have worked on developing good communication skills. These skills can help strengthen our relationships with everyone from strangers to our closest friends and relatives. Sometimes it is more difficult to solve problems with those with whom we are most intimate than with strangers. This is often true because of the emotional ties we have with those with whom we are close. We often try to avoid anger. Or, we become angry too easily in our relationships. We may fear failing in our relationships. Our fixed expectations of the other person may keep us from having good communication with that person. For a long time we may have leaned on alcohol or other drugs to deal with the problems and feelings that come out of our relationships with people we love, people we work with or people we are responsible to.

Part of developing good communication between people in intimate relationships is to deal openly with sexual problems or issues. This is a sensitive area, and you may want to deal with some of these things in a separate session with your counselor and your intimate partner.

*REMEMBER, THERE IS POWER IN COMMUNICATION. IT IS THE POWER OF TALKING AND THE POWER OF LISTENING.*

### b. Let's recall the two basic communication skills that we learned about in Sessions 23 through 25 of Module 9.

1) *Active Sharing:* This is self-directed communication and is based on using the skills of:

- Sharing about yourself—using "I" messages;

- Receiving feedback from others about you.

2) *Active Listening:* This is other-directed communication and is based on using the skills of:

- Inviting the other person to share by using open statements or open questions;

- Reflecting back what you hear the other person saying so they know that you have heard them and are interested in what they have said to you.

Developing and keeping up good communication with people depends on your using these two skills. But also remember the two important parts of active sharing and active listening that we learned in Sessions 24 and 25:

1) *Starting conversations;*

2) *Giving compliments.*

These are also very important in keeping up good communication with people close to you.

### c. Good communication with a person close to you will:

- Help you feel closer to that person;

- Help both understand each other better and know the other person's point of view;

- Help you to solve problems and arguments that you have with each other and in life;

- Result in more positive feelings and less bad feelings toward each other. For example, if you are nagging at each other about money all the time, you may feel negatively about each other in other ways and stop expressing affection to each other;

- Result in you being less likely to start using substances or engaging in criminal conduct if you have an effective way to solve your problems in your personal relationships.

d. **Getting closer to your intimate partner:**

Here are some ways to get closer to your intimate partner or significant other:

*Don't let things build up; tell your partner what bothers you.*

- *Don't expect your partner to read your mind.* It is not fair to expect her/him to automatically know what it is you want or feel, or think. This is especially true in sexual matters where we may have been taught that there is something bad about the topic.

- *Don't let things build up.* It is easy to let things build up between you. To keep from being bothered about these things and to keep them from building up, tell your partner what bothers you.

- *Express your positive feelings.* Remember the skills of giving compliments (Session 25). It is important in any relationship to express things you appreciate about the other person. The positive must always outweigh the negative. Otherwise, it will be a negative relationship. All parts of the relationship are made better if the positive expressions are there. That is particularly true for sexual and physical intimacy. Sexual intimacy can't take place without positive feelings between the couple.

- *Be an active sharer:* Take part in story telling. Share your day. This brings you closer.

- *Be an active listener.* When you use active listening skills you are communicating with your partner.

e. **Very important: keep the balance between closeness and separateness.**

Remember the overlapping circles we looked at in Session 20, Module 7. A healthy relationship allows each person to have separateness while at the same time maintaining closeness. A relationship often gets so close, we feel swallowed up. When we feel we are losing our separateness and our uniqueness, we will fight closeness. Yet, you need to give part of yourself to the relationship. You can't have it all your way.

## Classroom and homework activities:

a. Do Work Sheet 42. Draw your relationship with your intimate partner or spouse using the two circles like we did in Session 20. Answer the Work Sheet questions.

b. Do Work Sheet 43. Share your findings with the group and with your spouse or significant other.

c. Thinking Report: CLOSE RELATIONSHIPS. Remember the parts of the thinking report: SITUATION, THOUGHTS, FEELINGS, BELIEFS/ATTITUDES, OUTCOME.

# WORK SHEET 42

## LOOKING AT THE RELATIONSHIP WITH YOUR INTIMATE PARTNER

Draw the relationship you and your intimate partner have. If you are not in an intimate relationship, pick someone you are close to in your life.

A. DRAW CIRCLES HERE:




B. REFLECT ON:

1. How do you feel about what you see?

_____

_____

_____

2. Why are things like they are?

_____

_____

_____

3. How would you like the relationship? Draw another set of circles below if you want a different balance between closeness and separateness.

# WORK SHEET 43

## LOOKING AT YOUR CLOSENESS AND SEPARATENESS

What is it between you and your intimate partner that makes you close? What are the things that you do separately from your intimate partner?

In one column, write those things that represent intimacy and closeness (for example, going to movies together). Then list those things that you do separate from the relationship that keep your own sense of self and identity.

| Things You Do That Bring You Close or Together | What Do You Do That Is Separate from Your Partner? |
|---|---|
|  |  |
|  |  |
|  |  |
|  |  |
|  |  |
|  |  |
|  |  |

# Session ③⑧ : Understanding Values and Moral Development

## 1. Objectives of Session:

➠ Understand prosocial values;

➠ Understand your own set of values and morals and look at your own ideas of morality;

➠ Look at what you see as the morals and rules of the community and society you live in.

## 2. Session Content and Process:

### a. Introduction to session:

We have learned that thoughts cause feelings and actions. We have also learned that our attitudes and beliefs are the basis of our thinking. Our values and our morals are two of the most important pieces of our beliefs and attitudes. You might say that we have not tried to directly teach you any particular morals or values in this program. That is in part true. Yet, throughout our program, we have continued to leave you with some very important ideas that have to do with values and morals:

- The value of *change:* We have taught the value of change. The skills you have been learning support that value;

- The value of *freedom:* Many of the skills that we have learned will help you keep your freedom;

- Building *positive relationships with others and your community:* we call this the value of being prosocial (the opposite of antisocial or procriminal values);

- Being *concerned about others:* This has been a clear but unstated goal of this program.

### b. Understanding the meaning of values and morals:

Before we go on in this session, it is important that we learn the meaning of the key words we are using in this session. Here they are:

- *Values:* Something that we see as worthwhile, that means a lot to us, that is important to us; guiding principles of our life;

- *Personal Morals:* Has to do with what you see as right and wrong in relation to human behavior or action; it is the good or correctness of our behavior or actions; it comes from our sense of what is right and what is wrong;

- *Community Norms or Standards of Conduct:* These are the rules or guidelines that we live by and which have to do with what is right and what is wrong in relation to our actions or behaviors in the community and society in which we live;

- *Prosocial:* Thinking and acting in such a way that we take part in and build positive family, community and social relationships.

### c. What are your values? Your morals? Do you live up to them?

**Exercise:** Using Work Sheet 44, in the first column, make a list of what you value most. List 10 of them. Then, in the second column, put a check if you feel you are living up to those values: check no, sometimes, or always.

**Exercise:** Using Work Sheet 45, list ten morals important to you that you live by. Then, as to whether you live up to each of these morals, check no, sometimes or always. See the definition of values and morals above.

d. **What are some basic norms or standards of conduct of your community and society?**

Use Work Sheet 46 to list 10 basic norms or standards of conduct that your society lives by. Now, how do you see yourself as to whether you have lived up to those norms or standards of conduct? Check no, sometimes or always.

e. **The value dilemma:**

This takes place when your values go against or conflict with your basic morals or the norms of your community and society. Think of some value dilemmas you have had in the past. Here are some examples:

1) The value of being loyal to a friend who wants you to go against your moral principle of upholding the law;

2) The value of wanting a lot of money yet living up to the moral of not stealing.

What are ways your values go against or conflict with your own set of morals? What are some ways that your values go against or conflict with the set of norms or standards of conduct you listed as most important to the society or community you live in?

**Exercise:** See which of the values you listed in Work Sheet 44 go against the morals you listed in Work Sheet 45 and the basic norms or standards of conduct of society you listed in Work Sheet 46. If a value in Work Sheet 44 goes against a moral or norm (community standard of conduct) listed in Work Sheet 45 and 46, then put the number of the value next to the norms you listed in Work Sheet 45 and 46.

## Classroom and homework activities:

a. Complete Work Sheet 44, listing the guiding principles of your life (values);

b. Complete Work Sheet 45, listing the moral beliefs that you hold;

c. Complete Work Sheet 46, listing your community norms or standards of conduct;

d. Do the exercise above where you note which of your values go into conflict with your own set of morals and the norms and rules of your community.

e. Again, look at your Master Profile. Do you see any particular problems in your MP that relate to the area of moral development and values that we looked at in this session?

# NOTES:

---

---

---

---

---

---

# WORK SHEET 44

## GUIDING PRINCIPLES OF YOUR LIFE

List of your 10 most important values—the guiding principles of your life.

| List of Your 10 Most Important Values | Do You Follow These Values? | | |
| --- | --- | --- | --- |
| | No | Sometimes | Always |
| | | | |
| | | | |
| | | | |
| | | | |
| | | | |
| | | | |
| | | | |
| | | | |
| | | | |
| | | | |

# WORK SHEET 45

## LOOKING AT YOUR MORAL BELIEFS

List 10 moral beliefs that you hold. Then, check if you live up to these moral beliefs:
No, sometimes, always.

| List of Your 10 Most Important Morals | Do You Follow These Values? | | |
|---|---|---|---|
| | No | Sometimes | Always |
| | | | |
| | | | |
| | | | |
| | | | |
| | | | |
| | | | |
| | | | |
| | | | |
| | | | |
| | | | |

# WORK SHEET 46

## NORMS OR THE STANDARDS OF CONDUCT

List 10 norms or standards of conduct that are held by your community and the society you live in. Then check if you live up to these norms: No, sometimes, always.

| List of Your 10 Most Important Community and Society Standards | Do You Follow These Values? | | |
|---|---|---|---|
| | No | Sometimes | Always |
| | | | |
| | | | |
| | | | |
| | | | |
| | | | |
| | | | |
| | | | |
| | | | |
| | | | |
| | | | |

211

# NOTES:

## Session ⓷⑨ : Understanding and Practicing Empathy

### 1. Objectives of Session:

➠ Continue to look at your ideals of morality;

➠ Understand the difference between sympathy and empathy;

➠ Learn to consider the position of other people—learn empathy;

➠ Through the moral dilemma exercise, experience how difficult it is to make moral decisions.

### 2. Session Content and Process:

a. **What is our common value?**

Values and community norms differ across all peoples and nations. Yet, there are laws across all nations that have one thing in common: *the safety and welfare of people and the concern for people.* This is basic to most communities and cultures. Basic to this concern for others is what we call empathy. Dr. Robert Ross, a person who has taught us much about how to help offenders change, feels that empathy is one of the most important values we can learn as we change our life from substance abuse and criminal conduct to prosocial living and responsible attitudes toward others. Dr. Ross teaches that the person will have a greater chance to change his or her criminal beliefs and thinking when he or she learns to consider the attitudes, feelings, and views of others. This means that we become more understanding of (empathy) and caring toward others.

b. **What is sympathy?**

Sympathy is different from empathy. When we have sympathy for another person, we:

- May feel sorry for that person;

- Have an understanding of the other person;

- Have compassion for the other person;

- Sense or feel another person's hurt or pain.

c. **What is empathy?**

Empathy goes one step beyond sympathy. It is not only understanding the other person, or feeling the other person's pain, but it is actually being able to put yourself in the place of the other person. That is a deeper experience, a deeper emotion. We can feel sorry for someone but not really put ourselves in the place of another person. When we have empathy for another person, we are able to:

*Empathy is one of the most important values we can learn.*

- Relate to or know another person's feelings, motives, ideals or situation;

- Feel concern for another person;

- Feel another person's pain and suffering...

*BECAUSE WE ARE ABLE TO PUT OURSELVES IN THE PLACE OF THE OTHER PERSON—WE ARE TRULY ABLE TO "WALK IN THE SHOES" OF THE OTHER PERSON.*

213

d. **Practice having empathy or feeling empathic:**

Work Sheet 47 gives four stories telling about something that happened to another person. Carefully read each story and then put yourself in the place of that person. Close your eyes when you do this and really feel what the person in that story went through. Then note in the second column what your feelings and thoughts were after you put yourself in the place of the person in the story.

e. **The moral dilemma:**

We can learn empathy by changing our thinking. We can do this by looking at what Dr. Ross calls situations that present us with a moral dilemma—or situations in which our ideas clash with those of other people. A moral dilemma may put you in conflict with a value or moral that you hold and a rule that is placed on you by someone other than yourself. It could be two moral beliefs you hold that are in conflict with each other. We will do an exercise in class to help us experience the moral dilemma. Your homework this time is to complete Work Sheet 48, which is to find a newspaper article that presents a moral dilemma and then for you to put yourself in the place of that person who is experiencing the dilemma and to see what you feel and what you would do.

## Classroom and homework activities:

a. Complete Work Sheets 47 and 48.

b. Read next week's session.

# NOTES:

_____

_____

_____

_____

_____

_____

_____

_____

_____

_____

# WORK SHEET 47

## PRACTICING FEELING EMPATHY FOR ANOTHER PERSON

Carefully read each brief story. Then close your eyes and put yourself in the place of the person in the story. How does the person feel? What is the person thinking? Then write the thoughts and feelings that you had when you put yourself in the place of the other person.

| Below are four stories. Each story is about a particular individual who has experienced something of great importance in his or her life. Read each story carefully. | Put yourself in the place of the person in the story. Then write down what you think the other person was thinking and feeling. |
|---|---|
| John is 9 years old. He was hit by a car and was in the hospital for two months. He lost his right leg in the accident. He loved baseball, was a very good player, and was feeling a great deal of sadness because he knew he would never play baseball again. | |
| Marie, who is 45 years old, struggled all of her life to make a living and support her family of four children. Her husband died just after the youngest was born. She works as a cook in a high school. Her oldest son is very smart and will be finishing high school this year. He wants to be a doctor, but Marie knows she does not and never will have the money to send him to college. The other day, her son came home and told her that he received a full four-year scholarship to attend college. | |
| Hank, age 30, a house framer and carpenter, was leaving work when a robber hit him on the head and stole his car. The robber then drove over Hank when getting away. Hank has been in the hospital for two months. He has severe spinal injuries and will have to be in rehab for many months, and he may never walk again. | |
| Karen is 48, has six children and does not work outside of the house. Her husband drives a city bus. Yesterday she bought a lottery ticket. She and her husband checked the numbers today and found that they won a million dollars. | |

# WORK SHEET 48

## MORAL DILEMMA

Find a newspaper article that presents a moral dilemma to the people involved.

1. Describe the situation.

_____

_____

_____

_____

2. Who was the central character in the event?

_____

_____

_____

_____

3. Why do you believe this is a moral dilemma?

_____

_____

_____

_____

4. What should have been done in the situation?

_____

_____

_____

_____

# Session 40: Responsibility Toward the Community: Reflection and Review and Driving Attitudes and Patterns

## 1. Objectives of Session:

➡ Reflect on your progress in the program;

➡ Reflect on issues around community responsibility;

➡ Focus on one area of responsibility—driving a motor vehicle.

## 2. Session Content and Process:

### a. Introduction to session:

We spent last session looking at our values and moral attitudes. We looked at the idea that an important value to hold, and one that will help us in our change process, is to have concern for others. In this session, we will take about 45 minutes to reflect on our values, our moral attitudes and just where we are in the program at this time. Then, we will look in some depth at one of the biggest privileges we have in our society: driving a motor vehicle.

### b. Recall the list of values you have learned in this program:

- The value of change;

- The value of freedom;

- Being prosocial—building positive relationships with others and with your community;

- Having empathy for and concern about others;

- Building a set of morals which provide us with a guide for rightness and wrongness.

### c. The Responsibility metaphor: Driving a motor vehicle:

The most dangerous activity we take part in is driving a car. More people are killed every four years than were killed in all of the four major wars (World War I, World War II, Korean and Vietnam) this country has fought. More than 60,000 are killed every year on the highway. Over 60 percent of the deaths are related to the use of drugs and alcohol. Driving requires more responsibility toward the community and toward others than any other behavior we engage in. When driving, we:

- have to be alert continually;

- are at risk and danger;

- have opportunity to be concerned and considerate toward others;

- have opportunity to test our good will and patience;

- feel emotions and stress.

It is a challenge. All of the lessons we have learned in this program can come to bear on our driving on the streets and highways.

### d. Driving attitudes and behaviors.

Research has shown that people are really different as to their attitudes around driving and their driving behaviors. What are your attitudes? What kind of driving patterns do you show?

**Discussion:** Take time to talk about driving habits, the stress of driving and feelings that people have when driving.

e. **The Driving Assessment Survey (DAS):**

**Exercise:** Complete the DAS and score it in class; then plot the profile. The profile is provided in Work Sheet 49. Then discuss the results in class. Talk about what driving attitudes, thoughts and behaviors you can change.

**Exercise:** Use Work Sheet 50 to make a list of the driving habits and attitudes the client can change.

## Classroom and homework activities:

a. Use Work Sheet 49 to plot your driving profile.

b. Use Work Sheet 50 to list those driving habits and attitudes that you can change.

c. Do a Thinking Report:

Think of a situation during the week when you clearly found yourself not acting responsibly toward the community. Remember the parts of the thinking report: SITUATION, THOUGHTS, FEELINGS, ATTITUDES AND BELIEFS ABOUT THE SITUATION AND OUTCOME.

# NOTES:

_____

_____

_____

_____

_____

_____

_____

_____

_____

_____

_____

_____

# WORK SHEET 49

## DRIVING ASSESSMENT PROFILE

Name:_____     Date: _____

Gender:   ❑ Male     ❑ Female     Age: _____

| Scale Name | Raw Score | Low | | Low-Medium | | | High-Medium | | High | | | Number in Norm Sample |
|---|---|---|---|---|---|---|---|---|---|---|---|---|
| | | **1** | **2** | **3** | **4** | **5** | **6** | **7** | **8** | **9** | **10** | |
| 1. POWER | | | 0 | | 1 | 2 | | 3 | 4 | 5 6 | 7 8 9 19 | 392 |
| 2. HAZARD | | 0 | 1 | 2 | 3 | 4 | 5 | 6 | 7 | 8 9 10 | 11 13 21 | 393 |
| 3. IMPULSE | | 0 | 1 | 2 | 3 | 4 | | 5 | 6 | 7 8 | 9 10 18 | 393 |
| 4. STRESS | | 0 | 1 | 2 | 3 | 4 | | 5 | 6 | 7 8 | 9 11 15 | 395 |
| 5. RELAX | | 0 1 | 2 | 3 | | 4 | 5 | | 6 7 | 8 | 9 10 15 | 395 |
| 6. REBEL | | 0 | | 1 | 2 | | 3 | | 4 | 5 6 | 7 8 17 | 393 |
| 7. CONVIVIAL | | 0 1 2 | 3 | 4 | | 5 | 6 | 7 | 8 | 9 10 | 11 12 22 | 395 |
| 8. GENRISK | | 0 1 2 3 | 4 5 | 6 7 | 8 9 | 10 11 | 12 13 | 14 15 | 16 17 18 | 19 21 22 | 23 27 42 | 385 |

**DECILE RANK**

| 0 | 10 | 20 | 30 | 40 | 50 | 60 | 70 | 80 | 90 | 100 |

**PERCENTILE**

## NORMATIVE GROUP

The normative group is made up of 395 individuals who were being assessed by the district court probation department after being convicted of an alcohol-related driving offense.

## SUMMARY OF DRIVING ASSESSMENT SURVEY SCALES

Scale 1: POWER measures the extent to which the driver experiences power when driving (e.g., feel powerful behind the wheel, feeling powerful when driving at high speeds).

Scale 2: HAZARD measures the degree to which an individual takes part in hazardous or high-risk driving behavior such as beating a red light, driving fast and outrunning other drivers.

Scale 3: IMPULSE measures the driver who is impatient and impulsive (e.g., honks horn, swears at other drivers, loses temper).

Scale 4: STRESS measures the driver who, when under stress or is upset, tends to have accidents, pays less attention to driving, is less cautious, gets annoyed when the light turns red and so on.

Scale 5: RELAX indicates that a driver uses driving as a means of relaxing (e.g., forgets pressures, blows off steam, calms down when driving).

Scale 6: REBEL measures the driver who feels rebellious toward authority, who breaks the rules, gets into fights and so on.

Scale 7: CONVIVIAL measures a pattern of attending drinking parties, drinking at bars, attending "keggers" and drinking with people away from home.

Scale 8: GENRISK is a general or broad measure of high-risk driving behavior. It comprises only driving-related measures.

Source: Adapted from *The driving assessments Survey (DAS)*, Wanberg and Timkin, © 1991 by K.W. Wanberg and D. Timken. Used with permission.

# WORK SHEET 50

## CHANGING DRIVING THOUGHTS, EMOTIONS AND HABITS

Describe your driving patterns and attitudes. Then list 5 driving thoughts, emotions and habits that you can change.

1. Describe your overall driving attitude:

_____

_____

_____

_____

2. Describe your driving behavior and habits:

_____

_____

_____

_____

3. List five driving habits or patterns you feel you should change:

_____

_____

_____

_____

_____

# PHASE III
# TAKING OWNERSHIP OF CHANGE

# PHASE III:
# TAKING OWNERSHIP OF CHANGE

Congratulations on achieving entrance into Phase III: *Taking Ownership of Change.* You have worked hard. You have come a long way. You have shown a commitment to comfortable and responsible living through your thoughts, attitudes and behavior. Yet having the skills to maintain a positive lifestyle through the years ahead is another matter. You have made the decision to continue a drug- and crime-free lifestyle. But we now need to learn how to maintain personal harmony and sense of purpose throughout the life span. You gave a lot of energy and time to learning the skills and attitudes necessary to relax, create and enjoy. Your work on building close and caring relationships allowed you to greet life's challenges with joy and grace.

During Phase I, *Challenge to Change,* you gained knowledge and facts about alcohol and drug abuse and the cycles of abuse. You learned about criminal conduct and the cycles of criminal behavior. You learned about the part that thoughts, beliefs and attitudes play in controlling behavior and action. You learned the rules of how thoughts and behavior are strengthened and reinforced.

Change begins with self-awareness. But self-awareness depends on self-disclosure and getting feedback from others about yourself. In Phase I you took many risks to talk about yourself and your problems. You opened yourself up to have others tell you how they saw you. You learned and practiced basic communication skills to help you in self-disclosure and to receive and give feedback. We focused on spotting thinking errors and cognitive distortions. In order to help you become more aware of yourself, you wrote your autobiography, wrote in a journal and wrote thinking reports.

Toward the end of Phase I, you learned about relapse and recidivism. You learned about high-risk thinking, high-risk actions and high-risk situations that lead to relapse and recidivism. You learned that recidivism and relapse start long before one actually uses drugs or takes part in criminal acts.

Finally, we brought Phase I to a close by helping you to make the methods of change work for you. You learned to spot thinking and behavioral targets that you could work on to change. You learned to spot and overcome the barriers to change.

Phase II, *Commitment to Change,* helped you to sort out and label your thoughts, feelings and actions. You explored these in great depth. You received feedback from staff and peers as to your AOD problems and your criminal history. You took action on your story. You went through 18 sessions to learn and enhance the basic skills for self-improvement and change. You learned skills to handle your problems. But, hopefully, more than that. Phase II helped you to feel better about your life. It helped you to make your life better for yourself and for those close to you and for your community.

Now you enter the last phase of your program: *Taking Ownership of Change.* This phase of change and treatment will give you time to reflect and think back. We want you to think back at the changes you have made and how these changes have helped you to develop the skills to live a life free of AOD (alcohol and other drug) problems. We want you to look at and think about the changes that have helped you to be a better citizen, to be prosocial in your beliefs and in your actions and to live in harmony with your community.

Each day that you remain free from drugs and criminal acts, you will feel power and strength. Your self-confidence will grow. This power and self-confidence will give you ownership of the changes you have made. But you will always need to keep in mind the high-risk thoughts, actions and situations that lead to relapse and recidivism. Taking ownership of change means that you take responsibility for the high-risk thinking, high-risk actions and high-risk situations that lead to relapse and recidivism. You learned how to handle these high-risk situations in Module 5. And during this program you have put to work the skills that prevented relapse and recidivism. We will again visit and review those important ideas about relapse and recidivism in Module 10.

Taking ownership of the changes you have made means you do your own thinking and you allow your own values and morals to be the guide for your behavior. The skills of critical reasoning and decision making will help you to do this.

Often, our values and morals are tested when we find ourselves in conflict with other people. Learning to manage and resolve conflicts will help you maintain those values and morals when you are challenged with conflict. Module 11 will help you learn the skills of critical reasoning and to manage and resolve conflicts.

An important part of maintaining and keeping ownership of the changes you have made is to make changes in your lifestyle activities. It may also mean that you need to improve your ability to manage your work and job situation. These two topics will be looked at in Module 12.

We know we take ownership of our self-improvements and change when we want to share the joy and power of the changes we have made with other people. There are two ways to do this. One is to become an example or model for other people who are starting to make changes in their lives so that they can live free of AOD problems and free of problems of criminal conduct. We will help you look at ways that you can become a mentor—a guide, or teacher or tutor—for others.

Another way we share the joy and power of the changes we have made is to be part of a group whose members support each other in the changes they have made. Being part of a support group is an important part of this Phase of the program. Module 12 will give us a chance to look at how we can be an example to others who are making changes and how we can be part of a support group to help us to keep the changes that we have made.

## Specific Objectives of Phase III

The main goal of this phase is to help you take ownership of the changes you have made and to keep those changes over time. Our more specific objectives are:

◆ You will be aware of and manage the high-risk thinking, actions and situations that lead to relapse into AOD use and criminal conduct thinking;

◆ You will prevent mental recidivism and relapse from leading into alcohol and other drug use and criminal behavior;

◆ You will strengthen the changes you made by learning the skills of critical reasoning, decision making and managing conflict;

◆ You will have opportunity to learn how to be a mentor or example for others who are making self-improvement and change;

◆ You will begin to use the support of a group in strengthening the changes you have made.

## Time Structure

Phase III is a four-month program. The first five weeks will be spent in formal sessions. In the last session of Module 10 you will look back at your accomplishments and look forward to continued change and improvement. Then you will spend two months in a weekly support group. This group will meet for two hours each week. It will be mainly a reflection and support group, but sometimes you will review some of the things you have learned in the program. You have worked hard in this program. You have accomplished a lot. You are ready for the final phase of this formal program of self-improvement and change.

# NOTES:

# MODULE
# 10

## Relapse and Recidivism Prevention: Review and Strategies for Self-Control and Lifestyle Balance

# MODULE 10:
# RELAPSE AND RECIDIVISM PREVENTION:
# REVIEW AND STRATEGIES FOR SELF-CONTROL AND LIFESTYLE BALANCE

## Overview of Module 10

Each day that we live alcohol and drug free, we become stronger. Each day we prevent ourselves from taking part in thinking that leads to criminal conduct, we become stronger. Taking ownership of the power and strength in keeping away from AOD use and from criminal thinking is a way we prevent relapse and recidivism (RP).

In Module 5 we learned that relapse and recidivism takes place long before a person starts to use drugs or takes part in criminal conduct. We learned that relapse into AOD use and abuse is a gradual process of erosion that begins when you do *high-risk thinking* or place yourself in *high-risk situations*. These are thoughts or situations that have led to AOD use and abuse in the past. We learned that engaging in high-risk thinking or situations can be prevented through the use of mental and action skills. We also learned that a full relapse is when you once again become involved in a pattern of substance use that leads to abuse.

We also learned in Module 5 that recidivism back into criminal conduct is also a gradual erosion process. Recidivism begins when you become involved in criminal or deviant thinking or place yourself into situations that lead to criminal behavior. Full recidivism, or the actual involvement in a criminal act, always follows placing yourself in high-risk situations or high-risk thinking.

The ideas that we learned in Module 5 are so important that we want to spend two sessions reviewing them and strengthening our ownership of RP skills and actions. We will review the process and cycles of relapse and recidivism and the warning signs of relapse and recidivism. We will also have you look at how you have handled your high-risk thinking and situations in the past six months.

### Structure for Module 10

We will spend two sessions on RP review. The ideas that we learned in Module 5 may now take on a different meaning since by now you certainly have met many relapse/recidivism (RR) challenges. As well, you certainly have had many opportunities to practice RP. Part of the next two sessions will be spent looking at the RR challenges you have met and the successes you have had in putting to work the skills of RP.

# NOTES:

_____

_____

_____

_____

# Session 41 : Strengthening Relapse and Recidivism Prevention Skills

## 1. Objectives of Session:

➠ Review the basic definitions and ideas related to high-risk thinking and high-risk situations;

➠ Review the triggers for relapse/recidivism.

➠ Review of the RR process and steps (from Module 5, Session 15);

➠ Evaluate the high-risk thinking and situations that you faced in the past six months and identify those thinking and acting skills that you used to manage RR.

## 2. Session Content and Process:

### a. Review of RP Concepts and Ideas:

- Defining high-risk situations for relapse (AOD) and recidivism (criminal conduct): situations that have led to AOD abuse and criminal conduct in the past;

- Defining high-risk thinking for relapse (AOD) and recidivism (criminal conduct): situations that have led to being involved in criminal behavior and AOD abuse in the past;

- Defining relapse and recidivism: Relapse and recidivism begins when you engage in high-risk thinking or place yourself in high-risk situations;

- Relapse/recidivism prevention (RP): using the thinking and acting skills that replace high-risk thinking or avoid high-risk situations.

### b. Again, here are the high-risk situations you need to look for:

- conflict with another person;

- social or peer pressure;

- an unpleasant feeling of anger, depression or guilt;

- a change in self-image.

### c. Here are the steps in RR:

- High-risk situation and high-risk thinking;

- Lack of mastery skills and loss of self-confidence;

- What you expect AOD use and criminal conduct to do to you: expected outcome;

- Reaction to returning to AOD use or criminal conduct thinking (Rule Violation Effect);

- Relapse due to your belief you were weak and couldn't handle the thinking or situation;

- Increased chance of full relapse or full recidivism.

**REMEMBER: You are into Relapse/Recidivism when you place yourself in high-risk situations or begin to engage in high-risk thinking.**

### d. Evaluating the high-risk situations or high-risk thinking that you experienced in the past six months. How did you do?

- Using Work Sheet 51, make a list of the *thinking skills* you have learned and that have worked for you in avoiding relapse/recidivism (RR) or in managing high-risk situations which might have led to relapse or recidivism in the past six months.

- Using Work Sheet 51, make a list of the *action or behavioral skills* you have learned and which have worked for you in avoiding relapse/recidivism (RR) or in managing high-risk situations which might have led to relapse or recidivism in the past six months.

- Use Work Sheet 52 and list three high-risk AOD use patterns of thinking and two criminal conduct thinking patterns you were involved in the past six months. Then note the thinking skills or behaviors you used to deal with these thoughts.

- Use Work Sheet 53 and list three high-risk AOD use situations and two high-risk CC situations you placed yourself in the past six months and note the thinking or behavioral skills you used to deal with these situations.

## Classroom and homework activities:

a. Complete Work Sheets 51 through 53 in Workbook.

b. Make a note in your journal each day this week that describes confidence you have in yourself.

# NOTES:

_____

_____

_____

_____

_____

_____

_____

_____

_____

_____

_____

# WORK SHEET 51

## THINKING AND ACTING SKILLS

List your thinking and acting skills used to manage RR in the past six months:

| Thinking Skills You Used in the Past Six Months to Manage or Avoid RR | Action Skills You Used in the Past Six Months to Manage or Avoid RR |
|---|---|
|  |  |
|  |  |
|  |  |
|  |  |
|  |  |
|  |  |
|  |  |
|  |  |
|  |  |

# WORK SHEET 52

## HIGH-RISK THINKING PATTERNS

List  list three high-risk AOD use patterns and two high-risk CC thinking patterns you engaged in during the past six months and list the thinking and action (behavioral) skills you used to manage these thought patterns:

| High-Risk Thinking Patterns You Engaged in the Past Six Months | Thinking or Action Skills You Used to Deal with Each of These Thinking Patterns |
| --- | --- |
| | |
| | |
| | |
| | |
| | |

# WORK SHEET 53

## HIGH-RISK SITUATIONS

List three high-risk AOD situations and two high-risk CC situations you placed yourself in during the past six months and list the thinking and action (behavioral) skills you used to manage these thought patterns:

| High-Risk Situations You Placed Yourself in the Past Six Months | Thinking or Action Skills You Used to Deal with Each of These High-Risk Situations |
|---|---|
| | |
| | |
| | |
| | |
| | |

# NOTES:

## Session ④②: Relapse Prevention: Strategies for Self-Control and Lifestyle Balance

### 1. Objectives of Session:

> ➠ Learn how imbalances in your life can lead to relapse and recidivism when you face high-risk situations;
>
> ➠ Learn a self-control plan or strategy that can prevent relapse and recidivism.

### 2. Session Content:

#### a. How lifestyle imbalance leads to relapse and recidivism:

Living a drug- and crime-free life requires that you live a balanced lifestyle. Life can quickly get out of balance. You begin to feel pressured, hassled and controlled. You feel the pressure of the *shoulds* or the *oughts*. You begin to feel deprived and even cheated. You have no time for yourself. The demands of work, of family, of *everyone* become just too much for you.

Given all of this, how can you get your own needs met? You can do this by keeping a healthy balance between those activities that cause you pressure and hassles and those activities that bring you pleasure and self-fulfillment.

When life gets out of balance because of the imbalance of the *shoulds,* you begin to feel a strong desire to meet your needs right away, to indulge or gratify yourself now. As the desire to indulge increases, so does the need to get back the balance that you had with drugs and alcohol. This can lead to cravings and urges for drugs or even to commit a crime. When this happens, and after you have made a commitment to live a drug- and crime-free life, you have to make excuses for what you want to do. So, you say:

- "I deserve more than this"

- "I work hard and don't get nowhere"

- "They have more than I do—I deserve as much as they do"

- "I deserve a good time—a few drinks"

- "I have something coming."

This all can lead to relapse and recidivism. With relapse or recidivism, the payoff is quick. Both give immediate gratification and reward. But your choice to indulge may be hidden. You make choices that don't seem important. We call this Seemingly Irrelevant Decisions (SIDs). You even start to engage in high-risk thinking. You say: "I'll go down to the bar and chat with a couple of buddies." Or you put yourself in a high-risk situation (a friend drops by with some dope). These are all shown in the boxed parts of Figure 17 in the Workbook.

#### b. Developing a balanced lifestyle—Arming yourself with a broad relapse and recidivism prevention (RP) Plan:

1) *Arm yourself with a self-control plan:*

Remember, we make conscious choices to relapse or to reoffend. We are most apt to make these choices when our lifestyle gets out of balance. We have learned many skills to prevent relapse and recidivism, but we are always faced with high-risk thinking and situations that can lead to RR. It is important that we have a plan for self-control—that we don't have to come up with a plan every time we face a high-risk situation or every time we take part in high-risk thinking. We should have a plan ready to go. This is arming ourselves with positive actions or thoughts and having them ready when we need them. Figure 17 in our Workbook gives us such a plan.

233

2) *Filling in the spaces for a balanced daily lifestyle:*

The circled parts of Figure 17 in our Workbook give us general ways or strategies that help us handle the boxed parts of Figure 17. As can be seen in Figure 17, we can build a balanced lifestyle by building in daily activities that can give us positive feelings and gratifications. We should try to put those activities in each day of our life. When we do feel a desire to use alcohol or other drugs, we can put something else in their place. We call this substituting or replacing indulgences. We should be ready with those when we need them. These are activities that provide immediate self-gratification (such as eating a nice meal, sexual activity, getting a massage, etc.).

3) *Detaching and labeling:*

Cravings and urges are another thing. We might get urges when we smell alcohol, see people drink, notice a gang of friends on the street, or imagine committing a crime. The best way to handle these is to detach or remove yourself from those situations. You can also put a label on the urge and craving, and then tell yourslf, *ride it out*. The urge does go away.

4) *Don't make excuses and watch those decisions that don't seem important (SIDs):*

A powerful part of relapse and recidivism (RR) is making excuses, or denying you have the feelings or urges. Or, you might think that the small choices you are making that move you towards relapse or recidivism do not seem to amount to anything—or SIDs (Seemingly Irrelevant Decisions). You can do a number of things at this point. First, you can put a label on these as warning signs. For example, you can label "I deserve it" and call it "poor excuse" (PE). When you think this, it should warn you that you are close to relapse—very close. You can also look at the short-term and long-term good and bad parts of a decision to use drugs or to commit a crime. We call this your decision window. Or, you can just avoid those high-risk situations that are steps to relapse and recidivism.

**Exercise:** Work Sheet 54 provides a decision window. Complete the windows for both alcohol and other drugs and for criminal behavior. What do you get right now and later by not using drugs? What do you miss out on by not using drugs, both in the short and long runs? Do the same for criminal conduct. What do you get in the short and long runs by living a crime-free life?

c. **You highway map to recovery or collapse:**

Another plan that you can use to build a *balanced lifestyle* is to look at relapse and recidivism as a highway map. We talked about this map in Session 15. A picture of this map is found in Figure 18. During this program, you have found yourself on this highway several times. You have faced urges and cravings. You have resisted and stayed straight or abstinent. You may have lapsed (used drugs) once or twice. You may have done things or thought things that brought you close to committing a crime (what we call recidivism, but not full recidivism). But you have been set on staying on Road 101—to recovery city. Always keep this map in your mind. It is one of the best ways to remind you of where you want to go. But whichever direction you make—collapse city or recovery city— remember, it is **Your Choice**. You are in the driver's seat.

## Classroom and homework activities:

a. Fill in the bottom parts of the circles in Figure 17 with activitives that can be part of your self-control plan.

b. Complete the blank decision windows for AOD use and criminal conduct in Work Sheet 54.

**Figure 17**

**Relapse Prevention: Global Self-Control Strategies**

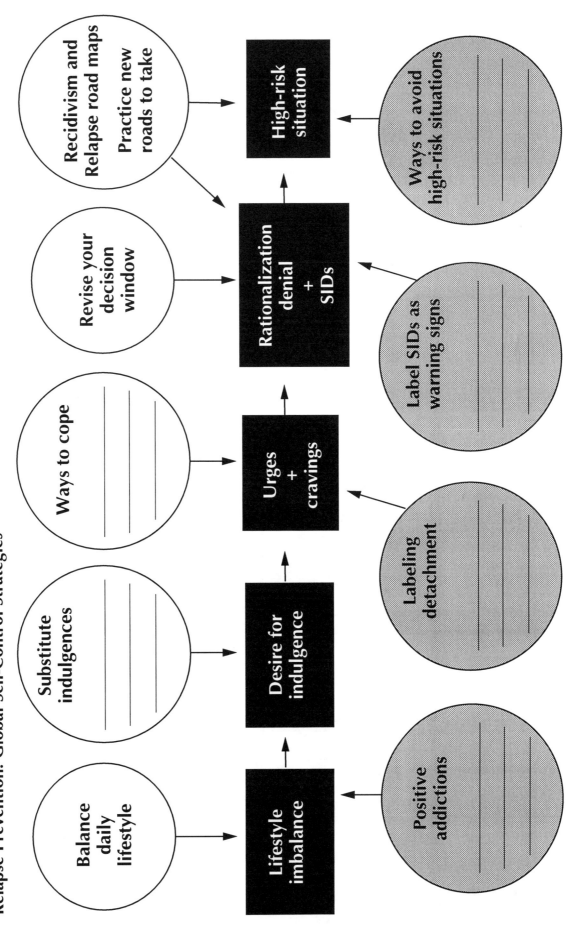

Reprinted with permission of the authors of *Relapse Prevention: Maintenance Strategies in the Treatment of Addictive Behaviors*, (page 61). Edited by G.A. Marlatt and J.R. Gordon, The Guilford Press, 1985.

# WORK SHEET 54

## THE DECISION WINDOW FOR AOD AND CRIMINAL CONDUCT
*Adapted from Marlatt (1985).*

### Decision Window: Example of Decision Window for AOD Use and Abuse

|  | IMMEDIATE OUTCOME | | DELAYED OUTCOME | |
|---|---|---|---|---|
|  | POSITIVE | NEGATIVE | POSITIVE | NEGATIVE |
| **Live an alcohol- and drug-free life** |  |  |  |  |
| **Continue to use and abuse alcohol and other drugs** |  |  |  |  |

### Decision Window for Criminal Conduct

|  | IMMEDIATE OUTCOME | | DELAYED OUTCOME | |
|---|---|---|---|---|
|  | POSITIVE | NEGATIVE | POSITIVE | NEGATIVE |
| **Live a crime-free life** |  |  |  |  |
| **Continue to commit crimes and offend** |  |  |  |  |

Reprinted with permission of the authors of *Relapse Prevention: Maintenance Strategies in the Treatment of Addictive Behaviors*, (page 58). Edited by G.A. Marlatt and J.R. Gordon, The Guilford Press, 1985.

## Figure 18
## Forks in the Road to Recovery

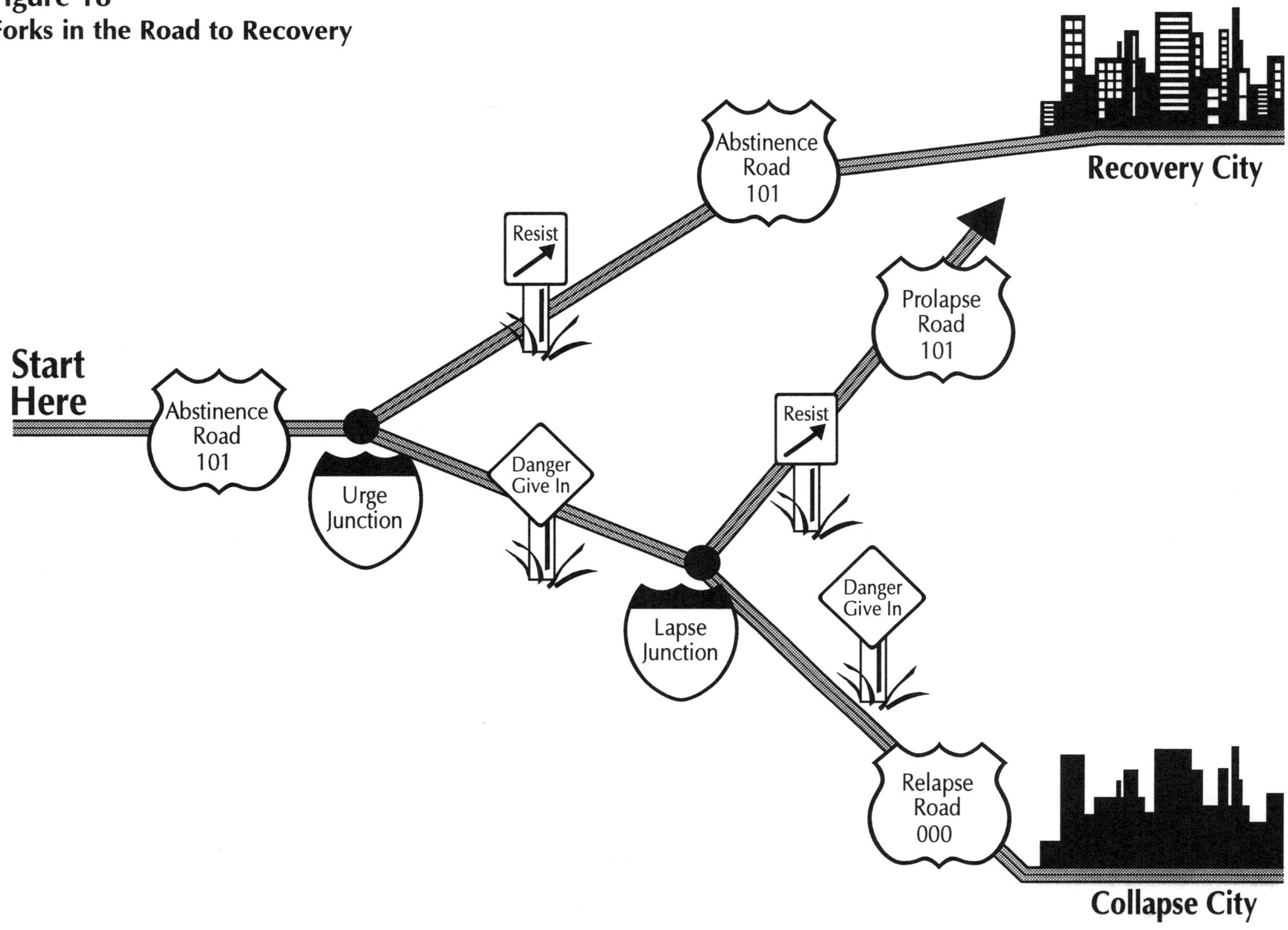

Reprinted with permission of the authors of Keeping "What Works" Working: Cognitive Behavioral Relapse Prevention with Substances–Abusing Offenders, G.A. Parks & G.A. Marlatt, In *What Works : Critical Issues Research and Best Practices in Community Corrections* (page 15). International Community Corrections Association Conference, Cleveland, OH (October 5–8, 1997)

# NOTES:

# MODULE 11

**Strengthening Our Ownership
of Change:**

**Developing the Skills of Critical
Reasoning and Settling Conflicts**

# MODULE 11:
# STRENGTHENING OUR OWNERSHIP OF CHANGE:
# DEVELOPING THE SKILLS OF CRITICAL REASONING AND SETTLING CONFLICTS

## Overview of Module 11

An important key to this phase of change is taking ownership of the changes you have made in your thinking, your beliefs and in your actions. Ownership of change is based, in part, on being able to take part in critical reasoning and creative thinking. It will do you little good to have made changes in your beliefs and actions only to allow yourself to be talked into old beliefs and actions which caused your past problems with AOD use and with the law. You take ownership when you allow your own internal values and morals be the guide for your behavior.

It is nearly impossible to live without having to face some conflict with others. You may find yourself in conflict because of the changes you have made in your beliefs and actions. You may find yourself in conflict because you are now standing up for what you believe will make you a better person. Conflict with others can lead to stress, feelings of defeat and a feeling of not being in control of ourselves. Conflict can be a test to your sobriety and a test to your goal of living in harmony with others and with our community.

We have lived in a world where problems are solved by someone being right and someone being wrong. There is power in learning to settle conflicts where both you and the other person or persons feel good about the outcome. This is what we call a win-win situation. You feel more of a master of your own life and your own changes when you settle conflicts so that you don't lose—and the other person doesn't lose. Taking ownership, then, comes when you feel the power of resolving conflicts with other people while at the same time holding to what you feel is best for you. Session 45 will help you learn the skills of resolving conflicts in such a way that you will not give up the changes you have made.

### Structure for Module 11

You will spend Sessions 43 and 44 on learning the skills of critical reasoning and creative thinking. The skills of critical reasoning will be helpful for you in Session 45 where you will learn the skills of how to settle conflicts and negotiate positive outcomes. Both of these areas will help you improve your sense of mastery over the changes you have made and taking ownership of these changes.

# NOTES:

_____

_____

_____

_____

_____

# Session 43: Critical Reasoning: Decision Making and Creativity I

## 1. Objectives of Session:

> ➠ Learn the skills of critical reasoning;
>
> ➠ Learn the importance of listening to what is being said and how you can be conned in certain situations;
>
> ➠ Learn to carefully study and judge what is being said and not just accept the arguments of the other person;
>
> ➠ Tell the difference between fact and opinion.

## 2. Session Content and Process:

### a. Looking at all sides:

Studies have shown that many substance abusing offenders have problems in being flexible. We call this "mental rigidness." They have problems of looking at all sides of a situation. Mental rigidness keeps us from using new ways to solve problems or to deal with a situation. It keeps us from changing our way of thinking about how to solve problems or the way we think about things in general. This may not apply to you. But what we will do in this session may help you look at things differently. We are going to work on what we call critical reasoning and creativity. To be creative is to think of new ways to do things that give us a good outcome and a good experience.

### b. Critical and creative thinking:

Critical thinking is the art of thinking clearly about something, making sense out of something and getting the facts before you make a decision. We call this logical thinking. We also call it rational thinking. To think sensibly or critically we:

- *Always get the facts first.* You need the correct information. The goal is to come to conclusions that are based on correct information.

- *Do not let your emotions make the decision.* Sometimes you make a decision because you are angry. I'm not going to shop there again because the "clerk was a jerk." That shoots you in the foot if the store has what you want. Counter the thought: "It's just the clerk. He doesn't own the store. He couldn't care less."

- *Make sense of the facts.* See how the facts fit together; what do the facts tell you?

- *Are you being conned?* When you come to a conclusion because you have been swayed by the needs or wishes of other people you are being conned (fooled). You are conned when you let others persuade you to do something or believe something before you get the facts or before you can reason critically. Your friends might persuade you to use drugs. But what are the facts? "Every time I use drugs, I get into trouble with the law. Where will I end up?" Critical thinking will prevent you from being conned or conning yourself. When people try to convince you to agree with their way of thinking they are using what we call propaganda. Propaganda is a statement someone makes to persuade you that what they want you to believe is true. It may or not be true. When you buy into propaganda, you fail to reason critically.

*Sometimes you make a decision because you are angry.*

241

c. **Here are some ways people try to talk us into things. These are methods of propaganda:**

**ONE-SIDED ARGUMENTS:**

- EXAMPLE #1: Job placement worker to a recent high school graduate: "This is a great job, it pays well, and you are likely to get promoted to a management position within a year."

- EXAMPLE #2: Friend who is concerned about the high school graduate taking a job out of town: "This would be an awful job. You are going to be living in a one-horse town with nothing to do with all the money you are going to be making. Besides that, they aren't really going to give a green kid a job as a manager."

  In both situations, the high school graduate is hearing propaganda because each person is giving a ONE-SIDED argument. The job placement worker is giving only the good points of the job and the friend who wants to keep his buddy in town is giving only the bad points. Propaganda often features a one-sided argument.

**THE BANDWAGON APPROACH:**

- Another propaganda technique used frequently is the BANDWAGON approach, designed to make you believe that you are not well-informed or part of the in-group if you don't buy the product.

- EXAMPLE #3: Mark: "Let's get some speed and shoot up."

  Betty: "I would never do that. I don't believe using drugs is smart."

  Mark: "Everybody does it. Why are you so boring?

- EXAMPLE #4: Advertisement: "Women everywhere are discovering that Insta-Youth improves the texture of their skin within 10 days."

**REPETITION IS ANOTHER WAY TO CON YOU:**

- Advertisers use REPETITION to get their propaganda across. They mention the product name time and time again, or they show their ads repeatedly in the same hour of television.

- Tobacco advertisement will use this technique: LSMFT: "Lucky Strike Means Fine Tobacco."

**TRANSFER:**

- Another technique that is common is TRANSFER, where they associate a young and attractive person with the product they are trying to sell.

- Again in tobacco advertisements, it is common to show the attractive and young and healthy smoking cigarettes.

**TESTIMONIAL:**

- Sometimes the propaganda is presented by a famous person who presents a TESTIMONIAL for or against a proposal, hoping that the name of the famous person will result in transfer of loyalty to the product or issue that is being promoted.

- This is common in the sportswear industry where a famous athlete is using or wearing the product being advertised.

**EMERGENCY:**

- A popular sales tool is to tell the buyer that there is only a limited time in which they can buy the product or get it at a reduced price; or there is only a limited number of the items left for sale. This technique is EMERGENCY or CRISIS.

- "This offer is good until Friday." "Come down now or you'll miss your chance...."

**BARGAIN:**

- Sometimes the advertiser or salesperson will encourage you to buy because you will get something FREE or at a BARGAIN rate.

- "Everything is on sale at half price."

d. **How do your past AOD use and criminal conduct relate to these methods of propaganda?**

- First, learn more about the methods of propaganda discussed above by doing Work Sheet 55.

- Take each of the methods of propaganda listed above. How have they led you into AOD use and criminal conduct? Take the statement: "They all stop by for a few beers after work!" Does this sound like the BANDWAGON APPROACH? Now, do Work Sheet 56 to see how these various methods of propaganda are related to your past use of drugs or your past involvement in criminal behavior.

## Classroom and homework activities:

a. Complete Work Sheets 55 and 56.

b. THINKING REPORT—PROPAGANDA

Option 1: Think of a time you have "conned" someone else in order to get what you wanted. Do a thinking report on the incident.

Option 2: Think of a time when a friend has "conned" you. Do a thinking report on the situation.

Remember the parts of the thinking report:

SITUATION;

THOUGHTS;

FEELINGS;

ATTITUDES AND BELIEFS ABOUT THE SITUATION;

OUTCOME.

# NOTES:

_____

_____

_____

_____

_____

_____

# WORK SHEET 55

## PROPAGANDA ADVERTISEMENTS

Describe five different advertisements that you have seen either in newspapers or on TV. What technique did they use? Use the information in the Workbook above.

**Ad 1)**

_____

_____

_____

**Ad 2)**

_____

_____

_____

**Ad 3)**

_____

_____

_____

**Ad 4)**

_____

_____

_____

**Ad 5)**

_____

_____

_____

# WORK SHEET 56

## RELATING PROPAGANDA TO YOUR DRUG USE AND CRIMINAL CONDUCT

For each of the methods of propaganda listed below, write a statement as to how that method has led you to AOD use or criminal conduct.

| PROPAGANDA METHOD | How has this method been used on you to get you to use alcohol or other drugs or to get you involved in criminal conduct? |
|---|---|
| One-Sided Arguments | |
| The Bandwagon Approach | |
| Repetition | |
| Transfer | |
| Testimonial | |
| Emergency or Crisis | |
| Bargain | |

# NOTES:

# Session 44 : Critical Reasoning: Decision Making and Creativity II

## 1. Objectives of Session:

> ➡ Continue to work on the goals of the last session as to persuasive and clear communication;
>
> ➡ Continue to work on the skill of critical reasoning.

## 2. Session Content and Process:

### a. Introduction to session:

You continue on the journey of understanding critical reasoning. This is a difficult skill to learn. Your old beliefs, your old attitudes and your old ways get in the way. Every day you have to deal with issues that challenge your commitment to sobriety and to living a crime-free life. You may be persuaded by friends to *have a few,* to *do this one more time and we'll get rich,* to put yourself in high-risk situations. Critical reasoning helps you to make good decisions. In the last session you learned some of the ways that you can practice the skill of critical reasoning. The most important was to get the facts and be aware that there are always other people who try to get you to make decisions based on their need and not on your need.

### b. Let us look a little deeper at critical reasoning. Here are some more pieces of the puzzle:

1) **Words are important:** You live your life using talk and words. Words are important. "Sticks and stones may break my bones, but words 'can really hurt me.'" Words can hurt if we don't understand what they mean. The same word may mean one thing to you and something different to the person with whom you are speaking. If you use words that don't mean the same to each of you, you will not communicate with each other.

2) **People often don't say what they really mean:** Learn to recognize what people imply by what they say. People don't always say what they mean in a clear manner. Don't always assume. Sometimes assume means making an ASS (out of) U (and) ME. Ask questions if you don't understand. There is no dumb question, only dumb answers. Pay attention. Remember, few people are able to say what they mean in a CLEAR way. We often have to figure out what is being said. We do that by asking questions.

3) **Listen to what people are assuming:** Recognize assumptions. You now know a good deal about good communication skills and critical reasoning. Remember to listen carefully to the feelings that people communicate when they use a particular word. Pay attention to body language and facial expression.

4) **Fact versus opinion.** Once you have understood what the other person is assuming, it is important to figure out if what they are saying to us is based on fact or on opinion. Here are some clues:

   - Phrases that indicate an opinion: such as *"in my opinion," "I think",* or *"it seems to me."*

   - Emotional statements indicate that people are expressing an opinion rather than fact. "I hate that person."

   - Extreme statements are generally an opinion rather than a fact: "He always does that."

*The same word may mean one thing to you and something different to the person with whom you are speaking.*

## Classroom and homework activities:

THINKING REPORT—CRITICAL REASONING

Think of a recent event when you had a misunderstanding with someone you were talking with. Do a thinking report on what happened.

SITUATION;

THOUGHTS;

FEELINGS;

ATTITUDES AND BELIEFS ABOUT THE SITUATION;

OUTCOME.

## NOTES:

# Session 45 : Resolving Conflicts: Negotiation and Social Skills Development

## 1. Objectives of Session:

➠ Learn that two people can both be partly right in a discussion;

➠ Learn that an open-minded approach to conflict and problem solving can be the most fruitful way to reach a solution or to resolve the conflict;

➠ Strengthen your ability and skills to identify problems and their consequences, and to find alternative ways to solve those problems or resolve conflict.

## 2. Session Content and Process:

### a. What this session is about:

*One of the most important skills is having the self-control and ability to calm yourself during a conflict with someone.*

You have already learned many problem solving skills and to understand the outcomes of your own actions. One of the most important skills is having the self-control and ability to calm yourself during a conflict with someone or while disagreeing with someone. In addition, it is helpful to know that everyone experiences and views the world from a different point of view and their attitudes, values and beliefs should be respected. These differences don't always require that one person is wrong and the other right. Both persons can have a sound point of view and both can be partly correct. Let's look at ways that you can approach a problem situation or conflict and how you can find what we call *win-win outcomes*. But first we briefly look at ways people try to solve conflict which usually do not lead to good outcomes.

### b. Remember the three old ways you have used to deal with conflict or friction:

1) FIGHT: become aggressive and forceful to get your way, which only increases the conflict or friction;

2) FLIGHT: withdraw or remove yourself from the conflict or friction and nothing is resolved;

3) FAKE: you go along with the other person but then what you want anyway and things are left up in the air.

### c. Working for a Win-Win Outcome:

Here are some skills you can use to get a good outcome and to reach an agreement around a conflict or problem. These are what we call the skills of negotiation and bargaining with the goal of reaching a *win-win outcome*—everyone gains, no one loses completely:

• You tell the other person(s) your ideas about the problem or conflict.

• You ask the other person(s) their views of the matter.

• You tell them why you think your idea is better.

• If you are a good communicator, you give them a chance to consider what you have said before you expect them to make up their mind.

d. **The steps in negotiation:**

1) **DECIDE:** Are you having a difference of opinion with someone else? Tell the other person your position. Describe how you see the other person's opinion.

2) **LISTEN:** Did you understand the other person? Be open minded.

3) **THINK:** Think about the other person's position; What are the options that might work?

4) **SUGGEST A COMPROMISE:** Can you suggest a compromise?

5) **DISCUSS:** Discuss the options and decide which is best.

e. **Steps in making a complaint:**

Sometimes problems cannot be solved by negotiation or convincing the other person that your point of view is correct. You have to resort to making a formal complaint. This is not as easy to do as one might think. There are several steps that might help you in being successful in making a formal complaint.

1) Find a way to express your complaint clearly.

2) Who is the best person to complain to?

3) Where and when should you make the complaint?

4) How would you like to have the complaint resolved? TELL THE PERSON WHAT YOU WANT.

5) Listen to the person's response.

6) Try to offer helpful suggestions to resolve the problem.

f. **A guide for diagnosing how you approach a conflict:**

Dr. Reinhold Niebuhr wrote a prayer that has become known as the Serenity Prayer of Alcoholics Anonymous:

> *God, grant me the serenity*
> *To accept the things I cannot change,*
> *The courage to change the things I can,*
> *And the wisdom to know the difference.*

Diagnose each potential or actual conflict that you may be a part of. Ask yourself the question: Is the circumstance of such a nature that you can in fact change the situation or negotiate a settlement? Or, is it simply impossible to change what exists? If you decide that change and settlement is possible, then negotiate with strength and courage (courage is the word that AA has substituted for strength in the serenity prayer). If you truly see that change is not possible and there is no hope for negotiation, then accept what is with patience. But most important—use your best wisdom and intelligence to know the difference.

## Classroom and homework activities:

a. HOMEWORK—NEGOTIATION SKILLS. Use Work Sheet 57.

b. Do a thinking report on the situation you described in the Negotiation Skills Task in Work Sheet 57. Remember the parts of the thinking report:

SITUATION;

THOUGHTS;

FEELINGS;

ATTITUDES AND BELIEFS;

OUTCOME.

# WORK SHEET 57

## NEGOTIATION SKILLS

Describe a CONFLICT SITUATION in which you had the opportunity to practice your negotiation skills.

1. What did you want to resolve the conflict?

_____

_____

_____

2. What did the other person want?

_____

_____

_____

3. What were the options or different ways to solve the conflict?

_____

_____

_____

4. What did you give to resolve the conflict?

_____

_____

5. What did the other person give?

_____

_____

6. What was the outcome? Was it win-win; lose-lose?

_____

_____

_____

# NOTES:

# MODULE 12

## Maintaining Self-Improvement and Change:

### Developing a Healthy Lifestyle or Manner of Living

# MODULE 12: MAINTAINING SELF-IMPROVEMENT AND CHANGE: DEVELOPING A HEALTHY LIFESTYLE OR MANNER OF LIVING

## Overview of Module 12

The real challenge of this program is for you to keep up the changes you have made in the past nine months. In this phase of our program, we have been working on taking ownership of the changes that we have made. But how do we make those changes stick? How do we keep them going?

One important way to maintain the changes we now own is to integrate or unite them into a healthy lifestyle. What this means is that we are really changing our lifestyle, or the way that we approach our living. We have spent a lot of efforts in this program working on changes in our thinking, our beliefs, our attitudes and in our behavior. But now, we need to unite or integrate the changes we have made in these areas into the broader picture of a healthy lifestyle. This is making change in the very way or method that we live.

There was a time when the use of alcohol or other drugs was a central part of your lifestyle. There was a time when your involvement in criminal conduct was an integral or central part of your lifestyle. Now, you are challenged to develop lifestyle patterns as alternatives to using drugs and engaging in criminal conduct. Whereas before you had ownership of those aspects of your life, now, we want you to make lifestyle changes and then take ownership of those changes.

In this module, we will look at four alternatives to AOD use and criminal behavior which build a healthy lifestyle. These are the alternatives of play, of work or being productive, of sharing our strengths, and of finding support from others in our efforts to grow and change. We will first look at play or finding pleasure in our lives. We will then look at ways to manage our work and job issues in a healthy and productive way. Third, we will look at how we can share our strengths through being a mentor or role model for others who are searching for and making change. Finally, we will look at how we can find support in others to strengthen our healthy lifestyle and the changes we have made in our manner of living.

### Objectives of this Module

◆ Learn to identify and begin to practice lifestyle changes that will strengthen your drug-free and crime-free living;

◆ Learn to develop a balance among work, play, supporting others and getting support from others.

# NOTES:

_____

_____

_____

_____

_____

# Session 46: The Alternatives of Healthy Play and Leisure Time

## 1. Objectives of Session:

> ⏩ Understand the meaning of play;
>
> ⏩ Learn about the activities which bring you the most pleasure;
>
> ⏩ Discover that you have replaced activities involving alcohol and other drug use with healthy activities not involving AOD use;
>
> ⏩ Learn how you can plan and fulfill healthy pleasures through leisure time activities that become a regular part of your life.

## 2. Session Content:

### a. Introduction to session:

Your involvement in drugs and criminal behavior has been a central part of your lifestyle. At times, you probably have strong feelings of emptiness because of the time you did spend in your AOD use. Unless you replace that void with some pleasant activities, there is a greater chance that you will experience loneliness, boredom and depression. In maintaining a drug-free and crime-free lifestyle, the alternative of healthy play is vital.

### b. What is healthy play?

There are many definitions of play. Most important among these many definitions is the idea that to play is to take part in fun, to have pleasure, to be amused, to enjoy an activity or to take part in a recreation. An important part of the meaning of play is *to move freely within a space*. But the lifestyle alternative we are referring to is more than just play. It is *healthy play*. This means that play is wholesome, it is of benefit to us, and most important, when we have finished our play, we feel good about ourselves. We feel fulfilled.

### c. Play through fulfilling our pleasures:

We know that the number of pleasant activities you engage in is directly related to how positive you feel about yourself. People who spend all their time doing required activities, the things we consider "shoulds" and "oughts," will experience little reward in life and are likely to feel they deserve to reward themselves with a drink, a hit, or a night out with friends with whom they should not associate. One way to learn healthy play is to know what pleases you—or to know your pleasures.

If you know what pleases you or what activities give you pleasure, then you will know how to play and your play will be more fulfilling. One way to discover this is through taking the Personal Pleasure Inventory (PPI). The PPI is found in Work Sheet 58. Complete the PPI and then add up the score for each of the specific areas of activities. Then, with the help of your counselor, use the PPI Profile on Work Sheet 59 and look at your profile. There are four broad areas of pleasure that you might fit into:

1) Physical expression;

2) Focus on the self;

3) Artistic or aesthetic activities;

4) Cooperative harmony or working together.

Where are your high scores? You can have high scores across all of these areas. Discuss your profile with your counselor, with the group and with someone close to you.

d. **Identifying specific leisure time activities that bring you pleasure allows you to play in a healthy way and replace activities which have involved AOD use in the past:**

1) Make a list of healthy play activities:

Using your PPI profile and Work Sheet 60, make a list of specific activities that will bring you pleasure and joy. How often do you do these? Are these part of your lifestyle? Are they now replacements or alternatives to AOD use or criminal activities?

2) Planning personal time for these healthy play activities:

Using Work Sheet 61, list play activities that you will take part in this week. Then, using the bottom part of Work Sheet 61, make a personal time schedule, and then plan what your activity will be in that schedule. This will help you to begin to develop a balance in life between work and healthy play. What kind of problems are you experiencing in finding alternative ways to fill your time? Have you been successful in finding new friends and acquaintances with whom to share leisure time?

## Classroom or homework activities:

a. Complete the PPI and plot your profile;

b. Complete Work Sheets 60 and 61. Discuss your findings in group.

# NOTES:

_____

_____

_____

_____

_____

_____

_____

_____

_____

_____

_____

# WORK SHEET 58

## THE PERSONAL PLEASURE INVENTORY

Using one of the five choices below, rate the following items as to degree of pleasure that you derive from each activity. Place the appropriate number corresponding to your choice in the blank line opposite the item. Then put the total score for each group of items on the line marked Total for Score.

0 = Never engaged in activity or no pleasure derived from activity
1 = Low degree of pleasure derived
2 = Moderate degree of pleasure derived
3 = High degree of pleasure derived
4 = Very high degree of pleasure derived

### 1. Athletic Prowess

____ Playing basketball.
____ Playing tennis.
____ Watching sports.
____ Playing softball.
____ Going to football games.
____ Playing golf.
____ Playing football and soccer.
____ Playing volleyball.

Total Score_____

### 2. Challenging Nature

____ Floating on a raft.
____ Canoeing.
____ White water rafting.
____ Camping out.
____ Hiking.
____ Skiing.

Total Score_____

### 3. Physical Fitness

____ Eating healthy foods.
____ Exercising.
____ Biking.
____ Stretching.
____ Walking.

Total Score_____

### 4. Sensuality

____ Making love.
____ Kissing and cuddling.
____ Giving flowers to your lover.
____ Erotic sex.
____ Going to the beach.

Total Score_____

# WORK SHEET 58 (continued)

## 5. Soothing Sensations

\_\_\_\_ Listening to soft music.

\_\_\_\_ Warming self by fire.

\_\_\_\_ Soaking in hot tub.

\_\_\_\_ Having back rubbed.

\_\_\_\_ Massage.

\_\_\_\_ Eating in a nice restaurant.

Total Score\_\_\_\_\_

## 6. Material Comforts

\_\_\_\_ Making money.

\_\_\_\_ Shopping.

\_\_\_\_ Spending money.

\_\_\_\_ Going out for an evening.

\_\_\_\_ Improving outward appearance.

Total Score\_\_\_\_\_

## 7. Seeking Adventure

\_\_\_\_ Driving to new places.

\_\_\_\_ Visiting different cities.

\_\_\_\_ Experiencing new places.

\_\_\_\_ Experiencing new things.

\_\_\_\_ Traveling to foreign cities.

\_\_\_\_ Visiting different cultures.

Total Score\_\_\_\_\_

## 8. Experiencing Nature

\_\_\_\_ Being in nature.

\_\_\_\_ Being in the woods.

\_\_\_\_ Watching wildlife.

\_\_\_\_ Watching the stars.

\_\_\_\_ Watching the sun rise.

Total Score\_\_\_\_\_

## 9. Domestic Involvement

\_\_\_\_ Redecorating home.

\_\_\_\_ Remodeling home.

\_\_\_\_ Working on home projects.

\_\_\_\_ Painting house.

\_\_\_\_ Gardening.

Total Score\_\_\_\_\_

# WORK SHEET 58 (continued)

### 10. Reflective Relaxation
____ Meditation.
____ Relaxation exercises.
____ Daily meditations.
____ Self-reflection.
____ Journal writing.
Total Score_____

### 11. Artistic Stimulation
____ Going to the theatre.
____ Attending symphony.
____ Creating art work.
____ Reading books.
____ Writing poetry/fiction.
____ Playing musical instrument.
Total Score_____

### 12. Mental Exercise
____ Playing word games.
____ Playing cards.
____ Solving crossword puzzles.
____ Solving mystery games.
____ Sewing.
Total Score_____

### 13. People Closeness
____ Helping family members.
____ Playing with children.
____ Being with family.
____ Spending time with friends.
____ Hugging.
____ Being with a partner.
Total Score_____

### 14. Religious Involvement
____ Spiritual thinking.
____ Worship.
____ Bible study.
____ Church work.
____ Going to church.
____ Praying.
Total Score_____

### 15. Altruistic Efforts

_____ Counseling others.

_____ Helping others.

_____ Teaching others.

_____ Volunteering services.

_____ Writing letters to friends or family.

_____ Total Score

When you have finished scoring all of your responses, place the Total Score for each scale on the profile Work Sheet 59 in the appropriate box under the Raw Score column. Then find the your raw score on the row for each scale in order to find your percentile rank for that scale. The percentile rank shows you the degree of pleasure that you derive from each orientation compared with others. For example, if your raw score for Material Comforts is 17, then you enjoy this pleasure orientation more than 80% of the sample population which is roughly typical of a mixed group of adults.

# WORK SHEET 59

## PERSONAL PLEASURE INVENTORY PROFILE

Name: _____   Date: _____

Gender:   ☐ Male   ☐ Female   Age: _____

Category headers (Decile Rank): Low (1, 2, 3) · Low-Medium (4, 5, 6) · High-Medium (7, 8) · High (9, 10)

| Group | Scale Name | Raw Score | 1 | 2 | 3 | 4 | 5 | 6 | 7 | 8 | 9 | 10 |
|---|---|---|---|---|---|---|---|---|---|---|---|---|
| PHY EXP | 1. ATHLETIC PROWESS | | 0 2 3 4 | 5 6 7 | 8 9 10 | 11 12 | 13 | 14 15 | 16 17 | 18 19 20 | 21 22 23 | 24 26 32 |
| PHY EXP | 2. CHALLENGING NATURE | | 0 2 3 5 | 6 7 | 8 | 9 10 | 11 12 | 13 | 14 15 | 16 17 | 18 19 | 20 21 24 |
| SELF FOCUS | 3. PHYSICAL FITNESS | | 2 5 6 7 | 8 | 10 | 11 | | 12 | 13 | 14 | 15 | 16 18 20 |
| SELF FOCUS | 4. SENSUALITY | | 1 6 8 9 | 10 11 12 | 13 | 14 | 15 | 16 | 17 | 18 | | 19 20 |
| SELF FOCUS | 5. SOOTHING SENSATIONS | | 4 10 11 | 12 13 14 | 15 | 16 | 17 | 18 | 19 | 20 | 21 22 | 23 24 |
| SELF FOCUS | 6. MATERIAL COMFORTS | | 4 7 8 9 | 10 11 | 12 | 13 | 14 | 15 | 16 | 17 | 18 | 19 20 |
| AESTHETIC DISCOVERY | 7. SEEKING ADVENTURE | | 4 7 8 9 | 10 11 12 | 13 | 14 15 | 16 | 17 18 | 19 | 20 21 | 22 | 23 24 |
| AESTHETIC DISCOVERY | 8. EXPERIENCING NATURE | | 1 6 7 8 | 9 10 | 11 | 12 | 13 | 14 | 15 | 16 17 | 18 | 19 20 |
| AESTHETIC DISCOVERY | 9. DOMESTIC INVOLVEMENT | | 0 1 2 | 3 | 4 | 5 6 | 7 | 8 | 9 | 10 | 11 12 13 | 14 15 19 |
| AESTHETIC DISCOVERY | 10. REFLECTIVE RELAXATION | | 0 1 2 | 3 | 4 | 5 | 6 | 7 | 8 | 9 10 | 11 12 | 13 15 20 |
| AESTHETIC DISCOVERY | 11. ARTISTIC STIMULATION | | 0 2 3 | 4 5 6 | 7 | 8 | 9 | 10 11 | 12 | 13 14 | 15 16 17 | 18 20 24 |
| COLLECT HARMONY | 12. MENTAL EXERCISE | | 0 1 2 | 3 4 | 5 | 6 | 7 | | 8 | 9 | 10 11 | 12 14 20 |
| COLLECT HARMONY | 13. PEOPLE CLOSENESS | | 4 11 12 | 13 14 | 15 16 | 17 | 18 | 19 | 20 | 21 | 22 | 23 24 |
| COLLECT HARMONY | 14. RELIGIOUS INVOLVEMENT | | 0 | 1 2 | 3 | 4 5 | 6 | 7 8 | 9 10 | 11 12 | 13 14 15 | 16 19 24 |
| COLLECT HARMONY | 15. ALTRUISTIC EFFORTS | | 1 6 7 | 8 | 9 | 10 | 11 | 12 | 13 | 14 | 15 | 16 17 20 |
| | **DECILE RANK** | **0** | 10 | 20 | 30 | 40 | 50 | 60 | 70 | 80 | 90 | 100 |
| | **PERCENTILE** | | | | | | | | | | | |

SOURCE: *The Personal Pleasure Inventory*, Wanberg, Milkman and Harrison.
Copyright © 1992 K.W. Wanberg and H.B. Milkman.

# WORK SHEET 60

## LEISURE TIME ACTIVITIES

List the leisure time activities that you are now taking part in. In the second column, write down how many times a month you do these activities. In the third column, check the activity if that activity has replaced drinking alcohol and drug use time or activities.

| LEISURE TIME ACTIVITIES | Times a Month | Replaces AOD Activities |
|---|---|---|
|  |  |  |
|  |  |  |
|  |  |  |
|  |  |  |
|  |  |  |
|  |  |  |
|  |  |  |
|  |  |  |
|  |  |  |
|  |  |  |
|  |  |  |
|  |  |  |
|  |  |  |

# WORK SHEET 61

## PERSONAL TIME

First, write down several pleasant activities that you believe you would enjoy doing in the next week. On the following chart, plan 30 to 60 minutes each day that you reserve as your own personal time. Make the time for this in advance. When the time comes, decide which of the things from the above list you want to do and take time to do it. Write down what you did and how it felt to do something for yourself.

_____

_____

_____

_____

_____

|                | Personal Time | Activity and Reaction |
|----------------|---------------|------------------------|
| Monday         | _____ | _____ |
|                |               | _____ |
| Tuesday        | _____ | _____ |
|                |               | _____ |
| Wednesday      | _____ | _____ |
|                |               | _____ |
| Thursday       | _____ | _____ |
|                |               | _____ |
| Friday         | _____ | _____ |
|                |               | _____ |
| Saturday       | _____ | _____ |
|                |               | _____ |
| Sunday         | _____ | _____ |
|                |               | _____ |

# NOTES:

# Session ⓸: The Alternative of Productive Work: Managing Work and Job Issues

## 1. Objectives of Session:

> ➠ Learn what your work is or what is your area of work;
>
> ➠ Learn skills necessary to take part in rewarding work.

## 2. Session Content and Process:

### a. Productive work: Our first alternative to AOD use:

We see productive and meaningful work as our first main alternative to AOD use and engaging in criminal conduct. Although you have most likely worked all of your life, you may not have seen your work and your job as a way to express yourself in healthy ways and as a way of replacing AOD use and involvement in criminal conduct. *There is a difference between your work and your job.* Your work is a physical or mental activity and effort that is directed toward accomplishing something. Your work is the means through which you practice your skills, fulfill your talents and earn your livelihood. Your job is what you go to in order to fulfill your work. You take your work to your job. You own your work. It is yours. You don't own your job; it is given to you in order to do your work. Work is one way you define your lifestyle.

### b. Being effective in your work:

Dr. Steven R. Covey has identified what he calls seven habits of a highly effective person. These habits can help you to be more effective in your work and in the job where you apply your work. These seven habits are:

1) *Be Proactive*®: Or to take responsibility for your life by having a *personal vision* of what you want to do and accomplish;

2) *Begin with the End in Mind*®: This means you think about what you want to do, and then you do it; you take *personal leadership* of yourself; you lead yourself in the direction you want to go;

3) *Put First Things First*®: This means that you manage your own time, your energies, your goals. It is *personal management* of what you do;

4) *Think Win-Win*®: We have spent time talking about win-win. This is the key to your *personal relationships* and a key to how you solve problems and settle conflicts;

5) *Seek First to Understand*®: This is putting yourself in the other person's shoes; this has to do with empathy, with *empathetic communication.* Remember, you put empathy to work when you take part in active listening. You are effective in your work when you use empathy with people with whom you work;

6) *Synergize*®: This means working together in a cooperative way *for the common good.* The whole of things is more than the sum of its parts. By working together, we cause things to happen that go beyond the sum of each person's efforts;

7) *Sharpen the Saw*®: This is *renewing your personal self;* it is refreshing yourself across your physical, emotional, mental and spiritual being. You can do your work in productive ways when you keep yourself renewed and refreshed in these four areas. This is not something you do just at work; it is keeping a balanced lifestyle—a balance between your physical, emotional, mental and spiritual worlds.

c. **Defining YOUR work:**

Use Work Sheet 62 to identify what your work is. First, give a name to the work you do. Then write down as many things as you can that define your work. For example, a person may write down: Truck Driver. Then, what is involved in that work? Being safe? Listening to the sounds of the truck as it is running? Driving the speed limit? Being on time for a delivery? Maintaining the vehicle? Now, feel a sense of pride in your work. Now, think about approaching your work using the Seven Habits discussed above. How can you improve your work by applying these Seven Habits? Discuss this with your group or with a close friend. Again, feel the pride in your work. You may not like your job but you can love your work. Feel power in that.

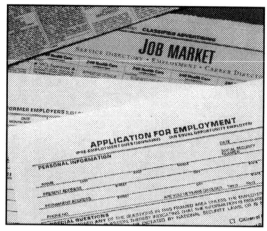

*Work is one way you define your lifestyle.*

d. **Skills in finding a job that matches your work:**

THINK ABOUT THIS: You may not have a job, but you have work. To prove this, just read what you did in Work Sheet 62. If you have a job, your job may not match your work. By doing this exercise, it may help you to see if your job matches your work. If you don't have a job, you can use this exercise in helping you find a job that matches your work—your work as you defined it above. Having or finding a job which matches your work is achieving an important lifestyle alternative to AOD involvement. Here are the skills needed to find a job:

1) **Developing a Résumé:** A resume describes your work history and desire for work. Make it look neat. It might be a simple letter or a more detailed document. The resume is the first step in finding a job that matches your work. Try not to leave large periods of time that you can't account for on the resume. Explain such periods by saying: "I was looking for a job that matched my work." It is important that the document be carefully typed and accompanied by a good cover letter. Your counselor and group will help you with your resume.

2) **The Job Application:** The job applicant needs to be able to emphasize personal strengths and strong job skills.

3) **Job Leads:** Make a list of 10 possible jobs and employers. Use Work Sheet 63. Job seeking is a full-time job in itself. Go after each one until you succeed. Talk about your disappointment with friends, family and group.

4) **Developing Telephone Skills:** Rehearsal of proper skills is an important step in finding a job. When making phone calls, *introduce yourself* properly and ask to *speak to the person in charge of hiring for the company.* When you speak with that person, *introduce yourself again.* You may say that you have heard that the company is a good employer and that you would like an opportunity to discuss a possible job. Set up an appointment. If you are unable to speak with the appropriate person the first time you call, ask for his/her name so that you may ask for the appropriate person when you call back. Practice your phone skills with a friend or in your group.

5) **The Interview:** Rehearse the job interview. Be prepared for success and failure. Remember: you have work to sell. You own that work; you can sell it. You can't buy the job; you sell your work.

6) **Set Goals:** Where are you going? What are your short term goals? What are your long-term goals? Look at your plan for school and/or work for the next three years. Use Work Sheet 64.

a. Complete Work Sheet 62 in class.

b. Complete Work Sheet 63, your Job Search Plan. Do this even if you have a job. Then prepare an up-to-date resume or letter of introduction. Do Work Sheet 64, your plan for school and/or work for the next three years.

# NOTES:

_____

_____

_____

_____

_____

_____

_____

_____

_____

_____

_____

_____

_____

_____

_____

_____

_____

_____

# WORK SHEET 62

## WHAT IS YOUR WORK?

First, give a name to your work. The following are some examples: Truck Driver, Tile Setter, Bookkeeper, Sales Person. Then, write down everything you think of that defines your work or the important parts of your work. Use extra paper if you run out of room in this Work Sheet.

NAME OF MY WORK_____

| LIST WHAT DEFINES YOUR WORK OR THE IMPORTANT PARTS OF YOUR WORK |
| --- |
| |
| |
| |
| |
| |
| |
| |
| |
| |
| |
| |
| |
| |
| |
| |

# WORK SHEET 63

## JOB SEARCH PLAN

Make a list of 10 possible jobs including the names of companies, address, phone number, and details of what happened to you when you made the call. If you have a job, complete the Work Sheet, but you may skip making actual calls unless you want to.

| Name of Job | Name of Employer | Date Contacted | Contact Names & Numbers | Notes |
|---|---|---|---|---|
| 1. | | | | |
| 2. | | | | |
| 3. | | | | |
| 4. | | | | |
| 5. | | | | |
| 6. | | | | |
| 7. | | | | |
| 8. | | | | |
| 9. | | | | |
| 10. | | | | |

# WORK SHEET 64

## SCHOOL AND WORK PLAN FOR THE NEXT THREE YEARS

List your specific objectives for education, schooling and work for the next three years. We will use this work plan in our next session.

| LIST SPECIFIC OBJECTIVES IN SCHOOL AND WORK PLAN FOR NEXT THREE YEARS |
|---|
| |
| |
| |
| |
| |
| |
| |
| |
| |
| |
| |
| |
| |
| |

# Session ④⑧ : Role Modeling Change

## 1. Objectives of Session:

⮕ Review the homework you did using Work Sheets 63 and 64;

⮕ Review the résumé you wrote;

⮕ Understand the power of being a role model or mentor for others who are working to change;

⮕ Begin to take part in partnerships with other persons who are trying to make changes in AOD use and in criminal conduct.

## 2. Session Content:

### a. Maintaining change through being a role model or mentor:

It is well known that the changes people make in their lives become more stable and permanent when they become teachers and mentors of that change. But it is only when we own something that we can share it with someone else. When we have full ownership of our self-improvements and change we feel secure enough to share with other people the joy and power of the changes we have made. One way to do this is to become an example, a model or sponsor for other people who are starting to make changes in their lives so that they can live free of AOD problems and free of problems of criminal conduct. This is the wisdom of the 12-step program. The 12th step is to become a sponsor or mentor of others in their effort to change. In this session, we will look at ways that you can become a mentor—a guide, teacher or tutor—for others.

### b. Two kinds of mentorships:

There are two ways you can be a mentor for another person:

*We become models for other people who are starting to make changes in their lives.*

1) Informal mentoring or role modeling: This means that you do not formally mentor or sponsor another person. It is informal. You present yourself as someone who has changed, who has control of your life with respect to AOD use and criminal conduct. Other people will see this, will identify with you and want to be "like you."

2) Formal mentoring: This is when you formally sponsor someone who has now been challenged to change. You make yourself available for supportive contacts and involvement. But you must be ready for this. You must be secure in your own change first.

### c. The steps of formal mentorship:

Here are six very simple steps in becoming a mentor for others who are making changes in their lives:

1) First, feel secure in your own change and in your ownership of that change;

2) Identify what are your strengths at this time in your life as to the changes you have made;

3) Identify the areas you are most vulnerable or the weakest in and keep track of these as you mentor others. For example, if you see yourself as vulnerable when you are in a bar, then you need to keep that in mind when you are sponsoring or mentoring another person;

4) Find someone who is in need of support in the changes they are making. **Be available to them** in their struggle to change. Use all of the skills you have learned in this **program in developing** a supportive and healthy relationship with that person.

5) Find your own mentor, counselor or sponsor whom you can get support **from as you mentor** or sponsor another person.

6) Go slowly and lend yourself to support only one person to begin with.

## Classroom and homework activities:

a. Use Work Sheet 65 to identify the strengths of your change that you can bring **into a mentorship** or sponsorship with another person who is being challenged to change. Use **Work Sheet 66 to** identify the areas you are most vulnerable in or your weakest areas. These **are areas that you** need to watch closely when you are mentoring or sponsoring someone else.

b. Write in your journal this week about your strengths and weaknesses.

c. Look for opportunities for both informal and formal mentorship and modeling. **Make notes in** your journal about these opportunities and then discuss them in the next **session.**

# NOTES:

_____

_____

_____

_____

_____

_____

_____

_____

_____

_____

_____

# WORK SHEET 65

## YOUR STRONGEST AREAS OF CHANGE AND SELF-IMPROVEMENT

Make a list of those areas in which you feel the strongest and most permanent with respect to the changes you have made.

| LIST SPECIFIC AREAS IN WHICH YOUR CHANGE IS THE STRONGEST |
|---|
| |
| |
| |
| |
| |
| |
| |
| |

# WORK SHEET 66

## YOUR MOST VULNERABLE OR WEAKEST AREAS OF CHANGE AND SELF-IMPROVEMENT

Make a list of those areas in which you feel most vulnerable or the weakest with respect to the changes you have made.

| LIST SPECIFIC AREAS IN WHICH YOUR CHANGE IS THE WEAKEST |
|---|
| |
| |
| |
| |
| |
| |
| |
| |

# NOTES:

# Session ④⑨ : Preparing for Maintaining Your Changes: Exploring Self-Help Groups and Other Community Support Programs

## 1. Objective of Session:

> ➠ Review your homework from last session as to your work in looking for opportunities for mentoring and sponsoring another person;
>
> ➠ Learn to find support in community self-help programs and other community resources.

## 2. Session content:

### a. Learning to seek outward for help: Exploring self-help groups and other community support programs:

In this program, a big part of our effort has been to seek inward to find help in our efforts to change and improve ourselves. But we have also learned that we gain help in our efforts to change by seeking support and help from outside of ourselves. This is often difficult to do. During our growing up years, we were often taught to solve our own problems, to do it on our own, to not take our problems outside of ourselves or to "not hang our dirty linen in public." But when we are committed to making change, or when we feel true ownership of that change, we feel secure enough to reach out and seek help and support from other people, from groups that are set up to help people and from our community. We have done this within our program group and with our program counselor. There are, however, many outside resources to help you keep up the changes you have made. One of the most important sources of such support is in the self-help groups in the community. We have found that when people seek the help of others who have problems similar to ours, we find the kind of support which helps us to continue our change and maintain the changes we have made.

### b. Finding self-help groups which meet your needs:

Each person has different needs and different problems. There is probably a self-help group in the community which will meet your needs to keep up the changes you have made. For some, Alcoholics Anonymous may be the kind of group which will best meet your needs. It may be that you will find the support you need in a group which focuses more on a specific drug pattern such as cocaine. In that case, Cocaine Anonymous may be the best choice. There are many other groups which may be good choices for you. These may include Narcotics Anonymous, Overeaters Anonymous, Al Anon, and many others. One of the objects of this session is for you to explore those groups.

### c. Exercise: Use Work Sheet 67 to help you explore the different self-help groups that are in your community. Make a list, and then call some of these groups and talk with one of their members. Make notes as to how the conversation feels. Do you think this group can be of help to you? Go to a meeting and try it out. Discuss what you found in next week's session.

## Classroom activities and homework:

a. Start working on Work Sheet 67 in this session. Continue to work on it during the week.

b. Write in your journal some feelings that you had when you did reach out to others for help.

# WORK SHEET 67

## PREPARING A LIST OF SELF-HELP GROUPS

Contact friends and use the Yellow Pages and any other source to make a list of self-help groups which you might be able to use in maintaining your lifestyle of being alcohol and other drug free and free from taking part in criminal conduct.

| NAME OF SELF-HELP GROUP | PHONE NO. | DATE CONTACTED | YOUR REACTIONS AND COMMENTS |
|---|---|---|---|
| | | | |
| | | | |
| | | | |
| | | | |
| | | | |
| | | | |
| | | | |

# Session **50** : Preparing for Your Program Change Support Group

## 1. Objective of Session:

> ⮞ Look back at your changes and self-improvement;
>
> ⮞ Prepare for your change support group.

## 2. Session Content:

For the next three months, you will attend a weekly group to reinforce and strengthen your changes and living a drug-free and crime-free life. This is your last formal program session. We will spend time during this session talking about what you have learned from the program and reviewing many of the skills and concepts you have learned in the past nine months. Much of the session will be devoted to your sharing where you are in your life at this time and what is different now compared to where you were a year ago. We will then do these things in this group session:

a. **Review the important skills learned in the last nine months;**

b. **Review the Johari Window as a model for ongoing group involvement;**

c. **Review the active sharing and active listening skills;**

d. **Review the changes we have made in the past nine months.**

## Review of homework for the coming week:

a. Write in your journal the most important things you have learned in the program. Just let the thoughts and feelings come.

b. Do a thinking report on what was the most difficult thing you did in the program. Remember the parts:

SITUATION

THOUGHTS

FEELINGS

BELIEFS AND ATTITUDES

OUTCOME.

## CONGRATULATIONS FOR A JOB WELL DONE. GOOD LUCK.